Poetry of Place

Other books by Jeremy Hooker

Poetry

The Elements
Soliloquies of a Chalk Giant
Landscape of the Daylight Moon
Solent Shore
Englishman's Road
A View from the Source: selected poems
   1967-1979

Criticism

John Cowper Powys
David Jones: an exploratory study
John Cowper Powys and David Jones:
   a comparative study

Editor of *Poems '71*
Editor (with Gweno Lewis) of
   Selected Poems of Alun Lewis

JEREMY HOOKER

Poetry of Place

Essays and Reviews 1970-1981

Carcanet Press · Manchester

First published in Great Britain 1982
by Carcanet Press
330 Corn Exchange Buildings, Manchester
SBN 85630 4090
© copyright 1982 Jeremy Hooker

Poetry of Place *is published with
the financial support of the Welsh Arts Council*

Hooker, Jeremy
  Poetry of Place.
  I. Title
  82   PR6058.0/

ISBN 0-85635-409-0

Photoset by Anneset, Weston-super-Mare
Printed in England by
Short Run Press Ltd,
Exeter

For Roland Mathias
and Ned Thomas

Acknowledgments

I owe a special debt of gratitude to Roland Mathias, who, when editor of the *Anglo-Welsh Review* encouraged my critical writing and gave it its first outlet. I am also indebted to Meic Stephens and Sam Adams, formerly editors of *Poetry Wales*, to Ned Thomas of *Planet*, and, more recently, to Michael Schmidt, editor of *Poetry Nation Review*. All of the essays and reviews which I reprint here were first published in these magazines, with the exception of the following:

'Brut's Albion' first appeared in *David Jones: Eight Essays on his Work as Writer and Artist*, ed. Roland Mathias (Gomer Press, 1976); 'An Autobiographical Essay' was my contribution to *Artists in Wales* 3, ed. Meic Stephens (Gomer Press, 1977). 'Edward Thomas' is the Introduction to *Edward Thomas: a centenary celebration*, with etchings by Arthur Neal (printed by Sebastian Carter at the Rampant Lions Press, Cambridge, and distributed by Eric and Joan Stevens, 1978). 'English Auden', first published in *Poetry Wales*, was reprinted in *Poetry Dimension* 3, ed. Dannie Abse (Robson Books, 1975), and 'T. F. Powys: "The Bass Note"' first appeared in the *Powys Review* 4, ed. Belinda Humfrey. My thanks are due to the editors and publishers.

There is some overlap of material between 'Ends and New Beginnings' and 'On *The Anathemata*' and my *David Jones: an exploratory study* (Enitharmon Press, 1975), which is currently out of print, but neither merely repeats what is said in the book.

Acknowledgements for permission to quote from works in copyright are due to:

Carol Brown for quotations from John Riley's *Collected works*.

Chatto & Windus Ltd and the Author's Literary Estate for quotations from the work of T. F. Powys; and with Raymond Williams for short extracts from *Border Country*, *Second Generation* and *The Fight for Manod*.

Faber & Faber Ltd for quotations from W. H. Auden's *Collected Poems*, *The Dyer's Hand* and the original edition of *Look Stranger* (1936); for quotations from *North* by Seamus Heaney; for extracts from *In Parenthesis*, *The Anathemata* and *The Sleeping Lord* by David Jones; and with Myfanwy Thomas for extracts from *Collected Poems of Edward Thomas*.

Gomer Press for lines from 'Rhydcymerau' in *Eples* by D. Gwenallt Jones.

David Higham Associates Ltd for quotations from *Outside the House of Baal* by Emyr Humphreys; and on behalf of the Literary Executors of the Estate of Frances Bellerby for quotations from her poems.

The Literary Executors of Charles Olson's Estate for quotations from poems in *Archaeologist of Morning*.

Oxford University Press for poems and extracts from *Collected Poems of Ivor Gurney*, ed. P. J. Kavanagh (1982).

And to Philip Pacey for quotations from *Charged Landscapes*.

Contents

Introduction	11
Matthew Arnold: On the Study of Celtic Literature (1978)	17
Edward Thomas: The Sad Passion (1970)	20
David Jones: Ends and New Beginnings (1972)	32
On *The Anathemata* (1973)	41
Brut's Albion (1976)	53
Philip Pacey: Landscape of Fire (1979)	66
Seamus Heaney: *North* (1975)	71
John Cowper Powys: Welsh Ambassador (1972)	75
T. F. Powys: The Bass Note (1979)	80
Emyr Humphreys: A Seeing Belief (1977)	93
Raymond Williams: 'A dream of a country' (1980)	106
Edward Thomas (1978)	116
Honouring Ivor Gurney (1980)	120
Frances Bellerby in Place (1980)	130
English Auden (1974)	137
Charles Olson: To Open the Mind (1971)	148
John Riley: *The Collected Works* (1981)	153
Living in Wales (1974)	159
An Autobiographical Essay (1977)	169
Poem and Place (1981)	180
Bibliography	191
Index	195

Introduction

'MOST of it has never been seen.' Roy Fisher's words about Birmingham, in *City* (1961), may be applied to places throughout England, from the smallest locality to cities and regions. It may be objected, however, that English places have been seen, with the receptive and creative romantic imagination, or in the great pioneering work of nineteenth century novelists and social critics; and indeed that English literature has shown from its beginnings a constitutional inclination to start with the here and now. Yet it still remains for individuals in every generation to see where *they* are, and to know the real from the superficially familiar. The difficulties in the way of this in the twentieth century are formidable.

A conviction outlined in some of the essays and reviews gathered together in this book, but standing behind all of them, is that images of a false unity imposed throughout Britain by a national or Anglo-American 'centre'—in fact, a consciousness and the institutions supporting it—are the principal causes of dull or conventional vision as far as the actual and potential life of particular places and the problematical reality of modern Britain are concerned. The same image-making processes are responsible for the valuation of places for their local colour, as picturesque deviations from the centralized norm or picturesque contributions to a generalized variety. In both cases, what is at issue is the truth of images of reality—which I take to be a writer's first concern.

There is much talk nowadays about growing cultural uniformity throughout Britain. Of course there is truth in this—more or less according to area, though all are subjected to the same political and economic system, the same centralized consciousness. But the talk is often vitiated by being an expression of the condition it ostensibly deplores, when it shows complete ignorance of the degree to which cultural, regional and local differences still affect many people's sense of themselves. The truth is rather that in the relatively small space of these islands, there are great creative differences, as well as grievous social tensions, but a bland centralism takes much for granted, as if the places where we or other people live are thoroughly known, and essentially much the same as the centre's image of itself. Such assumptions in fact represent pressures to understand ourselves and our places in a certain way. The irony is that a dominant centre falsifies even its own locations, so that it is equally true of London, for example, that 'most of it has never been seen'. It is my belief that much of the best modern writing makes no such assumptions and resists centralist pressures. It may do so consciously, within a range of radically different politics, as with Raymond Williams and David Jones, or it may do so only because the writer is seeing with his own eyes the place where he is. It may be naturalistic or visionary, but it will resist regionalist stereotypes and other centralist formulations.

Outside England, but within the British Isles, Fisher's words usually—but not always—apply much less to the insider's than to the outsider's view. In Welsh-speaking Wales, for example, writers are usually highly conscious of their places as communal and cultural centres, and for some the Welsh nation itself is such a centre. For Saunders Lewis, 'Civilization must be more than an abstraction. It must have a local habitation and a name. Here, its name is Wales.' Wales has its divisions, but in feeling, although not everywhere in the same language, people throughout Wales can affirm their national identity. I simplify; the situation in Wales is more complicated, more difficult, than this suggests. Yet there is an irony which is bitter for English and Welsh alike in the fact that the threatened culture of Wales informs a greater sense of national identity than is present in England, whose centralist pressures constitute the threat.

Beside Saunders Lewis's words I would set Nicolas Berdyaev's critique of imperialism in *The Meaning of History* (1936): 'Its will to universal domination disintegrates and melts the historical bodies of the national states belonging to culture. The British Empire is the end of England as a national state.' This statement, as with much else in this Introduction, and indeed my book as a whole, raises difficulties and questions which I cannot resolve or answer fully, if at all; they have rather to be lived. Berdyaev indicates a crisis I find expressed, integrally though sometimes unconsciously, in much English writing of this century, and of which I am personally aware. At least, there is no English national identity which can be taken for granted. But it seems to me that the recognition of this, disquieting though it may be, is infinitely preferable to the gap between absurdly sentimental national images and historical reality which characterized Edwardian poetry. But if England has ended as a national state, most of the English writers with whom I am concerned in this book draw upon sources in their country which confirm a deep-rooted if problematical Englishness.

Seamus Heaney in his brilliant essay 'Now and in England' (*Critical Inquiry*, 1977, III, 3), writing of Ted Hughes, Geoffrey Hill and Philip Larkin, has said: 'The poets of the mother culture, I feel, are now possessed of that defensive love of their territory which was once shared only by those poets whom we might call colonial—Yeats, MacDiarmid, Carlos Williams. They are aware of their Englishness as deposits in the descending storeys of the literary and historical past. Their very terrain is becoming consciously precious.' The truth of this has to be acknowledged—along with the bite of that two-edged 'precious'. But 'defensive love of their territory' did not begin with the poets Heaney considers. The contradictions for long present in a 'mother culture' which was also an imperial and industrial power, and which were given conscious expression in Blake's mythology, for example, were forced on to the consciousness of writers involved in or otherwise affected by the First World War. That, I believe, was the event that dramatically precipitated the complications of feeling about England in its dual identity, as compromised and disintegrating national state and locus of home territories. If, moreover, we recognize that 'disconnection' in all spheres of social and personal life in England, which to D. H. Lawrence was *the* wound caused by industrialism and war, it is difficult to say what is not involved in these complications and, therefore, in an experience of place.

The problems of an English writer defending a territory are similar in kind but different in degree to those of writers in the non-English cultures of the British Isles. In England, no less than in Wales, Scotland or Ireland, language is deeply implicated in the problems. Of course the English writer, unlike his Welsh counterpart, is not involved in a desperate struggle to save his language, or not in the same way. But he is concerned with its quality, and he has to find the words and forms in which the reality of his place and the integrity of his vision may be embodied, within a language that works increasingly to spread a uniform placelessness. It is surely more difficult than even Edward Thomas knew for English words to prove our love of the earth; less possible than David Jones recognized to affirm that the 'holy diversities' of these islands form a unity.

I begin the book with a critical view of Matthew Arnold's way of seeing Wales. This introduces one of its principal concerns—the importance of seeing places with understanding and sympathy and, therefore, with insight into the cultural, social, and linguistic factors that make them specifically human, as well as with feeling for their physical and atmospheric qualities. Arnold was sensitive to the atmosphere of Wales but insensitive to Welsh culture, and his aim was not to see but to exploit. He consequently represents, as he also fostered, all that is most dangerous, morally and aesthetically, in the movement from which so much modern writing about place comes. This is the movement by which sense of place has been greatly intensified for people who have been distanced from the places themselves—by education, work, social and geographical mobility. Thomas Hardy shared in this movement, and consequently saw a place as no one had before, and no one has since. But the movement which has sharpened the historical sense among modern writers has also heightened the tendency to transform place with the agency of myth, and for others, distance made their remembered hills unnaturally blue. Distance, however, does not necessarily give rise only to fanciful idealizations, and in any case, nostalgia may be an authentic subject. David Jones was no less romantic than Arnold in his vision of Wales, but his real inwardness with Welsh mythology and ancient and medieval history, and his genuine relation to Wales—the disconnection he consciously suffered—enabled him to create a significant ideal. In his work, as in that of Edward Thomas and John Cowper Powys, we see the tension between history and myth which is present in so much poetry of place. In some of the earlier essays, I take a less critical view of myth than I do later, but throughout the tension remains unresolved. I hope subsequently to consider it more fully in a study of Anglo-Welsh literature.

There is nothing simple about seeing or about place. My title has a rooted look, but I hope rather to unsettle fixed ideas of 'poetry of place' than to confirm its apparent stolid composure. Beyond the general description that this book is concerned mainly with writers who compose a poetic or fictional world from the elements of a place or places, much is problematical. All the writers have a sense of place; the places are, of course, different, but it is not even quite the same sense in any two cases. This is to be expected when the writers represent different traditions, and in bringing together essays on English, Welsh and American writers, and on fiction as well as poetry, contrast is partly what I am after. Yet I think it is not only differences that are revealed between Charles Olson and David Jones, or Emyr Humphreys and T. F. Powys. In other cases, differences may appear marked where less expected. But there is a sense in which their differences are what some writers have in common. For example, Edward Thomas, Ivor Gurney, Frances Bellerby and W. H. Auden in the 1930s, all draw on the same English traditions, and each is distinguished by his or her individuality. The unrepeatable personal 'voice', composing and speaking from a poetic world based on an actual historical landscape, but indelibly marked with personal experience, is indeed an important characteristic of their traditions. There is, of course, no contradiction between originality and tradition in this respect, for the personal is essentially the human.

In gathering together these essays and reviews written over a period of about ten years, I have tried not to rewrite past opinions—my revisions have been, as far as possible, only stylistic—but to let my changes of mind appear. These will be acknowledged in some cases, as in the second essay on Edward Thomas, but if they appear elsewhere as inconsistencies or contradictions, that will be because the book represents a continuing movement of thought and feeling around the problems with which it is concerned. The autobiographical pieces were each written for a series, which to some extent determined their shape, but they should help to give this movement a context and further explain its direction. This is exploratory criticism, but although it often begins with the need to explain to myself what it is in a particular work that moves or excites or puzzles or awes me, the end is to present the work in the light of my search. I have dwelt on difficulties and problems in this Introduction, but the writings which follow are mostly celebratory too. From almost every writer discussed in the book I have learnt to see places—cultural, social, *living* places—as I could not otherwise have done. The wish to share what they show is one of my main reasons for bringing them together.

On the Study of Celtic Literature

IN DECEMBER 1865, Matthew Arnold, Professor of Poetry in the University of Oxford, began his first of four lectures on 'The Study of Celtic Literature' by describing the views eastward and westward from Llandudno. First he showed his audience the eastern bay, 'alive with the Saxon invaders from Liverpool', where, 'putting aside the charm of the Liverpool steamboats, perhaps the view, on this side a little dissatisfies one after a while; the horizon wants mystery, the sea wants beauty, the coast wants verdure, and has a too bare austereness and aridity'. Then, evoking 'the eternal softness and mild light', the outline of 'mystic Anglesey', the mountains and the sea, he directed their attention westward—to 'Wales—Wales, where the past still lives, where every place has its tradition, every name its poetry, and where the people, the genuine people, still knows this past, this tradition, this poetry, and lives with it, and clings to it; while, alas, the prosperous Saxon on the other side, the invader from Liverpool and Birkenhead, has long ago forgotten his'. Given the discourse that was to follow, the present tense used in this celebration of the 'genuine' Welsh people has a sharp unintentional irony. But Arnold has prepared his stage. On one side, Saxons in their steamboats—a practical people, forceful and prosperous, without culture; on the other, mystery and beauty, mountains receding 'in an aerial haze' to where 'the sea, a silver stream, disappears one knows not whither'.

Clearly, in his description of two views Arnold has concentrated his idea of two national spirits or geniuses; his aim is to castigate English Philistinism, with its want of the mystery and beauty of Culture, by setting it against the Celt's possession of these qualities. In short, the lectures were to be essentially a tactical move in Arnold's campaign against the cultural, aesthetic and spiritual deficiencies of his fellow countrymen. Although in the event the move helped to achieve the limited objective of having a Chair of Celtic established at Oxford, it could end only in stalemate on the broad front. I do not mean this as a slight on Arnold, or on his achievement, but to acknowledge that, as an Englishman of his time, he was almost inevitably divided within himself. To my mind, *On the Study of Celtic Literature* is interesting today in several ways, most of which derive from its eloquent self-contradictions.

While Arnold criticized the Philistinism of a people whose

civilization had directed its energies to the subjugation of nature, and dominion over other nations, he accepted not only the inevitability of its success in these spheres, but also, on the whole, its desirability. He welcomed Progress but decried its soullessness; he did not see that it was incommensurate with the kind of soul in which he believed. One consequence of this was his view of Celtic cultures as belonging to the past, embodied in early literatures, and not as the expressions of peoples with a right to a continuing independent existence. Moreover, he used the sciences of philology and ethnology with their evidence of the underlying kinship of the peoples with Indo-European origins to reinforce his argument that there is a significant—and knowable—Celtic element in the English. He found this element in English poetry, and he wanted to reactivate it as a spiritual force. In this his aim was partially altruistic: he wanted the English to be far more sympathetic and understanding towards their Celtic 'possessions'—and in this respect Arnold was a knightly figure in the context of his country and his time; but he was principally concerned that the English should redeem themselves by becoming more cultured. He wanted them to enlighten their material success by gaining a soul.

Even considering Arnold's belief that 'the sooner the Welsh language disappears as an instrument of the practical, political, social life of Wales the better; the better for England, the better for Wales', and 'for all serious purposes in modern literature... the language of a Welshman is and must be English', I do not think that retrospective anger or scorn is relevant. For one thing, this emotion is a wasteful and dangerous luxury, and for another, it is too easy to judge past wrongs without considering whether, had we been there, we might not have said or done the same. But I think that it is relevant to understand the pressures on Arnold, and to distinguish between the letter and the spirit of his thesis.

Although he was condescending, in different ways, to both English and Celts, his criticisms of the former and his celebration of the latter were courageous too. The limitations of his knowledge (which he modestly acknowledged), as well as his confined outlook, made him treat Welsh literature as a thing of the past. He romanticized it, seeing the past colourfully and the present, apart from a disappointing Eisteddfod, not at all, but his romanticism gave him a true instinct for the antiquity of its roots. Consequently the most lyrical passages of *On the Study of Celtic Literature* are in praise of the oldest elements of *The Mabinogion*. As Rachel Bromwich has shown in *Matthew Arnold and Celtic Literature: a Retrospect 1865—1965* (1965) his critical instinct served him equally well in this, and other, respects. Arnold was a great critic; having read relatively little Celtic literature, he perceived large truths in the little he knew, and his general observations on poetry, together with his comments on specific passages, are still alive. Arnold the poet is also much in evidence in this study. His colouring of 'mystic' Celtic landscapes with feelings provoked by ancient literature, and his concepts of melancholy, 'natural magic' and Titanism, in particular, are distinctive signs of his romanticism. These ideas or emotions are as perilous as they are suggestive. In Arnold's case, the tension between his regard for all that the English empire was, and his worship of the qualities it excluded, led him virtually to resolve the Celtic nature, which he found in their early literature and in English poetry, into the suppressed soul of the English. And in the Celtic countries themselves, to which he denied the right of a real existence, through their languages and political and social institutions, outside greater England, this left little more than the mystic landscapes haunted by an irrecoverable past. In short, the 'spirit of place' of a decadent romanticism, which dissolved the lived-world of particular communities into atmosphere. Since Arnold's time a romantic, but usually less insidious, feeling for the spirit of place has intensified, and several Anglo-Welsh writers, for example, have explored the intimate relationship between living culture and landscape that he denied. He, however, was under pressure to divorce the present from the past in Celtic nations, and to create overall a generous and enlightened English unity. Of course it worked no more than an ungenerous and unenlightened form of unity has worked, but Arnold's version did at least have the virtue of being founded on his belief in 'the substantial unity of man'.

The Sad Passion

TO READ and re-read the *Collected Poems* of Edward Thomas is to become aware of two principal themes, which are indeed not so much themes as mental and emotional experiences that have coloured the poet's mind so thoroughly that they dye almost all his utterances. First, one realizes that these poems, written in the shadow of an annihilating war, have some of the darkness of that shadow in them. Reference to the war is explicit in a few, but in many the shadow is palpable. Its cold touch makes more urgent the poet's self-questioning; it provokes by its constant mementoes of a real human predicament the struggle of his mind from self-consciousness to the self-awareness which is also, inevitably, his awareness of others, and leads him to express with increasing directness his fears, his loves, and his failures in love and the achievement of wholeness. One feels, too, that the death this war has made him foresee, not as dream but as dung, has compelled him to write, thus acknowledging himself to be the poet he has always been too modest, too proud and too afraid to acknowledge before. To the influence of Robert Frost in making Thomas know himself a poet must be added the war's influence in actualizing the ever-present sense of death that is, too often in his prose, more literary than real. As if to acknowledge the debt, as Keats does in his Odes, death is frequently a presence in these poems.

> Rain, midnight rain, nothing but the wild rain
> On this bleak hut, and solitude, and me
> Remembering again that I shall die
> And neither hear the rain nor give it thanks
> For washing me cleaner than I have been
> Since I was born into this solitude.
>
> 'Rain'

Secondly, and as this quotation shows, by no means divorced from the companionship of death, we are made aware of Thomas's 'solitude'—less poetically, his loneliness—which is much more than the sense of solitude common to most lyrical poems and demanded by the medium. In part this is because, although he writes three poems called 'Home', he has no real home—and we must take the force of the word's metaphorical sense. He is homeless, I believe, partly because of his Welsh ancestry and his consequent pain at exile from a tradition which, though he loves it, he cannot be absorbed by wholeheartedly; and he is also homeless for other reasons which I shall try to define: in the broadest but most pressing sense he feels himself to have no place in human society.

In Richard Jefferies this same dreadful loneliness, exacerbated by his illness, is sometimes revealed in hysteria—in the overwrought hymns to life of a dying man in *The Story of My Heart* (1883), in the violent intensity with which he dedicates his whole being to nature. These are the outcome for a deeply emotional man of his experience of life without a society to embrace and sustain it. It is what Thomas calls 'the modern sad passion of Nature'. It is notable, perhaps, that both Thomas and Jefferies, when their imaginations are enkindled by the intensity of their love for nature, embody its beauty as a woman, often as a goddess.[1] It should at once be said, however, that to mention this peculiarity is not to suggest any interpretation as crudely simple as the inhibition of erotic impulse or its transference to the solitary communion with nature; for it is also a survival of the mythopoeic mode of perception, known in the Bronze Age and earlier, wherein nature is the great Mother, not the desiccated neuter of modern thought. Moreover, a further stimulus suggests itself in the idealism, the yearning to have and to behold perfect physical beauty, which Jefferies and Thomas, who were both too often nervously exhausted, passionately entertained. But what it all adds up to is loneliness and the projection on to nature of what cannot be possessed in the actual human sphere; and as such it is a poison when indulged to excess, because, as with Yeats's fantasies, the heart grows brutal with its fare: the glamour of dreams becomes a substitute for the more difficult task of loving what is imperfect. In 'Sedge-Warblers', for example, Thomas records the working out within himself of the problem this habit of mind creates, so that he is able to see things as they are and love them for being what they are.

But the idealizing tendency is only one aspect of the loneliness. What one feels very strongly in some of Jefferies's essays is the hysteria which derives inevitably from the love of nature becoming an end in itself. He is free from this in his books on country people and their condition, in *Hodge and his Master* (1880), for example, and also in his studies of animals, such as *Red Deer* (1884), and in the best of his fiction and reminiscence, but where he is alone with nature the vivid intensity of a love that is more than half pain cries aloud his need for a measure of ordinariness, of human contact and a work-a-day role in communion with people. In my view, the lack of these things contributes to his

---

[1] This occurs in Thomas's 'The Fountain' (*Rest and Unrest*, 1910), which in this respect may be compared to Jefferies's fine essay 'Nature in the Louvre' (*Field and Hedgerow*, 1889). There are other examples in Thomas's prose, but the opening of 'Sedge-Warblers' is a significant instance in his poetry.

nervous exhaustion, for he knows, perhaps unconsciously, that there is no place for him, as a writer, in rural society. The worship of nature that transcends nature or is diffused in it, in Wordsworth, becomes in Jefferies and Edward Thomas, concentrated in it: it is an egress of emotion, a bleeding away of energy, that offers in return only a fugitive—and sometimes shattering—ecstasy. They find in their own work little normality, such as that found in the fellowship of a common labour, in which to recover bodily, mentally, and emotionally their expenditure of energy. In Hardy, on the other hand, the nervous friction of loneliness—even this word is inadequate to describe the desolating isolation I am trying to define—is less evident, but this is due not only to the toughness corresponding to his sensitivity, but to the fact that he was not so irrevocably alone as these other writers. He was sustained by a network of family relationships and by the presence around him of 'friends beyond'; the society with which he could identify himself was much less of a chimera than in the case of Jefferies and Thomas. To put it bluntly, Jefferies was a man whose father and forefathers had definite roles within rural society, but in his own short life there grew in him—his nerves knew it, if his mind did not—the realization that he was essentially cut off. He did not till the soil; he had no relationship with it other than that of an overwrought sensibility: the more he worshipped and the more he observed, the more he felt himself to be insubstantial, a ghost. Spiritual parasitism developed in place of the symbiotic relationship between the man who works the earth and the earth that works upon him, subduing his body and mind to the rhythm of the seasons, and giving to him the culture of rural society, while he helps it towards the fulfilment of growth. And Edward Thomas was in almost exactly the same position as Jefferies, except that he was a countryman at heart and by choice rather than by birth; but he was not of the country as the agriculturist is, naturally and by right, so that his love of the gypsies and vagrants of his poems is also a deep longing to be like them, to be of the country without being 'brother to the ox'. What Thomas represents spiritually is the writer banished by his trade from Eden. Yearning for the wholeness of the relationship with nature of the man who follows the plough, he finds himself, pen in hand, divided by his work and selfconsciousness from that at-one-ness. Only consider the distance from reality of Thomas's Oxford and of the kind of work he was forced to do, and set against it the anguish of his intense spiritual life. One can then see how the loneliness of a man whose deepest, most permanent concern was faith in life and his relationship to the natural order with its cycle of birth, fruition, death and decay, who was—like D. H. Lawrence—a deeply religious man, must have been exacerbated by his social milieu, whose very existence was the denial of that life his instincts craved. Although he also lived to write, we know he felt that much of the writing he had to do in order to live was a spreading blight on his principles. The wonder is not that Thomas became sick, but that he survived his milieu and its demands with his integrity intact and the sharpness of his religious needs unblunted by cynicism. Like Birkin, in *Women in Love* (1920), he could still acknowledge that he was sick in the basic matter of the whole ordering of his life—the religious problem of disorder in the matrix of all man's relationships; and is there any modern writer to whom we still listen who does not *start* with this admission?

A brief examination of 'The Owl' should help to clarify the perspective I am trying to establish. In the first place one notes that the poet in the poem figures as a traveller, as he often does in Thomas's work—in 'Lob', for example, where he travels 'in search of something chance would never bring'. His travels are presented as actual journeys and also as symbolic quests for wholeness, so that the image of the hiking Georgian is neutralized by the unearnest seriousness, the lack of posture, in Edward Thomas. And the actual journey is freed from the hackneyed formula of Journey-Quest by its particularity, and thus achieves translation into metaphor simply because it does not flourish its symbolic significance. In 'The Owl' the poet-traveller is, as usual, alone. Significantly, the feelings stirred in him by the owl's cry are of sympathy for his fellows from whom he is cut off by his own charmed solitude. His heart goes out to 'soldiers and poor', victims of a society to which he is peripheral and from which they too, though abused by it, are isolated. But the full significance of the poem is conveyed by Thomas's use of one telling word. At the inn

> All of the night was quite barred out except
> An owl's cry, a most melancholy cry
>
> Shaken out long and clear upon the hill,
> No merry note, nor cause of merriment.

These lines, principally in the use of 'merry', deliberately echo Shakespeare's 'Winter' ('When icicles hang by the wall') at the end of *Love's Labour's Lost;* but in echoing it Thomas reverses the meaning—the whole order of thought and feeling—of Shakespeare's poem. For Edward Thomas, on this occasion, the owl's cry is 'no merry note, nor cause of merriment'. But in 'Winter' Tom, Dick, Joan, and Marian, though the tracks are foul and their blood is 'nipp'd', have their individual roles to fulfil in the natural order from which they receive their identity; and one notes how Shakespeare in evoking them assigns to each an occupation essential to the general good. For them—and the beautiful poem as a whole bears this feeling—the owl's cry is a seal, as it were, upon their security in relation to each other and to nature. Indeed, the archetypal pattern of feeling to which Shakespeare appeals is of the child safe in bed at night, with its parents close by, which feels its happiness increase the more the weather rages about the home. 'Winter' is a poem to which the beautiful word 'homely', in its fullest sense, can be applied. It may seem portentous to say that Tom and Dick and the others are at home in the world, but that is the supreme sense of well-being expressed by the poem, (and might we not say that this sense with its implied wholeness gives the full meaning to our homely expression 'safe and sound'?); and it is this sense which Thomas evokes, in order to reverse it. The soldiers and poor of 'The Owl' testify to the essential inhumanity of the society which exploits them. The natural order of the world of Shakespeare's poem has become a society of isolated classes and isolated individuals, which is, therefore, diffuse but also rigid. Thomas's conscious use of 'merry', then, evoking its Shakespearian context, as well as the potent image of 'Merry England' (in 1915–16!), brings into the poem an historical perspective which places critically the desolating nature of modern society. The poet has been made to feel the loneliness of his fellows, and their isolation is his, too. It is not, of course, simply the loneliness courted by a melancholy temperament—which we poeticize by calling it solitude—or the loneliness of a remote inn; it is a state fundamental to the poet's society and it expresses itself as his deprivation of a role within that society, and society's imposition—in its own basic fear—of a negative role upon its soldiers and poor. In my view, one feels in this poem, though it is only alluded to, the presence of the war by which the poet's mind is coloured; it is there in almost all the poems, as it is present in *The Rainbow* (1915). Again, it may seem a pity to thrust upon a beautiful lyric the suggestion of such a weighty metaphysic, but it is there, nevertheless, in the poet's selection of words.

In a sense the England loved by Edward Thomas had begun to die between two and three hundred years before his birth, but remnants of it survived (and still survive), to provoke in him a painful love. Indeed, in 'The Manor Farm', the other England, so different from its industrial successor, is seen to exist still, but its continuation can be expressed only as a state of timelessness, as a dream that lives on in the stones of a village, undisturbed by the gross temporal fact of change. There the poet sees it; he is nourished by it, but he is not part of it, nor is it reflected in a social order.

> But 'twas not Winter—
> Rather a season of bliss unchangeable
> Awakened from farm and church where it had lain
> Safe under tile and thatch for ages since
> This England, Old already, was called Merry.

As we have seen, Thomas can use 'merry', with its deep historical potency, to show its sad irrelevance to his own society, and also to show implicitly, I think, its bitterly ironic critique of a civilization deep in the mud of a hideous war. But he can also use it lovingly, of an England he can still perceive and of a continuity whose image is far removed from the object of Lucky Jim's shallow jibes. Indeed, the idea of continuity, and Edward Thomas's ambivalent attitude towards it, is a theme central to these war-darkened poems and sharpened in its poignancy precisely because the shadow of war does fall upon them. In 'Haymaking', for example, he sees the presence in the fields of an age-old tradition of beauty in the harmony of man and nature, and of the fulfilling labour of men on earth:

> All was old,
> This morning time, with a great age untold,
> Older than Clare and Cobbett, Morland and Crome,
> Than, at the field's far edge, the farmer's home,
> A white house crouched at the foot of a great tree.

It is characteristic of his temperament, however, and of its wisdom, to see the tradition as one which by its nature outlasts the individual men who serve it:

> The men, the beasts, the trees, the implements
> Uttered even what they will in times far hence—
> All of us gone out of the reach of change—
> Immortal in a picture of an old grange.

Confronted by these lines it would seem reasonable to assert, without reservation, that Edward Thomas saw the tradition of rural England as immortal, whereas it is difficult today not to be provoked by such sentiments into making a wry grimace, with the observation that the old grange is now, doubtless, a museum-piece coining its history, the men dwindled to a handful, and most of the implements used in the contemporary scene propelled by motors—all of which might be employed in an argument to limit Thomas's modernity. 'Haymaking' celebrates a rural life untouched by the war which all but completed its destruction. But it is by no means typical of Edward Thomas's attitude: the love it expresses is only one serene moment among poems which, while expressing no less love, regard the object of their emotion darkened by shadows. Only rarely, when he is betrayed into rhetoric, does Thomas see the future as the perpetuation of an England that he knows in his heart is already dying.

> Two witches' cauldrons roar.
> From one the weather shall rise clear and gay;
> Out of the other an England beautiful
> And like her mother that died yesterday.

But if rhetoric can be described as a deliberate working up of emotion whereby the resonance of certain words masters the intellect and transforms a core of genuine feeling into a bloated image parodying itself, then, in 'This is No Case of Petty Right or Wrong', we can perceive the exact moment at which the poet's sincere love of England, symbolized so movingly by the handful of earth he gave as his reason for fighting, betrays itself into a resounding echo of a journalist's roll of martial drums:

> But with the best and meanest Englishmen
> I am one in crying, God save England, lest
> We lose what never slaves and cattle blessed.

As usual the translation of genuine feeling into rhetoric is given away by the poet's ventriloquism, as when in this passage a Shakespearian note—from *Henry V*—usurps Thomas's own voice. But it is surely most human and understandable that even Edward Thomas, whose mind was no man's but his own, should, in preparing to sacrifice his life—and the poems show he knew how slender his chances of surviving were—*willed* for his decision an assurance that did not belong to it instinctively. Moreover, in the shadow of his coming death the way of life he loved most dearly was illuminated by an almost supernaturally beautiful late summer sunlight.

> The fiery day had a kernel sweet of cold,
> And in the perfect blue the clouds uncurled,
> Like the first gods before they made the world
> And misery, swimming the stormless sea
> In beauty and divine gaiety.
>   'Haymaking'

But he must add *and misery* to his hymn of praise, showing how his honesty is the acknowledgement of psychological realism—of his own limited self and divided powers—even at the moment of exultation when his ecstatic temperament has found in nature and rural society a beauty corresponding to his need to love and adore.

Two quotations from *The Happy-Go-Lucky Morgans* will help to restate my view of Thomas's relationship to the countryside. In the first he describes the character Aurelius as 'the superfluous man' and he goes on to elucidate the description: 'the superfluous are those who cannot find society with which they are in some sort of harmony'. Again, when in the same book Mr. Torrance recalls his childhood, spent in the country, he concludes sadly that now 'there is nothing to rest on, nothing to make a man last like the old men [of his youth]'. Having 'nothing to rest on', the superfluous man's experience torments him with a sense of unreality. Furthermore, Edward Thomas, like his Mr.

Torrance, thinks continually of his own childhood, but he is also haunted by the thought that the ideal for which he yearns may prove in time to be the present moment which he undervalues by his yearning.

> This is my grief. That land,
> My home, I have never seen;
> No traveller tells of it,
> However far he has been.
>
> And could I discover it,
> I fear my happiness there,
> Or my pain, might be dreams of return
> Here, to these things that were.
> 'Home'

There are other reasons, too, for Edward Thomas's sense of unreality and life as dream. One of these is the experience he shared with Keats of finding that his responsiveness to other personalities and things bled away his own centre of identity. In 'Two Pewits', for example, his response to the birds, which possess both earth and sky, makes him feel himself a 'ghost'. As Thomas wrote of the temperament with which he had so much in common in his book on Keats:

> His morbidity of temperament was inseparably kin to the sensitive passive qualities without which his poetry would have been nothing. I do not mean that his poetry sprang from his morbidity simply, but that both had to do with the brooding intensity of his receptiveness.

Just as the whole passage might be autobiographical, so 'the brooding intensity of his receptiveness' can be applied fittingly to Edward Thomas, for, when the responsive imagination of the poet goes out to nature, he often feels that his own life, in contrast to nature's, is a spectre at the feast. Thus what he experiences inevitably, by temperament, is brought to an unnatural intensity in Edward Thomas by the haunting knowledge of his own superfluousness: the whole world conspires to reduce him to a disembodied spirit.

Another factor contributing to Edward Thomas's sometimes desolating sense of unreality is, I believe, the shadow of the war. In 'Gone, Gone Again', for example, he writes of a derelict house

> I am something like that;
> Only I am not dead,
> Still breathing and interested
> In the house that is not dark:—
>
> I am something like that:
> Not one pane to reflect the sun,

For the schoolboys to throw at—
They have broken every one.

The countryside bereft of many of its inhabitants, civilization engaged in an internecine feud that is undermining its very foundations, the poet left behind in a nation emptied of its young men—surely it is facts such as these, concentrated in the bleakness of the single image he uses, that make Thomas's statement more universal, less extravagant when applied to his personal predicament, than, say, Shelley's 'I fall upon the thorns of life! I bleed!'.

One of the best poems in Thomas's meditative, conversational mode, 'As the Team's Head-Brass', embodies much of what I have said about his relationship to the countryside, the shadow of war, his prescience of death, and the posthumous life which the last quotation, together with many of his poems, shows him to have been leading in wartime England. The conversation in this poem, between the poet and the ploughman, is, in marked contrast to the monologues in a poem roughly contemporary with it, T. S. Eliot's 'Portrait of a Lady', a true dialogue wherein the men are responsive to one another. Meeting casually, they are at once in touch, while the ploughman reveals in his speech the deliberation—a rhythm of thought related to the slow rhythms of nature—and the unassuming wisdom of some of Hardy's folk. The men are so easy in each other's company that this may be thought to damage my contention that Thomas was isolated. Indeed, a number of occasions comes to mind in which Thomas shows himself to be perfectly happy among country people. He was; but the isolation I refer to was also a basic condition of his life since it stemmed from his severance from the natural order: the breakdown in himself and within rural society itself of the natural order that stands behind Wordsworth's 'Nature' and is reflected in it. Wordsworth's vision is sustained from without by the existence of a culture—a world of thought, feeling and belief whose foundation is the land. But it is a feature of the modern world that it begins in the death of Wordsworth's vision. Looking deep into nature Edward Thomas may perceive images of his own anguish, images, too, of Wordsworth's vision and Shakespeare's world, but the latter are fleeting and they are of what is dying. Thus for him the love of nature becomes in itself an affair with isolation.

The talk, in 'As the Team's Head-Brass', is of the war, and this poem, more than any other of the period, reveals the effect upon England of the war. Indeed, its priority as the subject of conversation in such a rural fastness shows what I have said repeatedly, that the war is constantly in Thomas's mind as the background of all his thoughts and experiences. The poem brings the war home to England in a very simple and, in afterthought, obvious way: by showing the land empty of men who once tilled it, and implicit in its imagery is the recognition that the land can never again be free of their loss—and of the Pandora's box opened by what such loss in such circumstances means for the values by which the earth has been tended. Lovers pass by them at the beginning and end of the poem, forming as it were a frame for its desolation: like Hardy's rural scene these will go on 'though dynasties pass'. The procreative principle of life goes on—that at least was not menaced then—but life's form is undergoing a change so radical that it might be described as an image of the Fall (Thomas's imagery is of falling) in which the essential innocence, the naturalness, of the rural order is giving way to a life which the poet fears, but which, in his prescience, he knows he will not live to see established.

> The lovers came out of the wood again:
> The horses started and for the last time
> I watched the clods crumble and topple over
> After the ploughshare and the stumbling team.

Now it is characteristic of Thomas's method that the images here can all be justified naturalistically. The horses start 'for the last time' because they have finished ploughing the charlock; the clods 'crumble and topple over' because that is what ploughed earth does, and the team is 'stumbling' on the uneven arable terrain. But on a close reading of the poem in which the poet's tone is considered and, in particular, the way in which he sees what he is describing, it becomes clear that the naturalistic surface demands to be interpreted as metaphor. So 'for the last time' is recognized as valedictory: the poet is saying goodbye to a way of life he loves, for he, too, like the ploughman's mate before him, is bound for a war he does not expect to survive; but it is also his valediction to a way of life the war will help to end. The horses, too, are going from the land. Then, in the final images, we are shown the poet's premonition of a whole order on the verge of collapse. It is not only the clods which 'crumble and topple over', and the horses which 'stumble', but the civilization of which they have been the foundation. Nowhere else does Thomas express as movingly as in this poem his knowledge that he and what he loves are dying together.

It should be clear from the foregoing argument that where Edward Thomas differs from a poet like, say, John Drinkwater—a Georgian's Georgian—quite apart from the difference between a dead and living use of language, is in his understanding that the countryside, in terms of whose imagery he expresses his inner experience, is also, primarily, the foundation of a civilization, a 'cultural landscape'. There, as in the old mill, 'once men had a work-place and a home', and they do so still though both it and they are becoming derelict. Like our major 'nature' poets Edward Thomas knows that Nature is not picturesque, not a pastoral tapestry the poet can unpick to adorn his own fancy, or only a neutral source of imagery, but first and foremost the 'maternal stone'[2] of a civilization, and the home of the society which tends it. This knowledge is a shaping influence on his poetry. Thus he describes his exultation at the sight of fox-hounds chasing

> like a great dragon
> In Blooming Meadow that bends towards the sun
> And once bore hops.
>
> 'Tears'

And once bore hops: responding to beauty he recognizes instinctively that the land is where man lives and has lived, not by any means only a source for his own personal associations or spiritual experiences.

In *The South Country,* referring to his degree in History from Oxford, Thomas wrote, 'but I have forgotten it all, or it has got into my blood and is present in me in a form which defies evocation or analysis. But as far as I can tell I am pure of history.' On the contrary, the recognition exemplified by the lines from 'Tears' quoted above, *is* the historical sense and Edward Thomas has it in his blood. He is certainly not pure of what may seem parochial when called 'local' history, but which is, for many people, the source of what is most real for their sense of the past. He knows that a particular field or lane ('Women He Liked') gets its shape and name from the lives spent on it by individual men now dead. From a different point of view 'Swedes' is a fine example of how Thomas sets the natural order—the changing seasons—against the historical—the pharaoh—and finds the former living while the latter is dust.

Nevertheless, as I have reiterated, his isolation derives in part from his lack of a role within rural society; and it is for this reason, surely, that his happiest moments—when he is serene, not when he suffers the nervous strain of ecstasy—come when he is working in harmony with nature; when he is in touch with earth as in the poems 'Sowing' and 'Digging'. Then

> It is enough
> To smell, to crumble the dark earth.

His attitude to nature also has a direct bearing upon his aim as a poet, which was, he wrote to Eleanor Farjeon, 'to get rid of the last rags of rhetoric and formality which left my prose so often with a dead rhythm only'. Indeed, the aim is associated intimately with the attitude, for it is when he is least close to nature in his prose—when, that is, his literary eye swims cloudily from its object—that he is betrayed into rhetoric and formality. But in the poems, under the pressure of war, he is as it were

---

[2] In *Richard Jefferies* Edward Thomas said: 'He... was the genius, the human expression, of this country, emerging from it, not to be detached from it any more than the curves of some statues from their maternal stone.'

composing his last will and testament (see, for example, the lovely poems addressed to Helen and his children), so that, at the end, his love of earth itself, and of life, asserts itself over the ideal dissociated from the real. Thus he describes what he loves in lucid detail:

> The Combe was ever dark, ancient and dark.
> Its mouth is stopped with bramble, thorn, and briar;
> And no one scrambles over the sliding chalk
> By beech and yew and perishing juniper
> Down the half precipices of its sides, with roots
> And rabbit holes for steps.
> 'The Combe'

—even when the descriptions serve to express inner experiences that are both ambivalent and unhappy. Embodied in imagery of the particular the expression of his inner self sheds the last embroidered rags of his least appropriate literary influences—Pater and Maeterlinck, for example. When we examine that inner life, from poem to poem, we find that it represents the quest for wholeness—the relationship of a whole man to human society and its home on earth—that will always be urgent, whether tractors or cart-horses plough the land, and whether trees or pylons ride over it. And in this quest he achieves one positive stage where his love of earth is embodied in clear, strong outlines, rising sharply from the haze which disfigured his prose style at its worst.

> I did not know it was the earth I loved
> Until I tried to live there in the clouds
> And the earth turned to cloud.
> 'Wind and Mist'

Ends and New Beginnings

[In the essays on David Jones I have used, where appropriate, the following abbreviations: *A* for *The Anathemata* (1952), *E & A* for *Epoch and Artist* (1959), *IP* for *In Parenthesis* (1937) and *SL* for *The Sleeping Lord and other fragments* (1974).]

AWARENESS of the present as a time of 'ends' is very strong in David Jones's writings. Indeed, all are concerned to some degree with war, but none with war only in its most obvious and limited sense of physical conflict. Already in *In Parenthesis*, the significance of the soldiers' war is apparent, not only as a hideous experience affecting individuals, but as a dramatic phase in the crisis of Western civilization. On one level this work is a very moving realistic narrative, but it also shows how the organization of men into units based on the principle of the machine is pitted against the survival of an order rooted in living cultural diversity. The latter gives full play to human identity, the former is concerned only with man's utility as an instrument.

In a passage evoking the North Sea which concludes the 'Angle-Land' section of *The Anathemata*, we are reminded that this poem, too, is a war poem both in the broad sense I have suggested, and more narrowly:

> I speak of before the whale-roads or the keel-paths were from Orcades to the fiord-havens, or the greyed green wastes that they strictly grid
> quadrate and number on the sea-green *Quadratkarte*
>   one eight six one G
>   for the fratricides
> of the latter-day, from east-shore of Iceland
> *bis Norwegen*
> (O Balin O Balan!
>   how blood you both
> the *Brudersee*
>   toward the last phase
> of our dear West.)

The chart which grids 'Cronos-meer', issued in 1940 by the German Naval Command, belongs to the same order of reality as the Draughtsman at Army, in Part 4 of *In Parenthesis*, 'who made note on a blue-print of the significance of that grove as one of his strong-points' (66). The grove is metamorphosed by one war into a blue-print, the 'greyed green wastes' by another into the 'sea-green *Quadratkarte*': both will now serve as parts of the military machine. But to the poet the sea and the wood are not only portions of nature but inseparable from man himself who has explored them, named them, told himself stories about them and made each an inextricable part of the culture in which his identity is rooted. Thus the physical violation of nature by war, and its reduction to a cipher, cannot be distinguished from the destruction of culture in the organization of both for subhuman ends. It is clear, however, that David Jones is not expressing an unthinking anti-scientific prejudice, which is a crude version of the Romantic-Symbolist reaction to the Industrial Revolution, but a unified Catholic belief concerning the relation of culture to nature, and man to God.

In the work-in-progress [i.e. *The Sleeping Lord and other fragments*] the deepening sense of crisis is one of the unifying factors. The prayer to the 'mother of us all', 'queen of otherness', in 'The Tutelar of the Place', is central:

> In the bland megalopolitan light
>   where no shadow is by day or by night
> be our shadow.

Intimately linked with this theme of the crisis of the West is the menace to the diversity within unity of Britain, in David Jones's apprehension of this otherwise compromised concept, of 'our Engle-raum'. This telling coinage occurs in 'The Lady of the Pool' ('our Engle-raum in this Brut's Albion' (*A* 164)) and its thematic connection with the 'Brudersee' of 'Angle-Land' places the war of the 'Fratricides' in a critical historical light. The effect of the introduction of Balin and Balan, while it does not soften the harsh image of the *'Quadratkarte'*, heightens the sense of the war's tragic pathos.

This theme of 'Engle-raum' also links *The Anathemata* with parts of the work-in-progress in which Wales is the embodiment of regenerative powers for Britain:

> In all times of *Gleichschaltung*, in the days of the central economies, set up the hedges of illusion round some remnant of us, twine the wattles of mist, white-web a Gwydion-hedge
>   like fog on the *bryniau*
>   against the commissioners
>
> and assessors bearing the writs of the Ram to square the world-floor and number the tribes and write down the secret things and take away the diversities by which we are, by which we call on your name, sweet Jill of the demarcations...

In the December of our culture ward somewhere the secret seed, under the mountain, under and between, between the grids of the Ram's survey when he squares the world-circle.'

'The Tutelar of the Place',

In this context of love of 'the diversities by which we are', it is interesting to note that the only great modern poem about London, apart from certain passages in T. S. Eliot's *The Waste Land*, is 'The Lady of the Pool' section of *The Anathemata*. In this evocation of the foundational things of the city the lie is given to the mental image, apparently nowhere more prevalent than in London itself, of the city as the capital of alienation and anonymity. But no Englishman reading David Jones can afford the complacency of regarding the destruction of cultural diversity as a process of which he is merely a passive victim.

As an artist concerned with the mythus of which he is himself a part ('one is trying to make a shape out of the very things of which one is oneself made' (*A, Preface*, 10)), David Jones is highly conscious of working in a time when 'dead symbols litter to the base of the cult-stone' (50). He is also aware that 'there are freezings-up and convulsions of many kinds, there are "ends" of all sorts of "worlds", as we in our age have reason to understand. There are also new beginnings and freeings of the waters' (note 1, 58). But the intensity of his preoccupation with 'ends' is a measure of his concern for the 'inner continuities' of those features of Western civilization that have shaped Britain and hence his own, necessarily conditioned, consciousness. His aim is not to make emotional capital out of a tragic sense of discontinuity, in the form of an all-too-familiar apocalyptic expressionism, but to explore the possibilities of regeneration and reconciliation through the creation of a time-perspective in which beginnings and ends and potential new beginnings are all present as facts of contemporary experience. His historical sense makes it inevitable that the perspectives he creates effect a dissolution of the 'Engle-raum' into 'the diversities by which we are'. Thus one of the most fascinating questions posed by his writings concerns the creation of perspective, and the methods by which the contemporary situation can be shown to coexist, in the 'present' of each work, with precise and highly imaginative renderings of historical period and even of geological time. For his admirers the writings are themselves 'new beginnings'. The forms are contemporary without annulling the historical sense that renders what is due to the differences as well as the similarities, the discontinuities as well as the continuities, present in time.

One way in which David Jones creates his time-perspective is through forms analogous to the dream, but to the dream as Private Clitus experiences it:

> In a sleep-dream you can dream of man sleeping and of a man

waking, there's no end to the recessions, nor to the superimpositions neither, in these dreams,... There's no end to the precision and exactitude of these dream-data....

...In these dreams the fates arrange no end of comings together.... There's no end to the unions these sleep-dreams can lend to things separate enough in wake-a-day.

...There's no end to the metamorphoses of these dreams.
'The Dream of Private Clitus'

This passage provides a metaphor that I think we can translate into a 'wake-a-day' prose in order to illuminate the writings' treatment of time. 'Recessions' and 'superimpositions', 'comings together' and 'unions' of 'things separate'—these offer a revealing description of the mental processes of the soldiers in *In Parenthesis*, and of the complex stratified images of *The Anathemata*. In the former work there is a close connection between chronology and narrative, but the 'wake-a-day' events also create and are given perspective by a 'dream'. As David Jones has written in a note to 'The Lady of the Pool', 'as with the individual psyche, collective myth cares nothing for discrepancies of time and circumstance' (*A* 168). Hence the time of *In Parenthesis* is both immediate and infinitely recessive since it is the time of the individual psyche, where immediate events give access, by means of shock and association, to historical and literary parallels, and to myth. But in the mind history and myth are as here and now as the events opening upon them. Thus the multiple allusions are integral to the work, not introduced arbitrarily to comment upon a present necessarily limited to the immediate. Only a view that confines the present to its immediate thoughts and sense-impressions could find fault with the principle on which this organization of material is based. All the same, one does need to accept that in many respects David Jones's war is mediated through a number of extraordinary minds. If one refuses to accept this, the relevance to the present of much that the war evokes will seem questionable. Thus as John Ball falls asleep on sentry duty, he meditates:

You can hear his carrying-parties rustle our corruptions through the night-weeds—contest the choicest morsels in his tiny conduits, bead-eyed feast on us; by a rule of his nature, at night-feast on the broken of us.
Those broad-pinioned;
blue-burnished, or brinded-back;
whose proud eyes watched
    the broken emblems
droop and drag dust,

suffer with us this metamorphosis.
    These too have shed their fine feathers; these too have slimed their dark-bright coats; these too have condescended to dig in.
    The white-tailed eagle at the battle ebb,
        where the sea wars against the river
the speckled kite of Maldon
and the crow
have naturally selected to be un-winged.

Now, while one can appreciate that a certain quality of mind will juxtapose the rat of the trenches with 'the speckled kite of Maldon' and 'the white-tailed eagle at the battle ebb' and even make a punning reference to Darwin as it contemplates the rat as a metamorphosis of these emblematic birds, which have 'naturally selected to be un-winged', one is acutely conscious that it is an extraordinary mind. But if there is a problem here, it is largely the familiar one of 'unshared backgrounds'. Isaac Rosenberg's immediacy is not generally felt to be weakened by his wide range of reference to his Hebrew inheritance, and to David Jones certain literary allusions and Celtic myth are no less immediate. On the other hand it may be objected that John Ball's name, which suggests qualities of representative ordinariness, is at odds with his sensibility; but why should a man be any the less common man for having an uncommon mind? A subsidiary reason for responding with excitement to David Jones's work is that it can teach one something, and what it teaches is more effective in undermining the mental 'Engle-raum' than any amount of scoriac Anglophobia.

'Precision and exactitude' describe the loving respect for things and disciplines *(disciplinae)* that roots each of the works in a richly textured and closely observed material world. Knowledge is through the eye of the artist and the hand of the craftsman. From boat-building to cleaning a rifle to the priest's vestments and act of manual offering, the contactual predominates. Upon the establishment of felt reality upon the material plane everything else in the work, including its numinous quality, depends. David Jones has an exact knowledge of what is proper to things, and to him all things, other than the merely utile, shaped by man are artefacts to whose making and use a precisely ordered and even ritualistic *disciplina* is essential. But since he is working with words the thingness of words, as in Hopkins, is a natural corollary to the thisness of things; and the thingness of words is a quality of sound as much as of texture, volume, shape and meaning. Thus, even at the level of 'description'—in fact, he enacts and embodies and re-presents, but rarely describes—there is a confluence of beliefs: each thing has its thisness, but each made thing also bodies forth the nature of its maker and his *disciplina*, and the act of making is not separable from man's identity. Also, between the artefact and the material of this planet out of which it is made the relationship is implicit of God to his Creation and the Creation to man. To this unified belief we owe one of the finest sustained passages of modern poetry—the enactment of geological stratification in 'Rite and Fore-Time' *(The Anathemata)* and the subsequent self-discovery of man the artist, 'whose man-hands god-handled the Willendorf stone', and his discovery of fire at the 'Easter of Technics'. A passage from the beginning of 'The Sleeping Lord' embodies a similar impulse:

> Is the tump by Honddu
>   his lifted bolster?
>   does a gritstone outcrop
> incommode him?
>   does a deep syncline
>   sag beneath him?
> or does his dinted thorax rest
>   where the contorted heights
>   themselves rest
> on a lateral pressured anticline?
> Does his russet-hued mattress
>   does his rug of shaly grey
> ease at all for his royal dorsals
>   the faulted under-bedding?
> Augite-hard and very chill
>   do scattered *cerrig*
> jutt to discomfort him?
>   Millenniums on millennia since
> this cold scoria dyked up molten
> when the sedimented, slowly layered strata
> (so great the slow heaped labour of their conditor
> the patient creature of water) said each to each other:
> 'There's no resisting here:
>   the Word is made Fire.'

Perhaps the most immediately noticeable feature of this passage is its conjunction of technical geological terms ('syncline', 'lateral pressured anticline') with the recreation of the material sensuously and imaginatively ('russet-hued mattress', 'rug of shaly grey'). The technical gives the passage an austere dignity but also creates a chilling sense of a non-human universe, measured and described by man in a way which places him outside nature. One notes that it is man's language that creates a non-human universe, just as it is his sensuous images that depict the landscape as a kindly place. Thus *cerrig* are stones in English but the use of this Welsh word 'incants' them as a cultural as much as a natural fact, so that the word gathers to the material all the associations of a particular culture in which *cerrig* are an essential part of man's identity in place. 'The patient creature of water' also emphasizes the creatureliness of matter, and 'the Word is made Fire' the belief in the Christian order implicit even in such potentially terrifying vistas of insensate matter violently rent as are suggested by 'this cold scoria dyked up molten'. 'The faulted under-bedding' conjoins kindliness and desolation. 'Under-bedding' images a rock adaptable to man's comfortable use, 'faulted' marries a geological term with a statement of the Fall, man's 'fault'. I would suggest that David Jones is genuinely moved by the cold beauty of the technical terms, but that he uses two kinds of language in the poem to create, according to one of his most characteristic techniques, an extended image of man's divided nature.

'The Sleeping Lord' effects the identification with Wales of Arthur, but of an Arthur who is both 'the young *nobilis*/the first of the sleepers of/Pretani' and a type of Christ. His sleep is the sleep of the regenerative powers that *are* Wales for David Jones, and whose stirring would result, in the words of the Lady of the Pool, in 'our Engle-raum in this Brut's Albion' coming 'to some confusion'. The land itself cannot be distinguished from its culture, nor is this culture independent of geology, and both land and culture have been wounded by industrial exploitation. But here the regenerative myth embodied in the primeval sleepers takes on a Christian significance in the identification of the wounded land with the wounded Christ. The time-perspective is created by a single image with complex associations: the Lord, like the land, is timeless and yet inseparable from his existence in and through time.

If it helps at all, in reading *The Anathemata*, to think of a consciousness encompassing the world of the poem, as we think of Tiresias's in relation to 'The Waste Land', then it is that of a man present at Mass sometime during the Second World War. However, it is the Mass itself which is important, not our sense of the mind confined in its own circle: the centrality of the Mass for David Jones is utterly dissimilar to the centrality of Bradley's philosophy for Eliot in his early work. In an invaluable letter to Saunders Lewis (printed in *Mabon* five), David Jones has written of *The Anathemata:* 'The action of the Mass was meant to be the central theme of the work for as you once said to me "the Mass *makes sense* of everything".' In a note to the poem he affirms that 'the whole Mass is an anamnesis'. And in another note he quotes from *The Shape of the Liturgy* (1945) by Gregory Dix:

> It (anamnesis) is not quite easy to represent accurately in English, words like 'remembrance' or 'memorial' having for us a connotation of something *absent* which is only mentally recollected.

But in the scriptures of both the Old and New Testament *anamnesis* and the cognate verb have a sense of 'recalling' or 're-presenting' before God an event in the past so that it becomes *here and now operative by its effects*.

The implication of this for the form of the poem is that its data exist on more than one level simultaneously: the historical event which is inseparable from its matrix in time is nevertheless present, here and now, during the sacred time of the Mass. Once again the form is analogous to the dream, but in the sense in which the dream, too, can be said to create an image of sacred time. As Mircéa Eliade writes in *Myths, Dreams and Mysteries* (1960), 'through the mystery of the Passion and of the Resurrection, the Christian dispels profane time and is integrated into time primordial and holy'. But there is no dispelling of profane time in *The Anathemata:* in the Christian view of history which it embodies, figural interpretation relates all events to the Christian order. The poem's metamorphoses are possible because the many are seen as one: a single order unifies cultural diversity, but the order requires diversity for its fulfilment. Thus the Lady of the Pool is many women and yet recognizably one through all her metamorphoses, for she embodies the feminine principle in relation to Britain and diversity is the nature of this principle. Similarly, the theme of geological stratification works by analogy for the theme of cultural stratification, but the Christian order is implicit in both.

It is obvious, however, that no poem could be an anamnesis as total as the Mass, since the poet can recall only what is available to his imagination. *The Anathemata* could not be inclusive of more than a fragment of the material relevant to its themes, and its selectivity has been made the occasion for adverse comment. Certainly the beginnings of British history do receive more attention than post-medieval times. Conversely, the whole poem is pervaded by a sense of crisis, and is addressed to the condition of late, megalopolitan Empire. In this respect the return to the beginnings is, as in any crisis, essentially regenerative. Moreover, the accumulation of historical data is in no sense David Jones's purpose, but rather the development of man the maker and its intimate relation to the Cross as the 'Axile Tree'.

For a Christian poet I suppose it can be said that a tragic view of history is, ultimately, impossible: the 'Sleeping Lord' is always there, and can never die. On the other hand there can be a tragic tension in his work between faith in the redemption and the knowledge that the culture which is the fruit of Christianity is being destroyed. This tension is also, ironically, creative and it is, I think, the mainspring of David Jones's work. The tension is present as a war within language itself, between the language of cultural diversity and the functional naming of parts in the world machine—more specifically, between what is available to the poet of the languages of 'Brut's Albion' and the increasingly standardized usage of 'Engle-raum'. From *In Parenthesis* to the work-in-progress this is the front on which David Jones has been engaged.

On *The Anathemata*

MY AIM in this essay is to discuss some of the themes of *The Anathemata* and to attempt to show how they affect the structure of the work and are integrated into its unity; but I must first stress the exploratory, tentative, and wholly provisional nature of the undertaking and make my own position, as a would-be critic of the work, perfectly clear. On this occasion it seems better to risk the accusation of trying to disarm criticism of my interpretations than the graver danger of assuming an authoritative tone where it cannot be justified.

In previous essays on David Jones I have set out to get certain ideas clear in my own mind at the same time as I hoped they might be of some use to those who were making a beginning with the work. In each essay I have started from the belief that *The Anathemata* is his major poem, and ended by pointing towards it; but in no instance confronted the poem satisfactorily. From the outset I have written as one who was attempting to explain to himself the causes of the intense excitement which the writings engendered, an excitement heightened by the fact that each reading has been a quest for further understanding, 'from the known to the knowable'. This continues to be so with *The Anathemata* above all. But, as T. S. Eliot wrote in 'A Note of Introduction' to *In Parenthesis*, 'understanding begins in the sensibility'. The truth of this observation should be a warning to anyone who may read this essay before first having felt 'that thrill of excitement' from reading *The Anathemata*, which, Eliot says, 'is itself the beginning of understanding'; for critical exegesis can be utterly confounding, and, worse, make the poem seem as dull and difficult as itself, while the highly original work speaks imaginatively to the imagination. Furthermore, though I am not a Catholic, the writings have involved me in discussions of the religious belief that is inseparable from their themes and, in the case of *The Anathemata*, from its form as well. It is probable that I have got some things wrong, but in writing about the poem's structure and themes this is an unavoidable risk. I can only apologize in advance for any errors I may make in this most sensitive of areas. While interpretation of religious ideas with inadequate knowledge may lead to the suggestion of unorthodoxies, these must be ascribed to the critic, not the work.

I

In a complex poem such as *The Anathemata* the way in which one enters the poem, through its opening words, is of the utmost importance, though it is often only in the context of what follows, or, indeed, of the poem as a whole, that the opening can be fully understood. Here the beginning is, at first sight, profoundly ambiguous:

> We already and first of all discern him making this thing other. His groping syntax, if we attend, already shapes: ADSCRIPTAM, RATAM, RATIONABILEM... and by pre-application and for *them*, under modes and patterns altogether theirs, the holy and venerable hands lift up an efficacious sign.

The reader is at once confronted by three questions: Whom do we discern? When? Where? It is clear, however, what is being done. *Adscriptam, Ratam, Rationabilem* are key words from the Prayer of Consecration in the Roman Mass: 'Which oblation do thou... ascribe to, ratify, make reasonable'. It is the priest, then, who speaks, setting the poem firmly in the context of the Mass? If this is so, the questions concerning person and place are answered. But one's normal sense of time, the desire to apprehend a specific When, has been disturbed by the infinitely regressive 'already and first of all'. Moreover, why should the priest's syntax be 'groping', and why are we told that it 'shapes', if the place and time of the opening words are the Mass some time in the present? The beginning of 'Rite and Fore-Time' poses such questions, but it is only in the context of what follows that we can attempt to answer them. Though the structure of *The Anathemata* is sequential at one level, it also reads back and forwards, round and about.

The second passage does concern the service of Mass in a modern church:

> These, at the sagging end and chapter's close,
> standing humbly before the tables spread, in the
> apsidal houses, who intend life:
>   between the sterile ornaments
>   under the pasteboard baldachins
> as, in the young-time, in the sap-years:
>   between the living floriations
>   under the leaping arches.
>
> (Ossific, trussed with ferric rods, the failing numina of columns and entablature, the genii of spire and triforium, like great rivals met when all is done, nod recognition across the cramped repeats of their dead selves.)

These rear-guard details in their quaint attire, heedless of incongruity, unconscious that the flanks are turned and all connecting files withdrawn or liquidated—that dead symbols litter to the base of the cult-stone, that the stem by the palled stone is thirsty, that the stream is very low.

Here, at the end of this passage, after using a characteristic military image, the artist embodies his apprehension of the modern cultural situation in metaphors of drought. This is the familiar waste land theme, as is made quite clear a few lines further on when he writes: 'The cult-man stands alone in Pellam's land'. But though the theme with its associated images is inseparable from its modern literary treatment and from modern interpretations of the original sources, it is essential to consider David Jones's use of it as a whole before questioning the extent of his influences. Significantly for the themes of this work, degeneration of the cultural tradition is linked with the degeneration of art forms, here Classical and Gothic architecture, which 'nod recognition across the cramped repeats of their dead selves'.

Thus the second passage of *The Anathemata* reveals the writer's view of the position of the 'cult-man' in a time when 'dead symbols litter to the base of the cult-stone'. It is clear from the *Preface*, however, that the term cult-man includes the artist (David Jones invariably uses this word in speaking of himself as a writer, perhaps to avoid the association with 'poet' of limited notions of self-expression) as well as the priest. Thus in the *Preface*, he writes of the artist: 'He has, somehow or other, to lift up valid signs; that is his specific task.' The affinity of artist with priest is made even clearer when he writes of the former: 'Rather than being a seer or endowed with the gift of prophecy he is something of a vicar whose job is legatine—a kind of Servus Servorum to deliver what has been delivered to him, who can neither add to nor take from the deposits.' The *Preface* tells us precisely how David Jones regards his role as artist, and distinguishes it from modes of self-expression: it is as one who 'deals wholly in signs'.

If the artist is related to the priest it is because they are both dependent for their signs upon the same mystery of the Christian revelation; in particular Christ's institution of the sacraments. It is essential to add, however, that David Jones does not confuse their roles, nor ascribe to the artist that quasi-mystical aura which, among poetasters at the decline of the present culture-phase, as in the past, can hardly be distinguished from ego-mania. (But we must also distinguish this trend from the profoundly religious apprehension of the imagination to be found in, for instance, Coleridge and Blake.) On the contrary, he sees the artist's signs as dependent upon the signs lifted up by the priest. But this is one of those sensitive areas in which I have already admitted the limitations of my understanding and I can suggest, only tentatively, that *The Anathemata* is related to the Mass in three principal ways.

The first suggestion has the authority of the artist himself. In the *Preface*, he writes: 'In a sense the fragments that compose this book are about, or around and about, matters of all sorts which, by a kind of quasi-free association, are apt to stir in my mind at any time and as often as not "in the time of the Mass".' In a letter to Saunders Lewis, printed in *Mabon* five, he has elaborated this remark: 'When I say somewhere in the *Preface* that one can think a lot of things in the brief moment it takes the celebrant of the Mass to move the missal from the Epistle to the Gospel side of the mensa domini, I literally meant that. The action of the Mass was meant to be the central theme of the work for as you once said to me "the mass *makes sense* of everything".' Now one implication of this is, I think, that the whole poem is circumscribed by the Mass and exists 'in the time of the Mass'. As I have argued elsewhere (in 'Ends and New Beginnings'), this access to sacred time gives the recalling of prehistorical, historical and geological events its special quality of recession *and* immediacy: these events both exist in their own time 'long, long, long before', and are present 'here and now'.

My second and more tentative suggestion is that the 'anathemata', those 'things set up, lifted up, or in whatever manner made over to the gods', available to the artist himself, from his own mythus, are represented by analogy with the signs of the Mass. Thus in a note on page 76, David Jones writes:

> In the rite of the fourth-century Egyptian bishop, Serapion, the eucharist is regarded as a recalling of all the dead: 'We entreat also on behalf of all who have fallen asleep, of which this (i.e. this action) is the recalling'. Here 'all who have fallen asleep' refers to the departed members of the Christian community in Egypt and throughout the world, because no institution can, in its public formulas, presume the membership of any except those who have professed such membership. But over and above these few there are those many, of all times and places, whose lives and deaths have been made acceptable by the same Death on the Hill of which every Christian breaking of bread is an epiphany and a recalling.

If the Mass be regarded as a total *anamnesis*, as a recalling of 'all the dead', 'of all times and places', then *The Anathemata* itself is, by analogy and because it exists 'in the time of the Mass', a partial anamnesis: the poem is a recalling of those anathemata available to the artist's imagination which are brought to mind during the Mass and by those events, in time but of and for all time, celebrated in the Mass.

Thirdly, the words of the liturgy echo throughout the poem and liturgical cadences and antiphonies have a shaping influence upon its style. Thus in more than one way 'the action of the Mass' can be said to be 'the central theme of the work', as it can also be said to effect its unity.

This is a complex argument and I am conscious of struggling with ideas which may be perfectly obvious to anyone more familiar with their element. With these ideas in mind, however, I hope it may be possible to return to the opening words of the poem with a clear understanding of what is meant by 'already and first of all'. It seems to me that this first passage images the whole of 'Rite and Fore-Time', which is concerned with the beginnings of man as a sacramental creature through his enactment of identity as 'man-the-artist', and with the theme of geological stratification. In this sense it can be said that man's first works as a maker of anathemata foreshadow the Mass. But perhaps it would be more accurate to say that the Christian revelation is implicit in the beginnings, as David Jones shows the 'New Light'

> Brighting at the five life-layers
> > Species, species, genera, families, order.
> Piercing the eskered silt, discovering every stria, each score and macula, lighting all the fragile laminae of the shales.

Hence man above all is, in his first making of signs, participating, 'already and first of all', in the benefits of the Mass; but his early works are a groping towards and a shaping of the signs of the Mass, though the Mass, instituted by an act in time, is of all time. Thus among the things that the Mass recalls is all that has led up to, and prefigured, the moment in time when the Mass itself, operative for all time, was instituted. Viewed in this light, the opening passages of *The Anathemata* are a microcosm of the whole: they intimate the groping beginnings of what was to become the culture of the West, with the Cross as its 'Axile Tree', and present us with an image of its threatened end. Inevitably, then, there is within the poem a tragic tension between the degeneration of Western culture and the eternal revelation that shaped its development when the Word became flesh and hence operative in historical time. Now, though what the signs signify is eternally valid, their temporal validity is under assault. The time of the Mass is now and always, but the efficacy of a sign depends upon its nowness; it is what is happening in the present cultural situation that threatens the regenerative powers of the 'cult-man'.

II

In his helpful study, *David Jones: artist and writer*, David Blamires has referred to the 'pronomial usage' of *The Anathemata* and drawn out some of its implications. As his analysis shows, the metamorphoses of one figure into another and the fusion of many in one depend to a large extent upon the artist's use of the protean 'he' and 'she'; but this cannot be fully understood without considering his apprehension of the male and female principles. One of the most haunting passages in 'Rite and Fore-Time' is invaluable to this end:

> Who were his *gens*-men or had he no *Hausname* yet
> no *nomen* for his *fecit-mark*
>   the Master of the Venus?
> whose man-hands god-handled the Willendorf stone
>   before they unbound the last glaciation
> for the Uhland Father to be-ribbon *die blaue Donau*
>   with his Vanabride blue.
> O long before they lateen'd her Ister
> or Romanitas manned her gender'd stream.
>
> O Europa!
>   how long and long and long and very long again, before you'll maze the waltz-forms in gay Vindobona in the ramshackle last phases; or god-shape the modal rhythms for nocturns in Melk in the young-time; or plot the Rhaetian limits in the Years of the City.
>
>   But already he's at it
> the form-making proto-maker
> busy at the fecund image of her
>   Chthonic? why yes
> but mother of us.
>
>   Then it is these abundant *ubera*, here, under the species of worked lime-rock, that gave suck to the lord? She that they already venerate (what other could they?)
>   her we declare?
> Who else?

This passage juxtaposes representations of different art forms from culture-phases widely apart in time, and, it may seem, with little in common in any respect. But the artist juxtaposes them in the belief that they are informed by a common impulse and embody the essential identity of man-the-artist. Thus the Willendorf Venus, at whose creation 'man-hands god-handled' the stone, belongs to the Aurignacian culture of 20-25,000 BC, but it is the same principle, in a more sophisticated form, that 'god-shapes' the church-music of the early Middle Ages. One of the prime associations I think we have to understand here is between the tutelars of each act of making, in the first instance Venus Genetrix and in the second the Queen of Heaven. The latter is both a development of the former and her redemption. I am afraid I can only describe this theme crudely, at the risk of giving offence: David Jones's art works to free the Virgin Mary from the association with virginity of all that is coldest, most ungenerous, unnatural, negatively prohibitive and essentially prurient in the puritan sensibility. He insists upon the creatureliness of the Mother of God, upon her Fiat and upon the fact that Christ was flesh of her flesh. As one of the sisters says, in 'Mabinog's Liturgy':

> Begetters of all huge endeavour we are. The Lord God may well do all without the aid of man, but even in the things of god a woman is medial—it stands to reason. Even the gigantic *dynion gynt* and mighty tyrannoi of old time must needs have had mortal woman for mothers, if demi-gods or whatever father'd 'em—it stands to reason. For these were of flesh and bone, not illusions men. So here also there is occasion for very flesh, for how should the eternal hypostases be conjoined with a flesh not substantial?

'Even in the things of God a woman is medial': this is a major theme of *The Anathemata*, though theme is a poor word for what is in fact one of the archetypes fundamental to this artist's apprehension of reality. Thus in all the writings, which are overtly concerned with male activities such as warfare, imperialism, and exploration, the role of woman, in stimulating or counteracting these activities, is emphasized: the interaction of man and woman, of the male and female principles, is an archetypal pattern shaping all his themes, whether political, historical, mythical or religious. Indeed, there are times when *The Anathemata* strikes me as a poem dominated by women (but not as *The Waste Land* (1922) is, negatively), until I am reminded that the Cross is its Axile Tree, the centre of its labyrinth, the still point of its dance. And here, in this mixing of metaphors, I am trying to convey an idea of the poem's form, that it is achieved on several levels simultaneously, all of which are related to the religious experience of initiation, in the labyrinth, the ritual circle, the Mass. But it should be clear that David Jones's fusions are not confusions. For instance, he does not confuse the Queen of Heaven with Venus Genetrix, but in his insistence on the creatureliness of the former we apprehend the latter as her prefiguration. (This principal theme, of development within continuity, would appear to have been strongly influenced by the argument of G. Rachel Levy's *The Gates of Horn* (1948).) And on the historical level there is a recalling of the spread of the cult of the earth mother, from the East to the Mediterranean, and its essentially prefigurative nature (of a culture, of a religion). In this way, too, the argosy theme of *The Anathemata* is linked with the theme of Christ's birth.

It is a significant paradox, which takes us close to the heart of David Jones's treatment of the female principle, that the 'form-making proto-maker' should be 'busy at the fecund image of her'. Thus in one of his earliest known works of art man is found to have created an image of that from which he himself derives, the woman, the chthonic, generative powers. The image is 'fecund' in two senses: as an early image of the earth mother it gave birth to a long line of similar, developing images, and the earth mother herself is fecund, giving birth to the image-maker. This theme of the interdependence of man and woman, foreshadowed in *In Parenthesis*, becomes devotional in the treatment of Christ and Mary; and it is a unifying principle of the work. Thus the image of the earth mother is followed through its diversification into different aspects of the female principle which have dominated the West in the figures of the 'delectable Kore', Helen of Troy, Guenevere, the Mothers of Celtic legend, Roma, Britannia, etc. Many of the female figures are inseparable from a male counterpart, and these are either types or prefigurations of Christ, or embodiments of the male will to organize and subdue cultural diversity. So an underlying theme of the poem traces man's developing image of woman, from the Mother of beasts and men, worshipped by the hunting peoples, through its diversification into the various beneficent and destructive images that have been a formative influence on the West, to their integration and purification in the figure of Mary, who is still The Great Mother.

When one attempts to spell out these themes, the inevitable crudeness or over-schematic nature of the exegesis is embarrassing to contemplate when contrasted with the delicacy and subtlety of their realization in the poem. It is at this point, in particular, that one comes to appreciate the considerable risks of sentimentality and dogmatism which David Jones has avoided by his treatment of devotional themes obliquely, by means of sophisticated techniques. For instance, the theme of cultural diffusion, by which various phases of Mediterranean civilization have had a shaping influence upon Britain, is unified with the theme of Christ's birth, death and resurrection through the argosy image common to both. As David Jones writes, in a note on page 106: 'What is pleaded in the Mass is precisely the argosy or voyage of the Redeemer, consisting of his entire sufferings and his death, his conquest of hades, his resurrection and his return in triumph to heaven.' The image of Christ as Argonaut is launched early on in 'Rite and Fore-time' when the table of the Last Supper is described metaphorically as 'the thwart-boards'. In 'Middle-Sea and Lear-Sea' the discovery of 'Britain' by the first argonauts is brilliantly re-enacted, and these men have their own tutelary goddess who is a prefiguration of the Virgin Mary. (They also open up the history-paths along which Christianity, following the cult of The Great Mother, will reach Britain.) Parallel to this theme, however, and also associated with it symbolically, is the extended metaphor of Christ's 'voyage' as noted above. This leads to some very complex symbolic effects in the recalling of the 'Skipper of the *Margaron*, sister-ship to the *Troy Queen*', and the 'master o' the *Mary*' in 'The Lady of the Pool'. The argonauts are described as 'precursors at the steer-trees', and the steer-tree is a sign for the Cross. Steer-Tree and Cross unite these two central themes and are thus the 'Axile Tree' of the poem, just as the Mass recalls the Cross as the Axile Tree of the universe. What is central to the Mass is also central to the poem's structure and themes, thus showing once again that one cannot speak of *The Anathemata* at any point without considering the Mass.

David Jones is clearly a devotional poet, but it is equally clear that he is also a 'Muse poet'—whatever Robert Graves might think of such a characterization, or David Jones of being associated with the argument of *The White Goddess* (1948). Nevertheless, the female principle in all its phases, from Venus Genetrix to the 'heath-hags' of *Macbeth* to the Queen of Heaven, is central to *The Anathemata*. Significantly, he creates, in 'The Lady of the Pool', a female persona for his expression of the foundational things of this 'Matriarch's Isle', and female personae for 'Mabinog's Liturgy'. The creatureliness of his art, its concern with otherness, with cultural diversity, cannot be understood in any other context. But it would be misleading in this context, above all, to give the impression that the poem's devotional character makes it solemn and humourless. On the contrary, a rich sense of humour pervades the work and is evident in the verbal wit of its puns, and in its personifications and the sheer ingenuity of some of its extended metaphors. The monologue of Clio in 'Middle-Sea and Lear-Sea', where she recalls Ilia's sexual submission to Mars at the founding of Rome, combines all these elements. So do 'The Lady of the Pool' and much of 'Mabinog's Liturgy'. It is clear from Clio's monologue, however, that the male principle is regarded, in one of its aspects, as the organizing power of Empire. The men in *The Anathemata* are the argonauts, the makers; but also the destroyers of diversity and otherness. Christ is the Redeemer and principle of beneficent order. The women are mothers, comforters, temptresses, tutelars of otherness, matrices of creativity. Thus the Lady of the Pool is tutelar of 'Brut's Albion', enemy of 'Engle-raum', guardian of Britain's cultural diversity.

III

In the final issue of *Scrutiny* (1953, XIX, 4), J. C. F. Littlewood placed himself among the select group of immortals who have damned a great work at its first appearance when he took up the alleged claim of enthusiastic reviewers that *The Anathemata* was 'a new (Roman

Catholic) *Waste Land* by a new (London-Welsh) T. S. Eliot'. He ended his review by adding that, 'although Mr Jones isn't absolutely sure that it's dissolution he wants to be a symptom of, the elucidators will find *The Anathemata* hardly less succulent pasturage than *Finnegans Wake*'. (Well, there are some who would prefer to be in purgatory with the later Joyce than elsewhere with Dr Leavis.) Despite the plain nastiness of the tone of these allegations, the derogatory comparison with T. S. Eliot, and the imputation that the work is a symptom of dissolution, must be taken up.

There are several allusions to T. S. Eliot's work in *The Anathemata*. These are evidence of admiration for the elder poet, and recognitions of his significance, but they also disclose a shared preoccupation with the waste land theme, which belongs to a culture, not an individual. Like *The Waste Land*, *The Anathemata* enacts a fusion of the quest motifs which embody a common archetype and are fundamental to the myths, romance, and religion of the West. Thus in 'Sherthursdaye and Venus Day', Christ and the Virgin Mary are identified with Peredur and his mother, and there is an unusual treatment of the familiar theme, Christ as the Grail hero. This theme continues the fusion of the Christian story with Welsh tradition that is central to 'Mabinog's Liturgy' but important throughout the poem. Naturally, water is the principal element associated with the waste land theme, and it is also *the* element of *The Anathemata*. Here again, though, there is a fusion of themes: the water of the seas on which the argonauts venture is linked with the waters of the womb and the restorative waters that are the object of the Grail hero's quest. Moreover, David Jones invokes 'the sign-stream', which he annotates as follows:

> The references are: to the term 'valid matter', used by theologians of the material water in the Sacrament of Water; to the material water essential to the Sacrament of Bread and Wine; to the water-metaphor used of all the seven signs; to the entire sign-world to which the metaphor of water flowing from a common source could apply; to the actual streams, our rivers, which are themselves signs of conveyance and themselves physically convey, which not only provide the metaphors but the material stuff without which the sacraments could not be.

Christ, 'Who primordially separated/this simple and fecund creature/*ab arida*', is invoked as 'Mandater of all the roundy-wells', 'Praefect of the strict conduits', 'Arglwydd of the Fountain', 'Magister of the Cisterns'. Hence the terrible irony that he, 'the *fons*-head', should utter 'his desiderate cry': SITIO (I thirst). Perhaps it is also worth noting, as an illustration of how this artist's imagination works, that the Lady of the Pool (of London) is also, like the divinity of a spring, tutelar of the source of signs that *are* the foundational things of Britain. As befits an island, these signs are mostly water-signs; but the full significance of this depends upon our realization that the archetype of baptism or initiation into many levels of individual and corporate being is fundamental to the work.

I would suggest that the treatment of the waste land theme in *The Anathemata* is radically different from that in Eliot's poem, not least because it explores it in greater depth and complexity, while using the same archetypes and sources. On the other hand, a sense of cultural dissolution is obviously central to both writers; but to move from this recognition to the charge that *The Anathemata* is a symptom of dissolution is a step whose logical progression I cannot follow. To my mind, David Jones is a poet of reconciliation, on more than one level.

Perhaps unintentionally, *The Anathemata's* subtitle, *fragments of an attempted writing*, recalls *The Waste Land's* 'These fragments I have shored against my ruin'. Both poems are concerned with the fragments of a culture, and shore against ruin with the values surviving in the fragments; but for David Jones cultural diversity is inseparable from the living culture of the West, and false ideas of order, especially the principle of mechanical organization, are the forces of destruction. Without making a comparative value judgement on the poems as poems, I would argue that *The Anathemata* is far more convincing than *The Waste Land* in its apprehension of what does constitute a living culture. Tiresias's fragments are primarily literary; David Jones's anathemata embody principles of social ordering, of the process of making a variety of artefacts, both utile and gratuitous, and, indeed, a unified religious philosophy of the creative and destructive forces in man: while the anathemata embody a profound conception of the elements of Western civilization, Tiresias's fragments are largely gestural. I have always felt that *The Waste Land* earns its despair on the individual psychic level; the selectivity of the cultural fragments it juxtaposes bears witness to the limitations of sympathy within which Tiresias is trapped.

Between these two poems there are similarities of method, and considerable differences. The differences of temperament are even more fundamental, as can be seen by comparing the way in which Eliot's poem embodies fear of the creaturely, and disgust at, as well as attraction-repulsion for, human sexuality, with the essential benefaction of sensuous particularities which is a dominant theme in all Jones's work. *The Waste Land* is characterized by a deep distrust of the female, and therefore by conflict within the bisexual Tiresias. This distrust manifests itself as a disturbance in the psyche, whereby the material world is cursed with an aura of unreality and all women appear sterile (or bestially procreative), neurotic, and predatory. This continues to be so until, in *Ash Wednesday* (1930), the female is subsumed under the redeeming influence of the Virgin. The ensuing friction is, indeed, a feature of the nervous power of Eliot's poetry, and it is the expression of this terrible conflict, rather than the more general theme of cultural dissolution, that speaks directly to us of our loss of relationship with a part of ourselves and a part of our world. At any rate, this is where I find the strength of his early work to lie, in fear, in the male will's baffled struggle with a world that is socially, ideally, and in its carnality, primarily female, with an unregenerate power that it can neither accept nor subdue. From the beginning, however, the female principle in all its aspects, even as mother of death on the battlefields of *In Parenthesis*, has been David Jones's Muse. The depth of his feeling for the creaturely can be gauged, surely, from the fact that his first impulse as an artist was to draw animals. I find it a singularly telling detail that both relates the first artistic impulse of the individual to the first artistic impulse of man himself, and indicates the remarkable continuity of David Jones's art: for *The Anathemata* is, among other things, a recalling of the infancy and youth of Western man. I can see no symptoms of dissolution in the work of an artist who has experienced, at first hand, the condition in which 'things fall apart', but, even without his belief, proof of reconciliation in the living presence of those anathemata he has lifted up. As the Lady of the Pool says, in a marvellously resonant phrase which embodies so much of David Jones's regenerative impulse, 'What's under works up'. If this is so it is, for the individual mind as for its sustaining culture, perhaps the last hope. It is what this artist has set against the modern tendency to suppress man's capacity for awe and tenderness, to seal every mouth giving access to the subterranean powers, that is the principle of dissolution.

Brut's Albion

I BEGIN WITH a note to the passage from 'The Lady of the Pool' which is central to the subject of this essay and which I shall quote later. Writing of the tradition of 'hidden guardians and strength-givers', like the head of Brân the Blessed, buried under London, David Jones says that 'vestiges of this deposit became a permanent part of English lore, whether folk or literary; to be felt in later centuries as a kind of ground-swell and sometimes as a present wind influencing such a deep-draughted ship of burden as the *Shakespeare* or the high-superstructured *Milton*' (*A* 163, note 3). Here he brings together two of his favourite metaphors, the ship and the deposits.

Among the many meanings that the former held for David Jones we find the ship as metaphor for the poetic imagination. The great imagination, influenced by winds from near or from far off in time, is the vessel of the culture to which the poet belongs. The burden proper to him, and indeed to man-the-artist, is the signs of his culture. It follows, of course, that the poet himself may not be fully aware of all that he bears; personal limitations or the limitations of the age may cause damage or loss to the signs. There is a marvellous passage in his *Introduction to the Rime of the Ancient Mariner* (1972) where David Jones in effect takes Milton to task for losing the traditional significance of one of his most impressive images. The tall pine, 'stepped for the great mast of a great ship', was traditionally a sign for the Cross and for Christ as Argonaut, bound like Odysseus to the mast, but Milton uses it to furnish 'the colossal spear-haft in the supposed almighty fist-grip of his god-damned Lucifer' (37). For all his humility and modesty, David Jones, like Blake, is not afraid of quarrelling with the great Milton. The ship symbol of *The Anathemata* restores this traditional significance to the sign.

Restoration of signifying power to the dominant signs of Western culture is one of the principal aims of all David Jones's writings. The *David Jones*, we might say, is, more consciously than any other, a sign-bearing craft; its voyage is a quest whose object is to release the power of the signs it bears by renewing their validity. Among these signs, those belonging to the deposits of 'this Matriarch's Isle', 'Brut's Albion', have a special importance.

In Parenthesis, like *Y Gododdin*, 'connects us with a very ancient unity and mingling of races; with the Island as a corporate inheritance' (*IP*, *General Notes*, 4, 191–2). The army brings together men from different parts of Britain in order to form them into an efficient military unit; by assembling them in one place, it unwittingly makes possible a different kind of order. *In Parenthesis*, no less than *The Anathemata*, presents the making of a culture. The culture of the trenches is both a form of adaptation to the primitive conditions, and a recovery of 'the Island as a corporate inheritance', with roots deep in history and native myth. In the following passage it is night in the trenches and the sentry keeps watch:

> And the rain slacks at the wind veer
> and she half breaks her cloud cover.
> He puts up a sufficient light dead over the Neb; and in its moments hanging, star-still, shedding a singular filament of peace, for these fantastic undulations.
> He angled rigid; head and shoulders free; his body's inclination at the extreme thrust of the sap head; outward toward them, like the calm breasts of her, silent above the cutwater, foremost toward them and outmost of us, and
> brother-keeper, and ward-watcher;
> his mess-mates sleeping like long-barrow sleepers, their dark arms at reach.
> Spell-sleepers, thrown about anyhow under the night.
> And this one's bright brow turned against your boot leather, tranquil as a fer sidhe sleeper, under fairy tumuli, fair as Mac Óg sleeping.
>
> Part 3

A note on this passage calls attention to 'the persistent Celtic theme of armed sleepers under the mounds' and to Plutarch's words about our islands: 'An Island in which Cronus is imprisoned with Briareus keeping guard over him as he sleeps; for as they put it, sleep is the bond of Cronus. They add that around him are many deities, his henchmen and attendants.' 'It will be seen', David Jones continues, 'that the tumbled undulations and recesses, the static sentries, and the leaning arms that were the Forward Zone, called up easily this abiding myth of our people.' He refers us to Blake's description of his picture, 'The Ancient Britons' (in *A Descriptive Catalogue*, V), where Blake lists the deeds of a cosmic Arthur, intimately associated with the prehistoric sites of Britain. 'And the sun of Britain set, but shall rise again with tenfold splendour when Arthur shall awake from sleep and resume his dominion over Earth and Ocean' (*IP*, note 36, 198–9). Thus Blake affirms the apocalyptic waking as a return to the original, uncontracted state of unity in being. For David Jones too, Arthur belongs to 'true, immemorial religion'. He is 'the Protector of the Land, the Leader, the Saviour, the Lord of Order carrying a raid into the place of Chaos' (*IP*, Part 3, note 42, 200–01).

The ancient images of sleepers and the earth as a womb, which are prevalent in David Jones's writings, embody a dormant creative power, a potentiality for renewal of the diversity within unity that the cultural deposits hold. In *In Parenthesis* the power is in the men themselves, in the culture which they create. But the military power which they are conditioned to serve brings them to destroy and be destroyed. It is a painful irony of *In Parenthesis* that 'the Island as a corporate inheritance' should be recovered outside the Island, in a situation brought about by forces of the same civilization that has imposed uniformity on the diverse cultures of the Island, and that its power should be spent, at least temporarily, on the battlefield. The images, however, are essentially regenerative. But of course these beautiful and uncanny images would be far less effective in the work as a whole without the down-to-earth response of the soldier woken by the sentry:

> Who cocks an open eye when you stamp your numbed feet on the fire-step slats,
> who tells you to stow it,
> to put a sock in it,
> to let a man sleep o' nights....
>
> Part 3

Considered within a tradition descending from at least the twelfth century, from Geoffrey of Monmouth through Malory and the Elizabethan poets, notably Michael Drayton, to William Blake and others, there is nothing in the least eccentric about an impassioned concern in the Matter of Britain, although a good deal of wilful eccentricity has fed on the materials. As a genuine tradition it has been hospitable to the individual imaginations of writers conditioned by different societies and times. If we consider the twelfth-century romantic chronicler, Geoffrey of Monmouth, the seventeenth-century poet Drayton, and Blake and David Jones, we can see that what they all have in common in their approach to this material is the need to define the identity of Britain in accordance with the truth as each saw it, in his time. It is not, of course, the same identity in any two cases.

Yet 'the Island as a corporate inheritance', or 'the unity of this island' (*E & A*, 'The Myth of Arthur', 216), as David Jones calls the theme elsewhere, is a curious concept to come upon in a modern writer; it may even seem to condemn him as eccentric precisely because it is traditional. David Jones knew well enough, of course, what the idea of Britain was being used for in his time; that for many people it was synonymous with England, that an especially virulent form, nourished at once by the British Empire and Little England, inspired the propaganda of the First World War. He saw, no less clearly than Blake in his time, the destructiveness of the contemporary national idea. Yet he was, as T. S. Eliot said, 'decidedly a Briton' (*IP*, 'A Note of Introduction', vii).

It is not easy for a poet in this century to be a Briton—not easy, that is, if the name is to be redeemed from the empty rhetoric of the Edwardian imperialists and from all forms of sentimentality, and if it is to distinguish what is at least a potential reality from emotive concepts culled from other ages. It is not easy for the modern poet who loves the things of these islands to lift them up as valid signs of a real unity. David Jones confronted this difficulty in his writings, and we should not shirk it in our reading of them. It was not difficult for Drayton, writing in the first decades of the seventeenth century, to use the Matter of Britain with a patriotism that embraced the whole island, for his patriotism did not differ in essentials from the national spirit of his age—and that spirit, as it is manifested by Spenser and Raleigh and Shakespeare too, was, despite its limitations, clearly a current of living feeling that flowed between writer and audience, and the historical and fabulous 'matter' of their native realm. For David Jones the London Welshman, on the other hand, there was total opposition between the 'corporate inheritance' which he loved, and the forms of political and economic organization that hold Britain together in the twentieth century. There was, in fact, total opposition between his apprehension of the culture proper to man, and the actual civilization, centred in megalopolis, that would impose a uniform system on the diverse traditions of the island, and has gone far towards doing so. As a Londoner he was necessarily a man of that civilization (as all of us, wherever we live, must to some extent be) and as a Welshman he felt its effects upon Wales most acutely. But of course there is more at stake here than different versions of Britain. The art and beliefs of David Jones and Blake are finally very different, but the national ideas whose tyranny each opposes also reflect constricting and destructive ideas of human potentiality. Those ideas represent mechanical systems, abstraction, man's instrumentality.

One intention of Geoffrey of Monmouth was, clearly enough, to show up the Saxons as barbaric invaders of a people with a long and glorious past. The Lady of the Pool's irony at the expense of John of Whethamstede, type of all those who have dismissed the *Historia* as 'totally fictitious'—

> for these learn'd be ever apt to
> burn phoenixes and are like to bury the cat that has much
> mousing in her yet, being but six times dead.
>   A

—certainly reflects David Jones's attitude to Geoffrey. He comments on the legendary city of Troy Novant, on the site of London, that Geoffrey of Monmouth 'made [it] an integral part of our national mythological deposit, whereby through the Trojan Brute, of the line of Aeneas, Venus and Jove, our tradition is linked with all that that succession can be made to signify; and seeing what we owe to all that, the myth proposes for our acceptance a truth more real than the historic facts alone discover' (*A*, 124, note 3). This observation may remind us of Virgil rather than Blake or any other English writer, and not only because it refers to Aeneas. *The Anathemata*, like *The Aeneid*, is about the founding and making of a culture. Consequently it presents the growth of a consciousness, of those signs shaped by Western man by which he has shaped himself, and its materials are drawn from myths which embody truths 'more real than the historic facts alone discover', as well as from history. David Jones uses history, legendary history, and myth with a Virgilian instinct for its shaping effect upon the consciousness of his people, but in the light of contemporary scholarship in these subjects. He starts from the Stone Age, as W. F. Jackson Knight would persuade us that Virgil did too, and he shows the marriage—often forced—between native traditions and traditions from without—from the Mediterranean, the near East, and the Christian West.

Brut's Albion is a traditional name—for example, it is found in Selden's 'illustrations' to Drayton's *Poly-Olbion*, where Selden tells us that an earlier writer called Henry V 'Protector of Brut's Albion'—and of course it links Brute, the legendary founder of Britain, with Albion, the earliest recorded name of the Island. The name occurs twice in *The Anathemata*, and is used on both occasions by the Lady of the Pool. The following passage comes immediately after her recalling of the 'hidden guardians and strength-givers' referred to above, 'the fathering figures... that do keep us all,' 'aged viriles buried under/that from Lud's clay have ward of us that be his townies—' She has just ascribed to them the qualities of protectors, fertility deities, and 'strong binders' who enable the loam to bear such a weight of masonry. And she continues:

> Though there's a deal of subsidence hereabouts even so:
>   gravels, marls, alluviums
> here all's alluvial, cap'n, and as unstable as these old annals
> that do gravel us all. For, captain:
>   even immolated kings
> be scarce a match for the deep fluvial doings of the mother.
>   But leastways
> best let sleepers lie
>   and these slumberers
> was great captains, cap'n:
> tyrannoi come in keels from Old Troy
>   *requiescant.*

> For these fabliaux say, of one other such quondam king
> *rexque futurus*.
> And you never know, captain
> you never know, not with what you might call metaphysical
> certainty, captain: Our phenomenology is but limited,
> captain.
> So of these let's say *requiescant*
> till the Sejunction Day!
> For should these stir, then would our Engle-raum in this
> Brut's Albion be like to come to some confusion!
> You never know, captain:
> What's under works up.
> I will not say it shall be so
> but, captain, rather I would say:
> You never know!

The phrase 'our Engle-raum', connecting England with the fascist idea, cannot but have a shocking effect, the more so when we recall how the blitz often brought other ages to light, ruins under the ruins. What the bombs did in a purely destructive way offers a gross parody—indeed, the negation—of David Jones's intention: to reveal 'what's under', not ruins but the creative principle buried in the mind and land of a people oppressed by contemporary civilization, 'our Engle-raum'. The phrase is, uncomfortably, all of a piece with the perception of the combatants of the Second World War as 'fratricides of the latter-day' (*A*, 'Angle Land', 45), and with the critical but profoundly humane historical perspective of this writer. The 'slumberers', Arthur and the rest, embody the dormant potentiality of Brut's Albion, the richly diverse culture proper to the island. The hope perceived, here as elsewhere in the writings, is that 'what's under works up', a key phrase that signifies the very opposite of the Tribune's 'only the neurotic look to their beginnings' ('The Tribune's Visitation', *SL*, 51). It implies much, only a little of which I shall be able to touch on here.

It is the river, 'the deep fluvial doings of the mother', that causes the subsidence whereby these 'immolated kings' might be awoken. 'Water', David Jones notes in the *Preface* (17), is in Britain 'unavoidably very much part of the *materia poetica*'. Drayton, in *Poly-Olbion*, personifies the rivers and streams of Britain, but his method is finally tediously naive; he simply makes them retell the stories belonging to the Matter of Britain. In contrast, David Jones, like Blake, both uses myth and is himself a myth-maker, but always basing his subtle and inventive symbols and analogies upon the doctrine of his faith. For him, our rivers 'sign the whole anatomy of Britain/with his valid sign' (*A*, 'Mabinog's Liturgy', 204). Christianity is an inescapable reality, its signs are incarnate in the very substance of the planet. Water likewise signifies the whole female principle, a power that is at once terrible and regenerative, destructive when denied, but ever working to erode purely utilitarian social and mental structures. In a haunting line in *Jerusalem*, Blake writes: 'And Albion fled inward among the currents of his rivers' (chapter I, section 19). The primal creative energy, temporarily defeated, takes refuge among forces that are part of the actual physical landscape. David Jones too restores a sense of contained dynamic power to the physical structure of the island, to its rivers and mountains. But for him it is essentially the same power that is locked in the signs themselves.

David Jones is a supremely confident poet. This is so despite the cry, 'I said, Ah! what shall I write?' and all it implies: his consciousness of living in a 'late' civilization for which not only the signs of Western culture but also the very idea of sign and sacrament are meaningless. It is true even despite the doubt which he sometimes expresses, as in his comment on *The Anathemata:* 'It may be that the kind of thing I have been trying to make is no longer makeable in the kind of way in which I have tried to make it' (*Preface*, 15). Yet the confidence is present where it really matters, in the poem, even in passages expressing anguished regret at the loss of conditions proper to man-the-artist. It is there in 'Middle-Sea and Lear-Sea', when the poet asks when again, if ever, we shall see the Word made stone:

> And when
> > where, how or ever again?
> > > ...or again?
> Not ever again?
> > never?
> After the conflagrations
> > in the times of forgetting?
> in the loops between?
> before the prides
> > and after the happy falls?
> *Spes!*
> > answer me!!
> How right you are—
> > blindfold's best!
> > But, where d'you think the flukes of y'r hook'll hold
> next—from the feel of things?
> > > > > > > > *A*

The impassioned directness of the questioning, the refusal of ironic under-statement and avoidance of rhetoric, the redemption from cliché of proverbial wisdom—these qualities bespeak supreme poetic confidence.

The confidence is in language, in the poet's native tongue, but also in significant words of Latin and German and Welsh, the other languages formative of Britain within the West. Indeed one way in which, in *The Anathemata*, David Jones restores the rich diversity of Brut's Albion to the island is by using words that signify the coming together of traditions from without, and *their* coming together with traditions from within. But this statement does not begin to show how his words generate power and make Brut's Albion more than the dusty name it is in Selden, and akin, in its potency, to the Albion of Blake.

Language as David Jones uses it, embodies

> The adaptations, the fusions
> the transmogrifications
>   but always
> the inward continuities
>   of the site
>   of place.
>
> *A*, 'Middle-Sea and Lear-Sea'

His imagination works through 'the precision and exactitude' of his data, through words and names in which the past has been deposited, bedded and stratified but also through the metamorphic qualities of his words and symbols. The Roman roads, he observes in 'Rite and Fore-Time', 'are not independent of geology' (*A*, 71), and for him the relationship between geology, cultural history and language is more than a metaphor. His places are always firmly located in a particular physical landscape, but the overall effect which he creates is of place as a specific cultural reality, adapted to its terrain but unmistakably the creation of a particular people or mixture of peoples. There is consequently a tendency in *The Anathemata*, which deals so much with the beginnings, to restore the island to the forces which first shaped its culture, but this is often combined with images that prefigure its future development:

> Before the Irish sea-borne sheet lay tattered on the gestatorial
> couch of Camber the eponym
>   lifted to every extremity of the sky
> by pre-Cambrian oreos-heavers
>   for him to dream
> the Cambroges' epode.
> In his high *sêt* there.
>   Higher than any of 'em
> south of the Antonine limits.
> Above the sealed hypogéum
>   where the contest was
> over the great *mundus* of sepulture (there the *ver-tigêrnus* was)

  here lie dragons and old Pendragons
     very bleached.
  His unconforming bed, as yet
    is by the muses kept.
  And shall be, so these Welshmen say, till the thick rotundi-,
  ties give, and the bent flanks of space itself give way
     and the whitest of the Wanderers
  falters in her transit
     at the Sibyl's *in favilla*-day.
              'Rite and Fore-Time'

Camber is the name of a legendary Trojan, the eponym of Cambria. From *combrox*, the singular of *Combroges,* the word Cymry, the Welsh people, derives. The passage releases from the names the significance buried within them, legendary history, but one which signifies the Celts' European inheritance, and therefore animates the cultural landscape in depth, by disclosing 'a truth more real than the historic facts alone discover'. Other words invoke the Roman occupation, and Welsh Nonconformity. Different ages are juxtaposed, not statically, as though bedded in successive strata, but as forces contributing to the making of a culture, and this in turn is set in the context of the geological making of the landforms and the world's final destruction by fire. Here David Jones, with what we might call a philological imagination, reveals the creative processes buried in names, in the names of a man-made culture, and the created landscape to which it has been adapted. 'The dragons and old Pendragons' are then felt, not as ornamental or quaint emblems, but as dormant powers, which wait, like the mountains themselves, to heave into life. His is an active universe, no less than Wordsworth's, and an active culture.

  David Jones's historical sense is, no doubt, something other than the scientific attitude would allow the phrase to mean. It is, nevertheless, precisely a sense of the living past which honours its pastness, its otherness. In the short 'Angle-Land' section of *The Anathemata*, for example, the words used are a showing of the Anglo-Saxon reality they name, because they are—in Professor Piggott's fine phrase—'radio-active with history':

    Past where they placed their *ingas*-names
  where they speed the coulter deep
    in the open Engel fields
  to this day.
      How many poles
  of their broad Angle hidage
  to the small scattered plots, to the lightly furrowed *erwau*,
  that once did quilt Boudicca's royal *gwely*?

foam. Past where they urn'd their calcined dead from Schleswig over the

★ ★ ★

>On past the low low lands of the Holland that
Welland winds to the Deepings north of the Soke
past where Woden's gang is *gens Julii* for Wuffingas new to
old Nene and up with the Lark
past the south hams and the north tons
past the weathered thorps and
the Thorpe...

Again the words incant and re-present history as a process of making. The south hams and the north tons invoke the places they will name. Past and future are equally present here, but past and future are not confused. The Latin and Celtic words signify cultures temporarily superseded by the Anglo-Saxon invasions but which will bring something important to the continuous making of England. Indeed, the Anglo-Saxon element is presented as only one of several contributory to the making of Britain within the West.

Much of what I am trying to say could, perhaps, be said more simply: David Jones restores this island to the Britons, the Britons to their European and Christian inheritance; to the English he restores a sense of what actually lies under their feet and under their tongues, in the land, in words themselves. Put thus simply, however, the assertions are far too confident. For him, 'the unity of this island' was a reality, but one that he knew to be at odds with the generally accepted ideas of Britain in the twentieth century. Hence the prevalence in his writings of images of regeneration that are, nevertheless, dormant, potential. The 'corporate inheritance' restored in *In Parenthesis* is abstracted from the island itself. There is an increasing tendency in the subsequent writings to invoke Wales as the sole repository of 'the foundational things'. This is countered, to some extent, by the fact that his language is English, that he uses English together with significant words belonging to the other formative cultures—Welsh, Latin, German—and thus presents, in English, writings which signify the 'corporate inheritance'. (It may be noted that the comparative fewness of French words in the writings, and of references to the Norman Conquest, indicates the centrality of the Roman occupation to his idea of unity.) He uses, in addition, an English that often differs widely from standard middle class usage, and embodies as much as possible of the past, including the deposits of folk-lore and literature in which the Matter of Britain is stored. But the potentiality of Brut's Albion lies dormant; and of course it could not be otherwise, unless he were blinded to the present by nostalgia, which was not the case. The opposition between two forms of power, and order, presented in *In Parenthesis*, is developed further in the later writings; there is no shrinking from the implications for man-the-artist of his understanding of modern civilization, nor from the implications for those diverse cultures that survive; his attitude towards Welsh culture becomes increasingly defensive, and yet offensive, on the basis of the values which it is seen to embody; there is an increasing tendency for the writings to assume the forms of prayer and requiem.

'The Tutelar of the Place' is partly in the form of a prayer to the 'queen of otherness':

> When they proscribe the diverse uses and impose the
> rootless uniformities, pray for us.
>   When they sit in *Consilium*
> to liquidate the holy diversities
>   mother of particular perfections
>   queen of otherness
>   mistress of asymmetry
> patroness of things counter, parti, pied, several
> protectress of things known and handled
> help of things familiar and small
>   wardress of the secret crevices
>   of things wrapped and hidden
> mediatrix of all the deposits
>   margravine of the troia
> empress of the labyrinth
>   receive our prayers.

★ ★ ★

> In the December of our culture ward somewhere the secret seed,
> under the mountain, under and between, between the grids of
> the Ram's survey when he squares the world-circle.
> Sweet Mair devise a mazy-guard
> in and out and round about
> double-dance defences
> countermure and echelon meanders round
> the holy mound
>   fence within the fence
> pile the dun ash for the bright seed
>   (within the curtained wood the canister
> within the canister the budding rod)
> troia in depth the shifting wattles of illusion for the ancilia for the
> palladia for the kept memorials, because of the commissioners
> of the Ram and the Ram's decree concerning the utility of the
> hidden things.
>   *SL*

The words chosen ensure that the prayer might be that of a Celtic villager at the edge of the late Roman Empire, or an Anglo-Saxon under the Normans, or any ethnic group under a totalitarian regime; but they also speak the heart of a London Welshman who is painfully aware of the effects of 'our Engle-raum' upon this Brut's Albion. 'The Ram's decree concerning the utility of the hidden things' has wide application, but among its many meanings it refers unmistakably to the threat to Welsh culture of English civilization and the forces of which it is the medium. Understood thus, the Ram is no less terrible than 'the English minotaur' of Gwenallt's poem 'Rhydcymerau' (in Anthony Conran's translation) about the destruction of a Welsh community. In this poem, and elsewhere, David Jones presents the Celtic world during a period analogous to the present; but he also presents it under the form of an Otherworld and in the image of a protective womb. These images may provoke misunderstanding unless we perceive that the Wales of the writings, deep as its roots go into pre-Christian myth, is quintessentially an earth-rooted, Christian culture. Thus it is an Otherworld precisely in the sense that its things, its 'kept memorials', are numinous; their 'magic' is therefore a signifying power possessed by objects that are not purely functional, and by the culture and the land itself. And the womb does not symbolize a negative retreat upon the pre-natal darkness, or the death-wish, but rather the genius of place, the female principle under the form of guardian of 'the holy diversities'.

'The Sleeping Lord' identifies the regenerative myth with Wales in the form of an Arthur who is both 'the first of the sleepers of Pritenia' (*SL*, 71) and the figure belonging to 'true immemorial religion', 'the Lord of Order carrying a raid into the place of Chaos'. So 'the abiding myth of our people', evoked by the sleeping soldiers in France, perceived by the Lady of the Pool in 'the fathering figures' under the clay of London, is finally identified not with the island as a whole, but with a part of it which embodies the creative principle required to renew the whole. David Jones's Arthur is a type of Christ; he is also 'decidedly a Briton', a Briton, moreover, who incorporates 'the remembrance of Rome as a European unity'. When we look back over the writings, however, we can perceive that virtually all the materials relating to 'the unity of this island' are mediated by the Welsh sources or embodied by Welsh figures such as Dai, or Aneirin Lewis, or the boatswain from Milford. Since this is so, one cannot help seeing a painful irony inherent in David Jones's attempt to reconcile the duality of his inheritance in a creative unity, for in his view the unifying forces are contained almost entirely in a tradition other than the English one, which is represented as being at once separatist and colonialist. The question must finally be raised, therefore, although it cannot be answered here, whether he ever looked steadily at what a total resurgence of the Celtic cultures in this island might mean for the kind of unity in which he believed.

Neither in 'The Sleeping Lord' nor anywhere else does he place any rhetorical confidence in the regeneration, only

>   you never know *what* may be
>   —not hereabouts.
>   No wiseman's son *born* do know
>   not in these whoreson March-lands
>   of this Welshry.

Which is much the same as the Lady of the Pool's 'you never know, not with what you might call metaphysical certainty, captain: our phenomenology is but limited, captain'. And powerfully as 'The Sleeping Lord' ends, it ends nevertheless with another question:

>   Yet he sleeps on
>   very deep is his slumber:
>   how long has he been the sleeping lord?
>   are the clammy ferns
>   his rustling vallance
>   does the buried rowan
>   ward him from evil, or
>   does he ward the tanglewood
>   and the denizens of the wood
>   are the stunted oaks his gnarled guard
>   or are their knarred limbs
>   strong with his sap?
>   Do the small black horses
>   grass on the hunch of his shoulders?
>   are the hills his couch
>   or is he the couchant hills?
>   Are the slumbering valleys
>   him in slumber
>   are the still undulations
>   the still limbs of him sleeping?
>   Is the configuration of the land
>   the furrowed body of the lord
>   are the scarred ridges
>   his dented greaves
>   do the trickling gullies
>   yet drain his hog-wounds?
>   Does the land wait the sleeping lord
>   or is the wasted land
>   that very lord who sleeps?

Landscape of Fire

CHARLES OLSON took 'SPACE to be the central fact to man born in America'. I take place, and therefore historical time, to be the central facts to man born in Britain—since the middle of the last century, in particular, but also since Anglo-Saxon times, when elegy and a pervasive sense of those gone before, in a landscape of ancient ruins, became our dominant poetic modes. To these, before widespread secularization, one would have had to add an apprehension of the eternal, not as a subsidiary fact, but as interacting with these: it is a matter of how the things of place and time dance round the still point, of how they are shaped to embody the aspiration transcending them, of how their darkness interacts with its light.

Place and time are facts which can inhibit the poet's sense of movement, and allow the dust of familiarity to settle on all things. When religion in its traditional forms no longer makes them new, the religious sense will attempt to do so by other means. There are several ways in which English poets have perceived energy in their time-bound world, and released it in their writing, at the same time as they have seen the world afresh. It is not my purpose here to attempt an historical sketch of these several ways, but to indicate two which the poet under review has found available, and which converge in his work.

One way of releasing the energy which can seem depressingly like an immovable fossil fuel in English places is to enact, in presenting them, the historical forces by which their present forms were shaped. To show a culture in process of making, while celebrating its 'mature' images and artefacts, was one of David Jones's great achievements. He was both sacramentalist and vitalist; for him, the temporal dance might have gone awry, but the eternal pattern could not. Philip Pacey has learnt from David Jones; he has learnt from him about movement, though his sense of the sacred is not the same. He has learnt, too, from one of the finest books published in England during the sixties, Ronald Johnson's *The Book of the Green Man* (1967). Ronald Johnson in this book has, in fact, something in common with David Jones. As an American, he was an outsider in Britain: he was not obliged to see the place as all grey, as on a pre-colour television screen, or to assume that its local colours must be those of picturesque postcards, for tourist consumption. David Jones, for other reasons, was equally outside modern conventional ways of seeing Britain. In consequence, both were outside a limited sense of the real, and could see myth, literature, and history as presences, as sources of creative possibility, in the land and culture they had helped to shape.

In writing this, I am aware of the selectivity of all traditions, of the choices love makes and of its blindnesses, and that the myths and histories and literatures of these writers are not identical, or sources from which Philip Pacey has derived naively, without guiding ideas and biases of his own. The sixties was also a time when anyone in Britain concerned to see where we are living, as Pacey evidently was, would have been aware of the work of Raymond Williams, E. P. Thompson, W. G. Hoskins, writers who in their different but complementary ways have restored a common history to places where, for people brought up on books of kings and queens, the uncommon had long reigned. For anyone responsive to them, the sense of place was invigorated; and in Johnson and David Jones there was delight, dynamic movement, clarity of perception, at a time when the dominant English poetic landscapes were either pinched by diminished hope or contorted by displaced agonies or a limited idea of brute power. There were other exceptions, of course—in Charles Tomlinson, Roy Fisher and Geoffrey Hill, for example; but it is evident that for Philip Pacey, it was principally David Jones and Ronald Johnson who offered alternative principles, both of seeing and of composition, to those of the dominant models, Philip Larkin, Ted Hughes and Robert Lowell. Johnson has behind him Emerson and Thoreau, Whitman, Pound and Carlos Williams; like Snyder, he renders the quick of nature, finds the names of real things alive with their significance, quotes other seers extensively in his work, observes the measure of a reality, including the preternatural, that is other than his self. In *The Book of the Green Man*, with birdsong, cloud, wind, and water movements, changing light and shadow, the land whose presences are also perceived as a living energy comes alive. And Philip Pacey, responding to this American's gift to England, has his native resources also, some of which nourished Johnson—in Wordsworth and Coleridge (who affected Emerson's way of seeing, which he, too, applied to England), Blake and Clare, Ruskin, Kilvert and Jefferies, Hardy, Hopkins and Edward Thomas, and the realist and/or visionary landscape painters (seeing clearly with the eye is, within this tradition, often a visionary act): Constable, Samuel Palmer, Paul Nash, and again, David Jones. The list is by no means complete, but sufficient, perhaps, to sketch a broad tradition, a way of seeing, which connects (for example) Pound with an English poet he disliked, Edward Thomas. Charles Tomlinson saw this early on, and the stupidity of opposing English to American poetry, or vice versa, as if there were only two poetries. Pacey, too, has seen this in his way, not via Tomlinson, as far as I can judge.

Landscapes seen not as finished, but as becoming; landscapes seen as in particular lights and weathers they are: these are the main ways of seeing brought together in *Charged Landscapes*. Without copying other writers, but by understanding their principles of composition and making a new (but traditional) poetry by adapting them to his needs, Philip Pacey has united elements from vital movements in English and American writing. His contribution is to the endeavour to see clearly which as theme, process and morality has characterized what I find the most hopeful and the most exciting English and American poetry of recent years, though written by poets with diverse beliefs and techniques, and even opposing ideas of their different societies. *Charged Landscapes* is a cycle of twenty poems. The landscapes are variously rural and urban, mainly English, from all parts of the country, but with two from the Welsh border and one called 'Scotland'. It is a live and inspiriting book, which can help us 'to see again in a world washed/fresh and clean', because, as I have already suggested, Philip Pacey shows us what he sees together with the process of seeing it, the revelation as it is revealed, the 'charge' as it startles the poet whose active receptivity is one of its poles.

The first poem begins:

> From the eye of the Uffington White Horse
> the downs' every feature. Spur, combe
> and fluting; lifted by low sun
>
> waves of a fossil sea, surging again
> as wind through barley, breaking
> on Berkshire's plain. The hand of man
>
> who cleared scrub—yew and juniper; felled
> trees below, exposing to view this land's
> form, kept cropped by sheep and cultivation.
>
>   'Uffington'

It is obviously the poet standing on the eye of the hill-figure who sees, and renders what he sees with immediacy, by recreating the original act of seeing. By retaining immediacy at the same time as he slips the time-bound point of view, however, he creates the life-giving illusion that this view is indeed 'from the eye' of the ancient symbolic figure, which, with a dynamism and breadth of vision not measured by the poet's 'I' or 'eye', sees the essence of the landscape it is part of. First there are the downs' physical features, given their proper, shapely, terms—spur, combe, fluting; then a cosmic perspective opens with the advent of the sun, and this is connected with geological time, but with the vast temporal dimension as a present energy, 'surging again/as wind through barley'. The named plain then introduces 'the hand of man', its human shaping agent, and so history. All is movement here. We in turn have been moved in nine lines through a *made* landscape (I think by association both of what W. G. Hoskins has shown us, and of R. S. Thomas asking, in 'The View from the Window', 'what eye... ever saw/This work and it was not finished?'): a made landscape, charged with the cosmic, geological, and historical forces of its making.

Inevitably, the particular landscapes seen disclose, in themselves and in their relationships, a view of Britain. They show love of wild nature, and equal appreciation of peopled places, like Rochdale, Shaw and Oldham, which accepts the industrial as 'hospitable to us', without romanticizing them; understanding of landscape as, in part, a cultural phenomenon, interacting with nature to form an excitingly various land; a sense of power in the land, certainly an energy of recreative delight, but also a source of continuing creation.

None of this would convince if one didn't feel the reality of Philip Pacey's landscapes, their particularity as dynamic physical forms, subject to skyey influences. This arises initially from his experience as a walker, with bodily knowledge of his landscapes, and then from his gift for translating movements, shapes, and sensations into words. With dynamic rhythms, internal rhyme and half rhyme, assonance and alliteration, he creates verbal music and texture that excite the senses, carry one with the poems, and into the moving landscapes they embody and enact. His verbal daring can be humorous as well as expressive, too:

> barbed wire, strand after strand festooned
> with cobwebs drops of moisture cling to,
>
> as if with tents of silk sextillion spiders
> sought to soften spikes to harmlessness.
>   'North Stoke'

Philip Pacey finds train journeys as capable as walking of making things new, and 'King's Cross to Grantham' is one of his most dynamic charged landscapes:

> vast fields in stubble, hedged
>
> at horizons hung with high palls of smoke
> where cornstalks combines left,
> not ricks fired by Captain Swing, smoulder
>
> and flare. We lean into a bend—flickering combs
> of flame; across the carriage
> explosions at the corners of windows
>
> snatch at our vision as the train speeds on,
> upstage the finite, diminished sun
> lowering through haze of a thousand fires

> cauterizing England. A man, a boy,
> with burning brand igniting straw
> set light to Lincolnshire—there! there!
>
> and there! at every touch, this side,
> that side, of their purposeful striding.

This presents stubble-burning vividly, but does so, of course, as a condition of doing far more. A charge passes between the eyes of the man in the hurtling train and the activity seen outside: its significance is simultaneously perceived and created, in a single action. The burning is present, and recalls other fires that have 'cauterized' England, as in the Swing riots, but not as a nostalgic review, rather as a passing recognition of that tragic, searing energy. This landscape is too historical to be a pastoral, too present to be only historical; in an image used later in the poem, it is 'a landscape of fire'. Here are flux and dynamic movement, history and a visionary moment—an image of what life centred on time and place actually is. And if it be objected that this is only a lively rendering of stubble-burning seen from a fast train in Lincolnshire, England, then I would ask, as I think the poem does, what is the reality of those names, and the potentiality of life's dangerous and exciting energies in those places? The poem, like the whole book, is the work of a discoverer of things that quicken and live, in a country so dominated by tired ways of looking at place and time, that it often seems as though only dusty surfaces or standing fields can appear. All seems told, the places have been regarded so often, that habit stales everything; then a fresh eye, seeing as others have done, perceives what is really here, not an essence to be abstracted, but landscapes of fire, charges to be borne responsibly, in attentiveness, charges to be released.

North

NORTH is, among other things, a searching and self-critical exploration of the growth of a poet's mind. The first poem in Part 1, 'Antaeus', which is also an early one (1966), may be read, on one level, as a mythical statement of Seamus Heaney's origins as a poet. We may then see, both in the poem itself and in its relation to those which follow, the conflict from which his power and his remarkable poetic intelligence have developed. 'Antaeus' is a boast of the cave-dwelling giant, whose strength was revived whenever he touched the earth:

> I cannot be weaned
> Off the earth's long contour, her river-veins.
> Down here in my cave
>
> Girdered with root and rock
> I am cradled in the dark that wombed me...

But Antaeus is aware of the threat represented by Hercules should he plan 'my elevation, my fall'. 'Hercules and Antaeus', the last poem in Part 1, concerns the giant's defeat by the 'sky-born' hero, who killed him by holding him aloft, 'out of his element'. The poems between these two manifest one kind of power; those in Part II show the poet confronting the destructive forces unloosed by a particular social and political crisis, but without using the regenerative myth that encompasses his earlier treatment of the same theme. What this means for the collection as a whole may also be expressed by saying that Breughel is the presiding genius of the first part, while the horror of Goya's 'Shootings of the Third of May' dominates the second. Seamus Heaney refers to both artists, but I do not mean to imply that his ways of seeing are other than his own; only that he moves from a realism which is capable of depicting both the enduring values and the hard facts of a particular social pattern, and which works through historical and mythical elements, to a sense of appalled but helpless implication in a communal experience of terror; and from this to a consciousness of unheroic escape 'from the massacre' as 'an inner emigré'.

From the start, Seamus Heaney's poetic strength has been nurtured by the Antaeus-like qualities of his imagination. He too is a 'mould-hugger', one for whom the boglands of Ireland are, in the phrase of 'Kinship', 'ruminant ground', not terrain from which he is detached as either observer or celebrant, but 'outback of my mind'. If, at the outset, this relationship with his subject may have suggested certain simple virtues and themes, his concerns are now no less than 'the diamond absolutes' and Ireland's 'love and terror'. If Patrick Kavanagh's *The Great Hunger* (1942) is the only Irish poem with which his feelings for earth and labour can be sensibly compared, in another important respect his recent work demands comparison with Yeats's quarrel with his 'blind bitter land'. Coming from a very different background, and having very different attitudes, inclinations and beliefs from Yeats's, Heaney nevertheless explores his national identity at a depth and with a poetic confidence that quickly bring Yeats to mind. Yeats is also brought to mind by this book because Heaney's quarrel is now partly with him, and partly with himself. But it is not the voice or the imagination or the loyalties of Yeats's Ireland of which *North* is reminiscent.

Part II consists of poems that confront the tragedy of Ulster more personally than anything which this poet has published before. In my view, it is, for this reason, less effective than Part I, although Parts IV and VI of the emphatically non-Byzantine 'Singing School' belie this opinion. It seems to me that, even in Part II, where he writes of the divided north and of his own self-division metaphorically, using his primary imaginative sources, he writes both more powerfully and with more effective directness. The tragedy is far too deeply rooted in his Ireland, in himself, for it to be expressible in either purely political or self-consciously personal terms. It is both political and personal, of course, but it is the roots of politics and personality, not their manifestation in political event or autobiographical detail, that Seamus Heaney can write about most effectively. It should be said, however, that the poems in Part II, which show him to be more conscious of his role as a national poet than previous work, may also indicate the new directions that an augmented sense of responsibility could make him take.

For Seamus Heaney, the division between north and south, between England and Ireland as influences upon these societies, is perhaps known most intimately as tension between the nature of his experience as an Irish Catholic and the language in which he expresses it. Certainly, many of his recent poems have been concerned with words themselves, especially with the Irish and Viking and English histories of Ireland as they are stored 'in the coffered/riches of grammar/and declensions'. His imagination has always 'inclined to/the appetites of gravity'; mole-like in its instinct to feed from the darkness under the earth, which is also the darkness of the creative unconscious, it has come increasingly to burrow into language itself. But the former inclination is more than a metaphor for the latter. Words take possession of things; things and the words which name them are equally the stuff of an historical, national identity, so that to have knowledge of words is to repossess the formative things, some of them far back in time, of a poet and a people. Consider, for example, how in 'Bone Dreams' the word 'bone-house' leads him back down to 'ban-hus', to the root, through the later history of England:

> Bone-house:
> a skeleton
> in the tongue's
> old dungeons.
>
> I push back
> through dictions,
> Elizabethan canopies,
> Norman devices,
>
> the erotic mayflowers
> of Provence
> and the ivied latins
> of churchmen
>
> to the scop's
> twang, the iron
> flash of consonants
> cleaving the line.

The possession of Ireland by England, by the language of the English poets Spenser and Raleigh, a possession which invokes the sexual metaphor, is a theme which is felt as a subterranean (and sometimes explicit) presence in *North*, as it is in *Wintering Out* too. But in his use of that tongue, Heaney recognizes both the local variations which are inseparable from his own origins, and all the violence of exploitation and repression by which it was imposed upon his country. It is, I believe, at the level of this kind of awareness that he really does confront the tragedy of the north, and the paradox of his position as a poet in the English language. Descending into himself, into 'our mother ground', he speaks powerfully and movingly of the whole complex tragedy. As when he sinks his imagination into the mud of Dublin, where the keel of the Viking longship 'stuck fast', he is able to speak with a directness that his more overtly personal poems do not afford:

> I am Hamlet the Dane,
> skull-handler, parablist,
> smeller of rot
>
> in the state, infused
> with its poisons,

> pinioned by ghosts
> and affections,
>
> murders and pieties,
> coming to consciousness
> by jumping in graves,
> dithering, blathering.

In particular, 'Funeral Rites', 'The Grauballe Man', 'Punishment' and 'Kinship' have a power to move that comes from their realization, in depth, of the tragedy in which he knows himself to be implicated.

Terror was present in Seamus Heaney's apprehension of the forces of nature from the start. Nostalgia, 'a dream of loss/and origins', has never been the controlling emotion of his work; and yet he has been close enough to such feeling to want to place it critically, in the form of a myth. Antaeus, when Hercules lifts him up, 'is weaned at last'. Although his real powers are dead, in death he generates, for others, an illusion of power. Hercules 'lifts and banks' his body,

> high as a profiled ridge,
> a sleeping giant,
> pap for the dispossessed.

'Pap' has a double meaning, which Beckett too has used. For those without effective political and social influence, the past, both their origins far back in a 'mother ground' and their childhood, may come to seem the source of a superior strength. Antaeus is then their 'pap'; their father-figure, their childish fodder. If Heaney were not a poet who draws imaginative strength from the earth, from childhood and the Irish past, he would not have been capable of this searching insight into the illusive compensations of the 'dispossessed', those who possess a dream. But it is also, surely, a way of saying that he believes his poetic gifts to be impotent to help or heal his people. If so, it would be a statement hard to quarrel with on that level. On the other hand, it would be sad to think that he feels the need to escape from what has been, so far, the very source of his imaginative power, in order to become a more overtly political and social poet. 'Antaeus and Hercules' may be a valediction to the kind of poem on which, to date, his achievement rests. Whether or not this is so, it would be extremely foolish to underestimate the re-creative powers of a writer with his poetic intelligence.

Welsh Ambassador

IT IS the centenary this year (1972) of the birth of John Cowper Powys, who was born in Derbyshire and spent the last third of his long life in Wales. Last year an attractive early book by Louis Marlow on the personalities of the three writers, John Cowper, T. F., and Llewelyn Powys, was reprinted (it first appeared in 1936), and its title, *Welsh Ambassadors*, raises the main question about John Cowper Powys's position as a writer that I shall attempt to answer in this essay.

The frontispiece to *Welsh Ambassadors* is a family photograph. At the centre of the back row, smiling benignly, stands the Revd. C. F. Powys, a man of powerful physique. To anyone familiar with the autobiographical writings of his sons, John Cowper and Llewelyn, he is a figure of mythical proportions, an inarticulate Titan of sublimated instinctive energies. Seated in front of him, at the centre of the group, wearing a melancholy, rather tense smile, his wife is a no less striking figure. Their ten children (the eleventh died in infancy) are grouped around them. William, the youngest son, sits in the front dressed in a sailor suit. A leafy shrubbery forms the backcloth. One can only imagine that John Cowper Powys's wife, who completes the tableau, must have had interesting feelings in the midst of this singular company.

It is a Victorian family-portrait, arranged in a very English upper middle-class pose, symbolic of a vanished social order. Clichés of nostalgic or resentful feeling are drawn to it as naturally as an old photograph acquires its yellow tarnish. But the work of the three writers who were to emerge from this family reveals the truth underlying the conventional image: this is no bastion of the old order, symbolized by the father's untroubled gaze, but, like so many families, an alliance of tradition and rebellion, of rooted certainty in established values and what Hardy called 'the mind adrift on change', later, 'the ache of modernism', fortunate in this instance to be united in the old form by love. Hardy was a guest in this household; he, too, adhered to the old form of conduct though his spirit had been divested of its assurances. It is all so very English in appearance. Looking at it, one thinks of the thousands of elegies for Queen Victoria. Later, T. F. Powys rooted his powerful, disturbing parables in Dorset; Llewelyn Powys celebrated the earth of Dorset; John Cowper Powys set his early work, which means, in this context, the writing he was doing until well into his sixties, in the Somerset and Dorset of his imagination. Why, then, the title of this book, *Welsh Ambassadors?*

Llewelyn Powys suggested the title. It is based on the belief, upheld by Louis Marlow, that the remote Celtic strain in the Powys ancestry was reflected in the individual members of the family: 'Although Powys derivations may be more Saxon than Celtic, every member of this family is, actually, more Celtic than Saxon: in mind, in emotions, and in appearance'. The urbane Louis Marlow had more than a little of that enthusiasm for romanticizing on the subject of racial inheritance that characterized John Cowper Powys, who found Jewish and Negroid, as well as Saxon and Celtic, blood in his veins. However, the point at issue is not the degree of Celtic blood possessed by Powys, but the use to which he put his affirmation of Welsh ancestry. It is also important to note that the theme of diverse racial inheritances, and the ensuing conflict or interaction of diverse temperaments, is central to Powys's major novels.

Llewelyn Powys made a further observation about the proposed title:

> You would have, he wrote [to Louis Marlow], to add an explanatory note. 'The cuckoo, the most poetical and scandalous of all British Birds, is known in certain shires as the Welsh Ambassador because its arrival used to coincide with the appearance of Welsh field labourers who came into England to be hired in the summer hay field', or something of that kind.

It would be easy, but grossly unjust, for a sceptic to invert the point of this item of lore by describing John Cowper Powys as a cuckoo in the Welsh nest, especially after he had settled in Wales in the mid-thirties, steeping his mind in ancient Welsh tradition and extending his fiction into the Welsh past. To understand Powys's position clearly we must first understand how deeply the imagination of Hardy, one of his masters, was affected by the Celtic foundations of the mid south-west of England, despite his revival of the Anglo-Saxon name for the area: the sleepers under Rainbarrow are Celtic, as is much of Hardy's folklore. From an early age, Powys, inspired by his father's pride in their Welsh ancestry, and with much more selfconsciousness than Hardy, sought to possess his Welsh inheritance, both as knowledge and according to what he took to be its teaching about the nature of Imagination. Two English novels of his maturity, *A Glastonbury Romance* and *Maiden Castle*, are concerned more with disclosing the Celtic roots still alive in Wessex than with the Anglo-Saxon present. By and large the Anglo-Saxon present can be said to have represented for Powys the kind of materialism infecting all areas of life, not least the human being's concept of his own psychic and emotional resources, which he hated as a man and could do little with as a writer (he can deal with ideologies, not with politics). On the other hand, the Celtic was virtually synonymous with Imagination. (Irish tradition, in contrast to nineteenth-century materialism, meant something rather similar to Yeats.) Powys's romances of the Welsh past, *Owen Glendower* and *Porius*, signify the return to origins that all his work up to that point had been seeking.

But whose origins? The Welsh past of the novels is, for all his learning, the present of Powys's imaginative development: it set him free to be himself. Ever since boyhood Powys had lived through his Victorian upper-middle class upbringing, which in externals was as conventional as the family-portrait, with the conviction that he possessed more than ordinary powers; which he sought to identify with the role of the magician in ancient Welsh tradition, with Taliesin and Merlin. But he was protean, and had humour: the *Autobiography* deflates each pretension even as the reader is about to choke on it. What Powys did have, certainly, was imagination, a faculty that in his case, as in many others, needed the natural world, and man in living relation to the natural world, for its expression. Moreover, as the *Autobiography* shows, John Cowper Powys's life was in large measure a deliberate process of self-creation, and the development of his imagination was urged on to fulfil the nature of this faculty as he interpreted it in ancient Welsh tradition. All this is consonant with his fiction, in which there are as many visions of reality as there are minds to recreate the external world in their own image. He believed in the shaping spirit of Imagination, and his awareness of the mind's creative power is such that his writings appear to have a supernatural dimension. Whether or not they do venture into realms of the occult is not the question under consideration here, though it might be observed that a corollary to extreme belief in the mind's power to create its own world is scepticism about the existence of any power outside the mind. At all events, the strangeness of Powys's mature work derives largely from the fact that he is not limited by a narrow conception of psychic power but is aware of the mind's creative ability to dissolve and remake the external world in a way that is akin, in the view of such narrow conceptions, to 'magic'. Naturally, the consciousness of his characters reflects the bent of his own preoccupations, but the reach of his understanding as to what consciousness is and the forms it can take exceeds that of any other modern writer. But his remarkable insights into the way in which obsessive instincts can affect the individual's recreation of external reality into the image of their delight or anguish, and into how the mind can become the object of its contemplation, are contained largely within traditional novel forms. Hence his novels are a peculiar mixture, sometimes a mismarriage, of originality and bookishness, eloquence and fustian, poetry and poeticism. He can be disturbing to read in more ways than one.

However, it is by no means adequate to answer the question concerning the 'origins' to which Powys returns (and returns us) by relating them to a personal quest for imaginative freedom, though in an essay of this length one can only touch on their significance for Wales as a whole. Powys is a great regenerative artist; he renews contact with sources of energy—of the spiritual power formative of a particular culture and inherent in the individual psyche—to which the bias of modern civilization is hostile. He does this partly through the nature of his material, partly through the understanding he brings to it (and, I would argue, through its mysteries which he discloses). In *Owen Glendower* and *Porius* this material is what might be called *the other world* of Wales, to distinguish it from the interpretation of national identity which dominates modern Anglo-Welsh writing and can be seen, at its best, in the poems of R. S. Thomas rather than in the work of Powys or David Jones. This other world is also the world of the *Mabinogion*, especially of its most archaic element which lies, like an elusive, strangely beautiful, strangely disturbing shadow under water, beneath the medieval surface of chivalry and romance; the element, that is, which hypnotized Matthew Arnold and happily interrupted his tiresome generalities.

These are, in more than one sense, dangerous waters; but there is no excuse for ignoring them. They are elusive, a source of weird transformations, of marvels, myth, and magic, but constitute teachings about life and death and initiation whose roots are in the mind—the *Welsh* mind, Powys might say. (The stranger, whether Arnold or Powys, is often eager to delineate national characteristics in a way which the native, perhaps wisely, is shy of.) Here, such remarks are necessarily vague and for their elucidation one must refer the reader to the portraits of Merlin and Taliesin in *Porius*, and of the 'wizard', Glendower, in *Owen Glendower*. Here, too, one might be wise to leave the matter, were it not for the stultifying limitations imposed on so much modern Anglo-Welsh writing by its neglect.

To my mind, the magical element in literature, those rites of passage by which the great writer conveys one from the shallows of a custom-staled reality to deeper levels, is what we most need, at present, to be reminded of. In Anglo-Welsh writing, in the prose of Edward Thomas and the poems of Dylan Thomas, for instance, it is often nostalgia, especially for childhood, that supplies this element. Though the beauty of much of this writing is distinctively Anglo-Welsh, its emphasis of nostalgia at the expense of other kinds of magic, related to the imagination as a principle of growth and of psychic integration, gives it a certain wistful ineffectualness and invests it with a glamour of the lost cause. Wales, it seems, is a wonderful place in which to be young, and then, a good sad place in which to grow up remembering what it was like to be young.

The butt of these remarks is neither nostalgia nor the necessary social concern of modern Anglo-Welsh writing; it is, rather, the neglect of those writers whose domain is the other world of Wales. Such neglect creates for the writer a profound sense of historical discontinuity, whereby the present is erected upon a platform whose supports go no deeper than the last two hundred years. Great modern artists (Picasso), and sculptors (Henry Moore), as well as writers (Lawrence, Eliot, Joyce) have found in the archaic a fertility of ideas and images that increases their relevance to the present. The same is true of Powys, for whom the source of fertility was specifically Welsh. This, above all, is the reason why neglect of his work makes the study of Anglo-Welsh writing seem rooted in much shallower soil than it really is.

Undoubtedly, what Powys understood imagination to be in the ancient Welsh tradition, and in great literature as a whole, formed the support of his own imagination in an unpropitious century, and after his attempts to embody it in modern societies, albeit incorrigibly Powysian and conceived in terms of archaic elements, he was drawn more and more to its source in the Wales of *Owen Glendower* and *Porius*. It is in the *Autobiography* that his art works most successfully in reviving the modern mind from its narrow and suicidal self-conception. Returning to the frontispiece to *Welsh Ambassadors*, a reader of the *Autobiography* sees the formal group in a unique light. The portrait dissolves; it is no longer a tableau of fixed social attitudes, but a pattern of living human relationships. Beside the strong elemental figure of the father, with his pagan zest for life informing a simple Christian piety, the eldest son is a like compound of natural forces, but wavering, protean, more mist than earth, his consciousness turned inwards upon a world of sensations, ideas, and turbulent psychic conflicts that is utterly remote from the father's concept of reality and yet draws its power from him. An aspect of the nineteenth century's version of itself, captured in the photograph, becomes something rich and strange, powerful and disturbing; which is what happens when a great writer's imagination works its alchemy upon conventional images of reality. To effect such transformations Powys needed the support of his Welsh inheritance, of what he believed the secret of that inheritance to be. Thus empowered, he transforms his reader's idea of the mind's resources, and therefore of the image of man and his ability to reshape the world that materialism deadens and makes desperate. His idea of Wales enabled him to step outside the narrow social world that the photograph portrays, rigid but shadowy in its shades of grey, and to disclose the strange life, rich in colour and light, underlying its flat surface. Yet Powys remains largely unread, and while he remains unread there are clichés, which his writings alone can dissolve, that continue to dominate mundane concepts of what individual identity can be. To leave a great writer unread, even if to read him provokes exasperation and revolt, is a culture's self-inflicted wound.

The Bass Note

> And the whole wonder of our Mother appeared unto thee, and the vision came unto thee, and said, 'It is good.'
> Through all time should this word of the Truth be remembered above all words.
> *An Interpretation of Genesis*

The word is about the earth, 'our Mother', and it is one of two closely associated words that must stand at the head of this essay to name T. F. Powys's fundamental affirmation and also that they may go on echoing where my necessarily limited focus of attention might otherwise seem to deny them. The other word is 'bless', addressed by Powys at the end of *Soliloquies of a Hermit* to Christian writers of the transition between 'the broken flesh and rotten carcass of human despair' and 'the New Heaven and the New Earth':

> ...let them bless the maiden and the young man that again loiter through the mead, for it is now evening, on their way home from the tavern; and let them bless the naughty child that lingered for one more solitary dance alone on the Green after all the others had gone.

It is really himself whom he addresses. Powys is the writer of this transition, looking forward and back; learning how to reconcile the goodness of Creation with the existence of evil; learning how to bless.

I

The Revd Henry Neville is one of the two characters—the other is his spiritual brother, Henry Turnbull—with whom T. F. Powys thinks and feels in *Mr Tasker's Gods*. But even if this were not so, there would still be abundant reasons for knowing that the following passage voices the author's intentions as well as his character's literary preferences:

> Mr Neville was not a great scholar, but he understood the soul of an author and he knew what he liked in a book: and that was the kind of deep note that Bunyan calls the ground of music, the bass note, that modern culture with its peculiar conceit always scoffs at. There was, besides this bass note, a certain flavour of style that he liked, a style that in no way danced in the air but preferred clay as a medium.

The terms used here are not the currency of 'modern culture with its peculiar conceit'. But not all moderns exhibit this vice, and it is not

Powys's celebrated irony alone that makes his mature art sophisticated in a distinctively modern way. This passage is itself more than the apprentice work of an artist who would become one of the most subtle modern stylists. Its central metaphor relates literature to music, a purer medium than language for intimating an order we may hear but cannot comprehend. Then 'a certain flavour of style' returns us to the senses of smell and taste, and by emphasizing their characteristic elusiveness, forms a link between metaphors that would otherwise contradict each other, when the tendency of music to dance in the air is brought down to earth by 'clay as a medium', a singularly palpable natural material, tacky and malleable. Thus the passage does more than sketch large gestures; in an as yet incompletely mastered medium, it partially sounds the note and enacts the style of which it speaks. Given the artist's skill in deploying the religious associations of his metaphors, we do not ask how a writer can make music from clay. Similarly, it is Powys's subtle artistry that enables a great mystic, an apparent anachronism, to express his vision in the forms of modern English fiction.

Henry Neville is a priest. Priests are legion in the novels and stories of T. F. Powys, where the figure is as important as the magician is in John Cowper Powys's writings. Many are false priests, ranging from the mildly harmful, who may change for the better, to agents of the Devil. Others are presented affectionately and with approval. They are capable of love. They may have a simple faith in Christ and live in 'humilitude', or they may be sceptics or even heathens, with a large measure of kindness. In either case, they embody some or all of Powys's moral values. Some are ordained priests and some are not. All are, in one way or another, fools.

It is more difficult to know whether any of them is a true representative of God. Of Christ, yes: Mr Hayhoe, for example, is certainly His representative, but Christ and God are rarely, if ever, one and the same in Powys's writings.

Powys is a moralist and a metaphysician. His morality and his metaphysics are, of course, related, and in any case I use the terms here for the sake of convenience; they must not obscure the fact that his art is their medium, a medium of revelation, which makes us see by delighting and moving us. But while his morality could be described, and is deep enough for Powys and simple enough for any one to live by, his apprehension of the Truth—the word he uses in *An Interpretation of Genesis* to avoid confusion with conventional images and ideas of God—is frequently reflected in his writings in ways that evade such nets as 'immanence' and 'transcendence', and even his own idea of conflict between Christ and the Father, and his apparently supernatural characters. Whereas John Cowper Powys creates a fictional multiverse to signify the multiverse, Theodore Powys creates a temporal world that opens on the limitless and the eternal. He uses his imagination to illustrate and confess its limitations, leaving us and himself in darkness, with faith if we have it, but knowing that even darkness is a human image of the unknowable. I think this is the metaphysical dimension of the moral virtue of 'humilitude', exemplified by the worm in 'The Blind Hen and the Earthworm':

> 'One of the first lessons that we are taught in our childhood is that of humilitude. We are told that we are nothing, and we are glad to believe it.'
> 'Surely that's easy,' said the hen, 'for a worm!'
> 'But 'tis with that nothing that God works,' replied the other.
>
> Fables

In *Soliloquies of a Hermit* Powys calls himself a priest, and interprets the priestly nature with a dramatic variation and combination of passionate involvement and scepticism. Here, we are at once in a world of paradoxes, inversions or original interpretations of conventional word usages and ideas, affirmations, negations and re-statements of belief.

> Am I a fool? Is not a fool the best title for a good priest? And I am a good priest. Though not of the Church, I am of the Church. Though not of the faith, I am of the faith. Though not of the fold, I am of the fold;... I am without a belief; a belief is too easy a road to God.

In this book, the idea that 'a fool [is] the best title for a good priest' gives an unironical meaning to the word 'good' and marks a change of emphasis from *An Interpretation of Genesis*. There, only one kind of priest is said to exist, and he is false. His wish is to be 'in the place of the Truth' and he interposes his falsehood between man and the Truth. In doing so for gain, he indulges in a particularly monstrous way the habit Powys sees all men as having: they make the object of their self-interest, desires and instincts a god, while even the good must necessarily conceive God within the limits of their understanding. 'In man a false desire ever bringeth him a false god', and man 'createth his god like to himself'.

This habit is deemed to be truly universal. In Powys's fiction all creatures, and the things he animates, devise a metaphysical system according to their natures and circumscribed by their limitations. For example, there is the mouse made homeless by Mark Only's plough:

> A mouse who had made its nest there, reasoning, no doubt, that land in that state could only have been intended by the creator of all things—to the mouse this creator was a rat—as permanent pasture. But the plough had turned over the little house, and the mouse became an infidel.   *Mark Only*

And each of Powys's characters—it is the basis of his characterization—
is obsessed by an idea; each inhabits the lesser or greater circle, harmless
or harmful to himself and others, of a consciousness turning round the
god he has made. (I use the masculine pronoun because Powys's women
and girls, though obsessed, should really be considered separately: they
cannot be usefully sketched in these general terms.) This god may be a
herd of pigs, or money, or lust, or ·'God', or something equally
extraordinary, but whatever it is, it will denote the nature of its
worshipper. ''Tis a world of wanting', says Mr Bugby in *Innocent Birds*,
(and he should know). Powys depicts a multitude of 'wanters', many of
whom, like Mr Clowes in the story called 'The Wanter' (*Captain Patch*),
discover that man cannot possess anything, not even his coffin—'that
we hold only in trust for the worms'. God's gift of death is central to
Powys's thought, not usually as a morbid preoccupation, but as the
focus of his mysticism; the gate between all that man is, and the God
whom he cannot conceive. Death is certainly absolute in the sense that
man can imagine only in terms of his existence.

Powys uses his characters' gods to illustrate their moral,
psychological and metaphysical implications and to create a wide range
of comic and tragic effects. He is a master both of pathos and of horror.
He shows deep, sympathetic insight into madness and he does not
measure sanity as the world does. With regard to the likes of Mr Bugby
and Mrs Vosper, he conveys a lively sense of diabolic possession by the
gods of their nature. God and the gods are all destroyers. Though there
are times when, for my taste, he overplays comic absurdity, he always
seems to have a reason for doing so. In *Innocent Birds* Mr Pim, though a
father, is for ever looking for someone to tell him how children are
made. I find this tiresome, yet, as Powys observes, procreation *is* a
mystery.... *The Dewpond* shows movingly and subtly the consequences
of Mr Gasser's deification of his credulity. In *God*, little Johnnie Chew
takes his father's hat to be God.

This story exemplifies Powys's mature art and his psychological and
metaphysical subtlety. We listen respectfully to the thoughts of John
Chew:

> Everywhere, where a man believes God is, there He is. God is no
> respecter of holy places; a mouse-hole may be heaven. There is
> nothing so small or so common that may not contain the whole of the
> Godhead. God is in no chuch or state; He is exactly and truly where
> the most simple think He is.   *The Two Thieves*

The word is surely Powys's as well as John Chew's. Is it his last word on
the subject? It may be. The hat is indeed the true provider, when,
'sacrificed', it discloses the money John's father has concealed in its
lining. Is there any reason why a comically absurd fictional ending

should not confirm a spiritual truth? The story may itself be just such a mouse-hole as that mentioned above, providing we are not too wise to its folly. Or we may conclude, as some do, that Powys was himself a sceptic. On the evidence of my readings I think otherwise: the darkness, though absolute, is everywhere too numinous for him to be fixed even in such a belief. He is gentle with his simple characters' faith, and fool enough not to be cunningly dogmatic, by depicting faith as an exclusively psychological phenomenon filling its objects with itself.

Yet 'a belief is too easy a road to God'. Belief beats the highway and leads to the images of 'child man', as Powys calls him in *An Interpretation of Genesis*—and all his characters are either child man or projections of child man's imagination. Not all of these images are false, not by any means, as *God* for example shows. But the priest who is without a belief is correspondingly more open to 'the mystic fear'. The good priest is a fool because he does not reason in the way most men do, from themselves to God, but attempts to know himself and others as moved by God:

> Man is a collection of atoms through which pass the moods of God—a terrible clay picture, tragic, frail, drunken, but always deep rooted in the earth, always with claws holding on to his life while the moods pass over him and change his face and his life every moment. The people of the earth are clay pieces that the moods of God kindle into life.   *Soliloquies of a Hermit*

It is, of course, impossible to see man as God sees him, while the great mystics, when uttering their apprehension of God, attempt to transcend language, and frequently use, as Powys does, images and symbols of light and darkness, fire and water, and speak paradoxically of death as life. But Powys is the good priest as artist, whose priestly duty is 'to dig in the clay through which the moods of God pass' and to 'foretell how the clay pieces will behave when the mystic winds blow through them', and whose artistic duty is to make the clay pieces. His thought is biblical yet also originally interpretative, viewing the Bible as our greatest 'story-book', or series of 'pictures', of figures moved by mystic winds that no words can trap. He is himself accordingly a maker of pictures. As novelist he makes a world with words: as good priest he makes it picture a reality beyond words. He attempts what to the rational mind seems impossible—like sounding the bass note with clay as a medium.

II

... new life ever wrestleth with the old and obtaineth life therefrom. Jacob wrestled with the genius of his forefathers and forced a blessing from that genius. We likewise have our forefathers in us, and we carry their burdens. With a great wrestling must we wrestle with them and force a blessing from them. *An Interpretation of Genesis*

Blessings received in living with a sense of the holy, and given again in his art—this is the act of Powys's maturity, but it was not made possible except by a prolonged and painful struggle of the kind described here. He was one in whom the dominant consciousness of a materialistic and conventionally pious age broke. He wrestled with the Bible, with writers in the mystical tradition, and it is clear to me that he went back to these, not only because of his upbringing and inclinations, but because the Church's orthodox ideas and its accommodation to an unjust and repressive society broke in him, while the new thought to which he was open, together with the fact of the Great War—and it is surely significant that his first novels, with their sense of savage cruelty and destructiveness, were written then—cast all into doubt, smashing conventional images of man, nature and God. His harsh satire on the ecclesiastical establishment recalls Hardy, but in his struggle partly to find and partly to create alternatives to the dominant order of thought and belief in his outward-looking society, he is more akin to Lawrence. Fabulous as his creations are, we should not overlook either his specific, damaging critique of English society or the alternatives he offers to the prevalent materialistic and idealistic modes of Western thought.

To Powys, man is again a mystery, broken out of his shell of customary concepts. He apprehends him in his early novels as deeply and unconsciously involved with the mysteries of God and Nature. In consequence *Black Bryony* is as it were his *Rodmoor*. It is a novel in which thought and technique are inchoate, and the connections between nature, sex, religion, and sin rather confusing and morbid; yet it is interesting, too, both for what it partially achieves, and for its disclosure of conflicts which are less visible in his mature art because it largely reconciles them. In the first three novels in particular, (which belong together, though *Mark Only*, a fine novel, is mature Powys artistically if not in vision), the characters are lived by a terrible force which the good may control in themselves but which the others do not even try to, thus maliciously destroying the good, and in some cases blindly destroying themselves as well. Self-destruction, most often by drowning, is however a dominant theme of Powys's mature work, developing in relation to his death mysticism and his treatment of obsessions. In the depths of their imaginations there are fascinating differences and affinities between Theodore and John Cowper Powys.

This terrible force, which Henry Neville's Christ suffers with man, Powys sometimes calls 'God'. This is 'The Ancient of Days' which possesses the tramp in *Mr Tasker's Gods*, 'the monster from below, the immortal beginning and ending of man's nature, ... even the everlasting mud'. In *Soliloquies of a Hermit* Christ is 'the stranger upon earth, He who was not afraid to call the terrible moods "Father", to take them into His life, to bear with them, to love them'. He dared 'to fall before His Father's terrible mood of blind rage working in men'. Though Powys's conception of this God is not, and could not be, wholly consistent and clear, he evidently felt Him, and found Him truly a savage God. The mellowness of the later novels, beginning with *Mockery Gap*, is then due in part to his ability to hold the balance between love and terror, or almost to resolve the conflict. He even comes to play with the idea of God.

Mockery Gap effects a partial resolution in a symbolic form, where the fisherman, a Christ-figure with his net of love, is the only character to live in harmony with the sea, as if he has learned to call the sea, focus of the fears of all and the longings of some, destroyer of all that man is, 'Father'. *Kindness in a Corner* is Powys's kindest novel partly because it virtually identifies Christ with God. Mr Turtle, however, thinks otherwise:

> 'Is there no way, then, to rid yourselves of your fear of death?' asked Mr Dottery. 'Cannot you trust in God?'
> ''Tain't wise to put one's trust in a murderer,' replied Mr Turtle.

The effect is comic, without suggesting either the nerve of cruelty in God, man and nature associated with this idea in the earlier work, or any sense of a tired, death-wishing, repentant God-figure such as we find in *The Only Penitent* and *Mr Weston's Good Wine*. *Kindness in a Corner* also contains, together with the finest dramatic meditations on death in Powys's writings, the following noble and witty passage, uniting Christ and God:

> God is still a carpenter. It was not for nothing that He was received into the family of Joseph. He can dovetail events, He can measure time, He can cut out a plank, so that it exactly fits the roof where He wishes it to go. He can do more than that. He can turn sawdust into bread. He can take a rude and knotty log—such as John Bunyan was—and plane him away until He gets a smooth surface to write His will upon, yet is able to leave the hard knots below, for He was never one to spoil by Art the rough matter of Nature. God knows how to use a jack-plane.

Far from ever mocking Christ, Powys devotes some of the most lyrical passages in his writings, notably in *Soliloquies of a Hermit*, to celebrating Him. Powys is like Mr Vardy in *God:* there are two things he never makes fun of—'poverty and love'. But like Mr Vardy he will 'even poke fun at death in a sly manner' and in his mature work he is one whom 'the thought of God often amuses'. Indeed Mr Vardy believes that God 'wishes to look a little silly at times just to make them [his children] laugh'.

'The true God,' Mr Vardy used to observe, 'must be a very foolish fellow, and as simple as any silk hat. He would gladly cover the heads of all mankind with His blessings, only none will permit Him to do so, for men only wish to make God as proud as themselves, and as righteous. The fools!' said Mr Vardy. 'What do they know about God?' *The Two Thieves*

In *Soliloquies of a Hermit* Powys writes, 'I do not object to any kind of story ... but it must be something with a soul. If it be a story, let it have a touch of human blood about it; what I want is a real mind's battleground, with sweat and agony.' His early novels are such a battleground, but his later ones are his playground, where humour and seriousness are indivisible.

Mr Weston's Good Wine is a comic masterpiece, with humour that is alternately broad and gentle, whimsical and subtly ironic. It is also a measured, beautiful and melancholy meditation on transience and death; a lyrical celebration of love and a terrible judgment on those who would destroy its erotic innocence; a satire, alternately loving and savage, on human follies. But above all it is an affectionate but disquieting comedy of man's traditional personification of God. This makes it quite different as allegory—if that is what it is—from *The Pilgrim's Progress*, where Bunyan's meanings are easy to decipher because his doctrine is unequivocal, and different again from a work like *Paradise Lost* which attempts a portrait of God as He is.

Who, after all, is Mr Weston? First, a character in a novel, the one who, together with his creator, most frequently reflects on the nature and power of art, and who says that it is wrong to be 'so firm a believer in the Bible' as Cowper was, 'for no poet should ever believe the words of another, however true he may think his own'. He is himself an author, with an author's vanity. His name is borrowed from *Emma*, from no knightly hero, but from a jovial, decent, limited fellow. So as author of the Bible and of Creation, he is still T. F. Powys's tribute to Jane Austen. His literariness as both character and fictional writer is emphasized, recalling John Cowper Powys's technique of calling attention in his fictions to their fictional nature, and hence to the destructive and creative power of imagination. Once again, but here in a consummate form, Powys is making wonderful comedy from traditional images of God deriving from the Bible and our childish pictures. Mr Weston had, as he tells Tamar, to leave 'much of the truth' out of his book in conforming to 'a capricious and ignorant public'. He is conscious of having sinned against true art. Powys on the other hand has necessarily to omit much of the truth, for he is a simple and foolish man who does not pretend to know it. Instead, he pictures the limits of imagination, thus both pointing to the unknowable reality and showing the 'humilitude' in which man acknowledges himself a creature, incapable of knowing his supreme Creator. There is, however, a knowable supreme reality—Christ's spirit—and I suggest that this is the true hero of the novel, working through Luke Bird and others, but above all, through the supernatural wine merchant's repentance.

III

Almost every passage in Powys's mature writings repays the closest attention. I have chosen to look at extracts from a short chapter of *Mockery Gap,* both because this novel is still curiously undervalued, and for reasons that should become obvious.

Chapter 4, 'A Warning', begins:

> The hill, or Mockery cliff as it was usually called by those who lived near, might have smiled, could a hill smile, at the fine visitors who had peopled it and then departed, leaving only their wheel-marks, and a scented handkerchief dropped by Miss Ogle, behind them.

The anthropocentric view of the hill is immediately qualified by juxtaposing it with clauses indicating the hill as it is. The former view is given by the naming of the hill—'Mockery cliff as it was usually called by those who lived near'—and the fancy that it can be personified—'might have smiled, could a hill smile'. The author himself personifies the hill, but in the perspective given by a way of seeing that sets man against land and sea, not land and sea in the fanciful and self-centred view of man. The tokens left by 'the fine visitors' bespeak their alien and insignificant presence, and make 'fine' ironical.

We are next shown the village below, where 'the land and the cottages grow into one another' and buildings may be seen 'if carefully looked down upon'. These include the vicarage and church which 'had settled meekly in the folds of the valley as hardly to be noticed, and even when seen they only appeared to point to Mr Pink's stone house that stood by the church lane, and to say that "it shouldn't have been there".' Hardly noticeable even on this portion of the earth, the ecclesiastical buildings are related ironically to Mr Pink, a truly meek man, of whom orthodox religion disapproves, thus making the word 'meekly' applied to them signify hypocrisy.

The next three brief paragraphs use a light but subtle irony to place man and his faith in the context of the cliff's geological movement inland from the sea, in 'one of God's moments'. Powys continues his personification of the hill in a way that detaches it from man's measurements of time and the world around him in terms of his own assumed centrality. Then the tone deepens:

> The mere daytime of prettiness departed with the town visitors, and now that they were gone the true look of the land, that had been hidden from them, came forth again to be seen by those who have eyes to see. The blind-cow rock, that alone of all natural objects had never been beguiled by the sunbeams into looking pretty, now took upon it as the sun declined, giving the true bass note to the colours of the evening, the blackness of despair. The blind cow now began to spread out her influence further than herself, the waves that struck the rock became intense and living. Its dead state, as the abodes of the dead will sometimes do, reached out hands to form, to grave, and to portray, and to cast over Mockery the feelings and the fears of the night.
>
> Clouds that earlier in the day had been but shining vapour, now became real and yet more real and grew sensibly darker. The cliff, the fields below, the church that waited for the night, even the tiny shining of the little water-brooks, were beginning to express the supreme loveliness of lonely silence—of the beauty that dies.
>
> Shadows, born of the shadow of the blind cow, began to creep here and there like monstrous toads and thick vipers. The shadows became more and more monstrous as the sun dropped, while some amongst them now showed a likeness to him that is called Man, a dweller upon the earth.
>
> And now the sea, more than any other emanation of eternal truth, changed its face. The sea darkened, the dainty spaces above the waters where the light was began to take up the shadows of the deep and to wear them as a garment, while the tumulus upon the cliff watched as if glad that the evening was come.

The passage immediately recalls Hardy's personification of Egdon Heath in *The Return of the Native* (1878), by which he conveys both its utterly non-human character and its accordance in certain moods with man's nature, as he interprets it. There is more than recollection, there is overwhelming evidence of strong influence. And Theodore Powys, like John Cowper, was influenced by more than Hardy's evocations of the mystery of nature. But here, as elsewhere, what we see is not an imitation of Hardy but a passage that though bearing the marks of his influence, is in itself and in context distinctively Theodorian.

Powys sounds the bass note here even as he names it, relating it to 'the blackness of despair'. But despair is too limiting to express all that he evokes, as, with a change of cadence, colour and tone, and using natural objects and elements with their biblical associations, he shows us time in a God-like perspective and reaches down to the ground of these forms of rock and sea, darkness and light. This is 'the true look of the land... to be seen by those who have eyes to see'. The chapter as a whole illustrates different ways of seeing and the importance of having eyes to see the true look, not of the land alone, but of 'Man, a dweller upon the earth', who is subject to time and natural processes, not their master. Yet the central elemental symbol is the blind-cow rock. This might be taken to intimate the blindness of the First Cause, a blindness giving rise to despair in one who perceives it, and therefore the perishing nature of himself and of all things. He might be thought to perceive despair as man's element, arising from the blind and obdurate ground of the flux of being. I do not myself think that it does intimate this. Powys is certainly profoundly conscious of time and hyper-sensitive to its manifestations and its effects on nature and man, and some of his finest passages, especially in *Mr Weston's Good Wine*, *Innocent Birds*, and *Fables*, are lyrical and melancholy concentrations of the seasonal cycle in a measured flight of images, and of man's life, fleeting as a shadow. Yet time is for him a mystery which he almost always presents as partially concealing and partially revealing a deeper mystery. As here, when the sea washing about the 'dead state' of the blind-cow rock which makes its waves 'intense and living', intimates eternity, while death, which has the same effect on life, cannot see the element in which it stands.

Powys personifies these things no less than Miss Ogle does, whose name describes her way of looking; but his personifications carry his melancholy and dread, expressing the vision of one who knows despair, 'lonely silence', 'the beauty that dies', the relation of life—imaged as being beautiful, delicate, monstrous, precarious—to death; who sees Man as a shadow deeply implicated in these, a shadow who can be monstrous and is not essentially what he conceives himself to be, but subject to 'the feelings and the fears of the night'. It is a mystic's vision, conveyed poetically, and despite the interpretation I have offered, no complete or wholly rational philosophy can be abstracted from it. The passage invokes 'eternal truth' without reducing it to an impossibly neat or logical meaning. Perhaps the closest we can come to saying in other words what Powys sounds and shows is to quote another, equally irreducible, passage:

'And he was afraid, and said, How dreadful *is* this place! this *is* none other but the house of God, and this *is* the gate of heaven.'   (Genesis 28: 17).

Yet in citing this, we have also to bear in mind another passage, which I shall quote later, concerning 'the golden gate of the grave'.

The chapter then returns from Man seen against this background to characters in the novel, and from the bass note to comedy which echoes its significance. The characters are thought of by the spirit of an ancient king hovering about the tumulus. One is a meddlesome know-all, for whom the spirit has no love; another is a greedy farmer who aims to dig for treasure in the tumulus. Another is a comic simplification of Powys himself.

This is Mr Caddy, whose name, perhaps not accidentally, recalls by association the words quoted by Sylvia Townsend Warner, (included in the extract from her work published in Kenneth Hopkins's *The Powys Brothers*, 1967), from an incident when Violet Powys 'broke into one of Theo's bouts of dilly-dallying with the exclamation: "Oh, get along with you, you old tea-pot!" ' But whether this recollection is relevant or not, Mr Caddy is certainly one of Powys's amusing self-caricatures. He tells stories, 'all of which contained night-time or, as Mr Caddy would have said, bedtime matters'. And he would sometimes 'mention his betters'.

> 'They do say,' Mr Caddy had been heard to remark, 'that wold God be everywhere—but 'E bain't where I be, and that I do know. Parson do a-preach of, an' even Mr Pink 'ave a-named 'E; and some do tell that 'twere God who made the wide roaring sea, and the more fool 'E to make en, so I do say. But I do believe,' and here Mr Caddy would wink slyly, 'that 'E did a-make each pretty maiden.'

Thus the chapter moves from the departure of its characters leaving the land and man's presence there to be seen as they are, to a Godlike view of man and the elements in time, back to the novel's characters, including a gently self-mocking portrait of the writer who has created this movement. The 'warning' is of the spirit's enmity to the greedy farmer, but it is universal too. As Powys frequently says or shows, 'we all feel so safe in the world', but—'How dreadful *is* this place!'

Humour and 'humilitude' are closely associated in Powys, for with humour he mocks himself and his designs, and takes us from the sublime to the ridiculous and back again, each being equally a way of resigning himself and his fictions to that which is beyond them, unknowable and unimaginable:

> And then as the light of day wanes and the darkness gathers, and we behold the far reaches of the deep, we are left to contemplate the grand vista of eternity. Then the dark waters gather tumultuously about the golden gate of the grave, behind which stands the Name, spoken with holy dread by all generations of mankind.
>
> Spoken with awe unfathomable. For whatever we may think of the injustice, the cruelty, the pain here upon earth, the Name, and the terror and love of it that hides so silent behind the tomb, must for ever hide, too, the ultimate truth. God, for ever and everlasting, life without end—God. *Mockery Gap*

The sea as a symbol of eternity we may be able to fathom, but not the awe that knows how dumb are its own finest symbols to utter the reality behind the Name. The silence of Mr Dottery, in *Kindness in a Corner*, may be the only possible answer to the question Mr Turtle asks about eternity: 'And what be that?' It is, however, silence named in a novel, and for Powys his mature art is both a sounding of and a playing upon the surface of a mystery which is not art, but which art may make us aware of.

We fancy ourselves as wise as the old gentleman who holds up his hand and points to heaven and its amusements that await the good.

We hold out our hands too and show the world Mockery Gap, and point out that there are pretty pebbles to pick up along the sea-shore.

Pebbles, that from the point of view of the Author of all things—and bow to Him we had better, or we may rue the omission—may as well be looked at as anything else that He has made. All life is but a looking, so why not stare at Mr Roddy?

Or, we might add, Mr Weston, or Tinker Jar, or even wise sexton Truggin. For all are the 'pretty pebbles' made by their great author from the clay of which he is himself made. Or 'a picture' which, as Mr Solly thinks of the passage of time, 'can show a vaster and a grander one behind it'. Powys's art is one great picture with many scenes, many tragic figures and more comic ones, which makes us see what we cannot see, and feel the source of terror and love: 'God, for ever and everlasting, life without end—God.'

A Seeing Belief

THERE are passages in which the dominant themes of *Outside the House of Baal* are revealed starkly, as in the scene in a London chapel during the Second World War, where the preacher urgently addressing a small congregation is interrupted by the siren. It is not the last words of his unfinished sermon—'The whole world will have to kneel...'—that bring most of his auditors to the floor, but the silence before the explosion of a flying bomb, which, falling close by, damages the chapel. Earlier he has asked, 'What if the love of power was really confronted with an organized power of love?'

The ironies are pointed, but are not heavy nails driven into the coffin of Christian efficacy by a despairing moralist. The preacher has borne witness, as has the congregation, which includes the hero of the novel and the son who most resembles him, good men, who suffer, and make those they love suffer, for their principles. The siren, though 'fixed to the clock tower of the town hall', announces a decisive moment, but not the end of time.

A conflict between the love of power and the power of love is at the heart of the novel. Revealed thus starkly at times, it is complex in its actuality, because shown in the living experience of individuals, in a society becoming ever more complicated in its multiplication of powers of organization, communication, and destruction. The problems of communication and community, which are intimately related to this conflict, are themselves inseparable; for a community is encompassed by a common language comprehending all its activities, but in process of fission self-interested social groups develop means of communication which emphasize the divisions between them, until apparently separate 'worlds' proliferate even in a small country, and through their atmospheres man speaks to man with difficulty, if at all. In the following scene, on the Eisteddfod field during the First World War, the young pacifist minister, J. T. Miles, urges his soldier friend to take him to deliver his petition for peace:

—The Plas Coch people are good Methodists. They'll let me talk to him, Griff. In our language. It could make a difference.
—You really believe that?
—Well, in the end, the dialogue is between man and man.
He stopped talking because of the expression on Griff's face.
—What's the matter?
—There can't be anything more defenceless. Not even a chicken in a cracked egg.

—Will you give me a lift?
—A chapel-bred Welsh poet, Griff said.
A chicken in a cracked egg.
—I'm not a poet.
—You should have been.
—Will you give me a lift? Yes or no?
Griff lifted his hand in mock alarm.
—Right, he said. I hope I've got enough petrol. Just think a cupful of petrol could stop the war. Come on.

The minister believes 'it could make a difference' if he talks to the Statesman in their common language—Welsh—for, 'in the end, the dialogue is between man and man'. He lives by this belief—'defenceless', more so than 'a chicken in a cracked egg', according to the soldier, who nevertheless knows what his friend is talking about. Griff has just saved him from a savage beating, as an alleged pro-German, by the authority of his military uniform, and will now use his motor-bike to help him to deliver the petition—'Just think a cupful of petrol could stop the war.' Which it does not, of course, any more than it stops the lovable and 'realistic' Griff being killed. At this time the irony of the situation cooperates with Griff's irony to underline J. T. Miles's ineffectualness, but not to show that his ideal or his action is wrong. The local ironies are subject to the judgment of history. J. T. Miles is right, not only about the war, but about the values inherent in the common language which many of those who use it betray, by cooperating with the war, some for worthy and some for unworthy reasons. He does not realize, however, the extent to which, even then, Welsh could no longer be assumed to be a language of shared beliefs among all its speakers.

The power of love, embodied in individuals, guiding their lives, is a power both affirmed, and explored and questioned by the novel, thus adding considerably to its subtlety, depth and complexity. The conflicts are not abstract, but present in individuals and a changing society, and complicated by the natures of these, offering no easy solutions or interpretations. Love itself is shown to be dangerous, mysterious, often ambiguous. Thus J. T. Miles, as a stretcher-bearer, acting on love's principle, personal responsibility, disobeys an order and both fails to accomplish his mission of mercy and is indirectly responsible for his comrade's death.

Outside the House of Baal contains several sermons but is none. It is a committed novel—with an artistic integrity comparable to the work of Joyce. Emyr Humphreys, a Christian and Welsh nationalist, offers no comfort to those complacent in either or both beliefs, or those complacent in their opposition. He is far more disturbing than Caradoc Evans in his portrayal of Wales, because of his deeper knowledge of

Wales, and the superiority of his intellectual power, moral, social and psychological insight, and artistic skill. Above all, because his regard for truth exposes, simply by being what it is, attitudes that romanticize, or falsify in any other way, the ideals to which he is loyal. This is not to imply that the novel does not celebrate, lyrically, values perceived in the Wales it presents; but the right to celebrate is paid for by revelations of ills which are far more painful than any that the most savage caricaturist or satirist could make. His is a seeing belief.

Before continuing to develop the main lines of this argument, it is first necessary to provide an idea of the novel's basic narrative and formal design, for without this the numerous apparent paradoxes of a novel that is simultaneously committed, lifelike, and a refined, 'objective' work of art will remain merely teasing.

The opening section presents the beginning of a day in the lives of a Calvinist Methodist minister, J. T. Miles, referred to usually as J. T., and his sister-in-law Kate, who looks after him, at 8 Gorse Avenue, on an estate off a holiday road in North Wales, some time in the mid-twentieth century. Alternating sections present the progress of this one day, from before breakfast until teatime, and the past that has brought the protagonists together, from separate childhoods at the end of the nineteenth century. In the past we see J. T. in boyhood with his alcoholic father; as an apprentice blacksmith; as a young minister opposed to the First World War, and a stretcher-bearer on the Eastern Front; married to Kate's sister, Lydia, with a ministry in South Wales during the Depression; in London during the Second World War after Lydia's death in an air raid on Liverpool; with his grown-up children. Kate we see as a girl and young woman with her sister and brothers on their father's farm, Argoed (of which he is at first the tenant); growing older in the service of Pa, who discourages suitors (all, but especially those who *laugh*); married after Pa's death to the feckless Wynne Bannister; widowed; with the children of her brothers and of J. T. and Lydia, and with *their* children. So the past moves towards convergence with the present, as the events of the one day unfold, and the novel encompasses four generations within the long lifetimes of its main characters. The past however is as present in the novel as its latest day, for the narrative consistently uses the past tense to render current actions; but as the novel progresses the effects of the past on the present are seen, and, with the ironies and knowledge that a widening retrospective view affords, the events of the past become increasingly poignant as they occur. The method reveals both the relationship between before and after, cause and effect, and the significance of the ever-present now, when the individual can either allow himself to be determined by worldly forces, or choose to act on principles bearing witness to another power. Similarly, the incidents of the single day, many of which would be seen in a conventional view as trivial, tedious, or absurd, present choices as decisive as the events of history.

The novel incorporates time in its shifting scenes, and uses it, mainly by juxtaposing past and present, and contingent or divergent events, as the medium of revelation. The novelist's technique is accordingly to *present:* to make his characters present, and to show them from the outside, so that they reveal themselves by what they say and do, or are otherwise revealed, except by explicit comment, now and in time. One of the novel's principal motifs is the clock or watch; another is the photograph or photographer. The latter creates the illusion that time can stand still, but only arrests appearances, suggestively or by belying the internal and external movements composing the living moment. Emyr Humphreys's technique has something in common with the photographer's, but more with the film-maker's. His scenes are observed from without, recorded faithfully, clear-cut with precise details, and framed alongside other frames; he shows; he is the master of time in his novel, cutting, selecting, arranging. He too is limited in face of his subject. One function of the photograph motif in the novel is, surely, to indicate the limits of its art: the lifelike is not life; the scene reveals through outer manifestations, but the novelist, respecting his characters as he respects the mystery and integrity of the life from which they have been drawn (which is not to say that they are portraits of actual people, of course) will not presume to know their unspoken feelings and thoughts; the 'still' which selects from the stream of the generations arrests its current. This humility before the subject affirms the necessity outside the novel of 'I-Thou' relationships (which are also operative in the novel, between the novelist and his characters), and is among the novel's principal strengths; in so far as parts of the novel are necessarily schematic, and all the characters are shown to be defined and determined *up to a point* by their cultural environment, it also preserves human personality and the dialogue between man and God which is called conscience as the mysteries they are.

For the most part, *Outside the House of Baal* works to present its revelations unobtrusively, and it would be a mistake to interpret the humility it incorporates as modesty of aim. The magnitude of its ambition is evident once it is seen to combine, with its own spirit and in an individual form, the concern of the great novelists of the last century, pre-eminently Tolstoy, with personal and national or social salvation, and formal devices developed from an understanding of modernist works, most notably *Ulysses,* which appear to be independent of their invisible creators.

Emyr Humphreys shows awareness of Joyce, without imitating him, in his verbal deliberation, his subtle incorporation of time (which is nevertheless progressive, and not cyclic), his contrasts and juxtapositions, but above all in his authorial invisibility, whereby epiphany replaces comment, and pointed word the act of pointing. The novel is Tolstoyan in its depiction of the movements of history on a large scale, in their passage through the lives of characters who struggle with the great problems of individual and national salvation. As Emyr Humphreys has said of Tolstoy and Dostoevsky in his radio talk 'A Protestant View of the Modern Novel' (*Listener*, 2 April 1953): 'These greatest of novelists looked upon themselves and upon all mankind as souls thirsting equally for salvation.' He finds that they have an 'I-Thou' relationship with their characters, and Joyce an 'I-It' relationship with his characters, or, strictly speaking, with the raw material of life from which the characters are drawn. Akin to Tolstoy in this respect, he is least Tolstoyan in the modernism of his form, and—to re-employ the hard-worked 'canvas' metaphor—in his skill in creating and arranging scenes which are, in their surface dimensions alone, miniatures, while appearing to be their distant spectator. There is loss here, of course, loss of the depth at which we know and experience with a Pierre or a Levin, and of the continuous unfolding of a broad canvas; and gain for the modern novel in its repossession of souls thirsting for salvation, alive in history and a nation.

The most lyrical scenes of *Outside the House of Baal* are set either before 1914 or during the war. In these a simpler, more intimate world is not simplified:

Just as the Reverend Benjamin Davies was about to pick up his fork, Pa said,
—Will you lead us in prayer, Mr Davies?
The whole family was assembled at supper after chapel. Outside, gusts of fierce wind made the windows rattle and doors bang. Benjamin Davies pushed back his chair and stood up with some difficulty. His white beard fanned out on his chest as he lowered his head.
—O Lord, he said in a muffled voice and then cleared his throat noisily, let us look out through the windows of life and watch the shadows approach and let us realize as we pull down the blinds that the night will be very long. Let us put our ears to the walls of the Universe and hear the planets thundering towards the void.
He paused as if to listen to the wind outside. Kate opened her eyes to look at the old man. All the other heads around the table were lowered... Pa's, Ned's, Dan Llew's, Griff's, Lydia's, Rowland's, Hugh's; and Mary Parry Rice stood in the doorway ready to serve and anxious to hear anything Benjamin Davies said. He was a preacher famous for his peculiar sayings, and Mary had a passion for memorizing as many as she could. She was listening so intently now she could not close her eyes and her ears were cocked like a gun-dog's.

—But glory be to thee, it will end. Yes it will end and the Sun of Righteousness will rise in all its splendour never to set again.
   He cleared his throat and shut his eyes very tightly, lifting his head so that his beard jutted forward.
   —We thank thee also for this quiet assembly of one of the families of thy church. And for this food. Amen.
   —I didn't get hold of that one, Mary Parry Rice said bringing in the bread basket.

The family are together at supper after chapel, each in his or her place around the table, and the servant, 'ready to serve and anxious to hear', both waits upon them and participates, her presence being as well-defined as the minister's. The order here is at one and the same time hierarchical and communal, and in this setting the minister's prayer, which is biblical, prophetic, and poetic, is not exorbitant, but in its proper sphere. His meaning may not be understood by all, or even by anyone; that is not relevant. The point is that in this room, among these people, young and old, being waited on and serving, of varying degrees of intellectual ability, at this ordinary supper after the usual attendance at chapel, the reverence, and perhaps even the recognition of mystery, is shared as naturally as other cultural and familiar bonds. This common world comprehends as a unity with its one language, 'Let us put our ears to the walls of the Universe and hear the planets thundering towards the void', and Mary Parry Rice's 'I didn't get hold of that one'. The familial setting is an image of the order encompassing it. Naturally, the minister likens human life and the universe to a house.
   After supper, 'the harmony of their voices helped to soften the metallic tone of the grand piano'. Benjamin Davies is heard to say: 'Best time of your life, children, remember that. Keep together in harmony. The only way to keep the storm out.' In the storm he recognizes, prophetically, the powers threatening their common, ordered world. The harmony contains discord, is enforced by rigid formalism (represented at this point by Pa's enunciation of the hymn's number), but arises from a form that defines its participants, offering them moral strength, and familial and communal loyalty. The singing releases both natural and religious impulses.
   Emyr Humphreys presents revivalism in a passage which, at once lyrical and down to earth, comprehends details of the rural, working world in which J. T. serves his apprenticeship as a blacksmith, the loss of some pigs entrusted to his fellow apprentice, Ifan Cole, the ecstatic singing of the young men returning from the meeting at night, the confession to J. T. by their leader, Parry Price, of his homosexuality, and J. T.'s study of the Holy Spirit in Dr Charles's *Welsh Biblical Dictionary* late into the night. This passage, like several others in the novel, is reminiscent of Thomas Hardy in its unforced combination of

diverse levels of experience—workaday and religious, communal and individual, comic and serious. Another passage calling Hardy to mind, though it could only have occurred where it does, beautifully unites the tenderness and physical passion of J. T. and Lydia with details of domestic work, and J. T.'s deep intellectual and spiritual questioning.

This, then, is what a common world of the kind under discussion is: containing diverse levels and elements of human experience in an order sustained by work and belief, which reflects in every facet the clear or distorted features of its religion, its language encompassing all values and relationships makes all mutually comprehensible. Its harmony both releases and contains related or opposing impulses in its forms of expression. It is not simple, or simply innocent. There is no simple innocence here, for example:

—You go on, my friends, Parry Price said, and God be with you.

He lifted his arm, and they went forward obediently as if they had been dismissed. The fingers of his other hand clutched spasmodically at Joe's shoulder.

—It was beautiful, Joe, he said. Very beautiful. But I tell you this, I was not called. I was not called.

—I think I ought to go in now, Mr Price, Joe said.

He looked up at the window of Mrs Isaac's bedroom. The forge was still and quiet. There was no sign of Ifan and the pony and trap. Parry Price gripped his arm tightly.

—I know why, Joseph Trevor, I know why. The sinner always knows why and I'll tell you why before I spend the night in an open ditch. And may the Lord hear me as you hear me and take pity. I try to punish myself. I don't hear the call, in spite of my gifts, I don't hear the call because I prefer the flesh of the male to the flesh of the female. This is my downfall.

—Well goodnight now, Mr. Price, Joe said.

—Tomorrow night. I shall call for you again tomorrow night and we shall go in search of the spirit together again? The Holy Spirit will seek us out again, Joe.

—If it's convenient for you, Mr Price, Joe said. Goodnight.

It is not shown whether or not J. T. understands and accepts Parry Price's confession, or realizes with what feeling the man clutches and grips him, or whether he is even listening. The confession however casts new light on Parry Price's intense fervour, and delight in comradeship. This does not invalidate either emotion, or his eloquence: 'Less than the thickness of a silk handkerchief... that's all that separates us from the world of the Spirit. Glory be to God. We can speak quietly and he can hear us. We can think and He can hear our thoughts.' Although this is not invalidated, it is shown to be—as eloquence often is in the novel—disturbed: the disturbed eloquence of a prophet or seer who sublimates outlawed passions and reveals lawful ones in his rhapsodic discourse, oratory or song. Again and again, the dangers of having a gift of words are revealed: in the presentation of the old minister who first inspired J. T. with the belief that 'there was nothing in life so exciting and interesting as doing good', but who cannot pray; and in J. T. himself, who becomes to Lydia an alienating man of words in his concern for others and material neglect of his family. Yet J. T. can be more truly described as the novel's hero in the traditional sense in that his capacity for passion and tenderness, and his devoutness and practical Christianity are not substitutes for one another.

That the harmony of communion can release dangerous passions alien to its spirit is shown most memorably at the shrine of Welsh culture, the Eisteddfod, where Emyr Humphreys reveals, with shocking effect, the general Welsh reaction to the First World War. Here the orator, addressing a large gathering, exploits Welsh ideals—of a crusade in defence of little nations, sacrifice, honour, the land and feeling for the land, and perhaps above all the art of oratory itself—to arouse ugly emotions and mass hysteria. When he finishes, 'the whole canvas pavilion seethed and hummed like a hive that had been disturbed', and he submerges 'his own voice in the united effort, an equal among equals to be seen sharing the pleasure of communal sound'. He releases a violence that finds its first object to assault in J. T., the solitary inarticulate interrupter, and is as vicious in the man who, 'in a sudden rage hammered at J. T.'s knuckles with a folded newspaper until shreds of its pages fell away', as in the zealots who, abetted by the police, attack him afterwards. This is not a 'mindless' violence, of course: the folded newspaper is the orator's ally and mentor, making idealism the fuel of brutal passions.

'The pleasure of communal sound' drowns the protesting voice of conscience. Idealism perverted (a crucial preoccupation of Emyr Humphreys since his first novel, *The Little Kingdom*), casting off personal responsibility, is shown to be a terrible force. There is nothing in Caradoc Evans's writings that is as shocking as this scene, because nothing as seeing, as realistic, and as truthful. Nor could that gifted comic and savage carver of gargoyles have equalled the scene in which J. T. is offered payment for the service he has performed, in chapel, by malicious and materialistic deacons, in an atmosphere of subtle corruption. Clearly the perversion of religion by worldliness—whether sexual frustration or deviation, or materialism in several forms—and the subsequent hypocrisy is one of Emyr Humphreys's significant themes. The effect of the instance in the chapel is strengthened by the sense of menace he conveys as the First World War approaches. This self-seeking is present within the common world, ready to cooperate with the forces threatening it from without.

The place of women in a patriarchal society is another theme which Emyr Humphreys shares with Caradoc Evans, and treats with incomparably more sympathy and understanding. The courtship of Kate by Archie Griffiths is presented as a monetary affair. When Kate as a young woman first hears J. T.'s voice she is at the sink: 'her hand covered with soapsuds clutched her father's drawers in a soft and slippery bunch against the washing-board'. A characteristic attitude. We are first shown her 'on her knees', not in prayer, but at the altar of the fire-place, her fingers 'stained with grey ash', working for J. T. while he is still in bed upstairs. Ill and uncomplaining, she is always working at the basic everyday tasks on which J. T.—and her father before him—depend. She has spent her life clearing up messes ('I had to clear up the mess', she says after her husband's death, referring to his debts and dishonesties). She is associated with domestic objects, which are presented effectively in precise and oppressive detail, but at which one would look in vain for naturalism similar to Arnold Bennett's, and hopelessly for the properties of a Joycean myth: these are the things she is close to, which she orders and animates, and which define the function she accepts. Although she is associated with life in every form except marital fulfilment, no easy conclusion may be drawn. From the patriarchal order that oppresses her she has drawn her strength, loyalty and devotion. She is the realist who does good practically, and a truth-teller; J. T. is the idealist, the theorist of doing good practically, who often does it impractically. But Kate is no Achsah, driven in a cow's halter for an airing in the fields. Masterly in his sympathetic treatment of old age and bodily decay, Emyr Humphreys is equally successful in presenting the diverse personalities and essential femininity of Kate and Lydia.

As the century advances the comprehensive language of the common world is shown to be replaced by the languages of contending ideologies and social classes, with loss of shared beliefs and diversification of the means of communication. This is a talking world, in which strangers, meeting casually or assembled for a purpose, debate ideas, and frequently misunderstand each other, even when they listen. It is also a world in which machines of many kinds, but especially devices which extend the range of the human person or voice, complicate the dialogue between man and man. So, at the declaration of war in 1914, announced in a newspaper bought at a station, there is the political argument on the train between J. T., who says little, the Marxist collier, and the conservative Professor Temple Morgan, who is proud of having climbed out of 'the pit of ignorance by education and effort'; and in the thirties there is the disagreement, of representative significance, between the socialist Bill Mabon, the Welsh nationalist Walter Silin, and the liberal

Bayley Lewis, who believes in reconciliation, and later commits suicide. Similarly there is division among the Calvinist Methodists between fundamentalists and social reformers, within families, and between the generations. J. T. in age is seen arguing with his son Ronnie in front of the Vice-Chancellor and a girl reporter, where, as in other instances, context and audience are as representative as the differences of belief. Ronnie is to be the university's first Professor of Sociology and Industrial Relations, and has published *Mobility and Social Structure;* J. T. has written the pamphlets *Jesus Today* and *Honesty and Dogma.* Their argument is a further illustration of the division apparent between the titles. Ronnie is able to mock his father's beliefs cleverly—with the rather manic smartness of the intellectual whose urge to win an argument, and to be seen to win it, is intensified by the fact that he is also talking his conscience to sleep—and, by using a sociological perspective and jargon, to make out a plausible case for regarding those beliefs as unrealistic and backward-looking. J. T. repeats his principle: 'Old Ambrose used to say that nationality was a question of loyalty'; 'How can there be any faith or meaning or purpose without loyalty? This is the basic question'; 'The treason of the intellectual... is to have no loyalties at all'. They are, of course, speaking different languages. Extending its setting into a society thus divided, a novel that is composed so much of dialogue must necessarily become more schematic in the presentation of its themes. In this respect, the later sections of *Outside the House of Baal* anticipate the design of *National Winner.*

Near the end of the novel, when a pigeon lands on J. T.'s arm as a young photographer is trying to persuade him and his contemporary, Mr Bowen, a retired schoolmaster, to let him take their picture, J. T. says: 'Is this a pigeon or a dove descending?' He would have been understood at Argoed, but to the young man it is as if he 'had spoken in a foreign language'. But to Mr Bowen, too, J. T.'s morality is equally foreign:

—My eldest boy, he's an inspector of police in Manchester. You wouldn't believe the things that happen.

—I know, J. T. said. We must try not to be afraid.

—But for law and order, I can tell you, this country would be worse than the Congo.

—Fear is a bad thing, J. T. said. It holds us down like a force of gravity. If we could conquer it, and keep our imagination as sensitive as a child's, I think we could walk on water.

—There is no substitute for a strong police force, Mr Bowen said.

If in this world, unlike that turning upon the chapel, the love of power cannot understand the language of the power of love, at least it cannot use it for its own ends—or not when it is used as sensitively as it is here.

The most moving and powerful scene where failure of understanding occurs is also set late in the present day of the novel, and involves J. T. and Dan Llew, men who know the same language—the Welsh of the chapels and the laws it embodies—but ascribe different meanings and values to its words. Dan Llew has been wandering—in his mind, and back to Argoed to see his long-dead father. Having been returned to his bungalow, also called Argoed (although only J. T. seems aware of the name's deeper historical and literary significance), and his housekeeper, Mrs Wilson, he and J. T. and Mrs Wilson are shown slides of Oberammergau by his son, Norman. He alternately insults J. T. and offers him hospitality, when he remembers the 'respect for the cloth' taught by his father. Mrs Wilson is pathetic and absurd in her coy girlishness, Dan Llew pathetic but tough; the novelist presents both compassionately. The argument begins over a slide of the Christ of the Passion play, when J. T. reminds Dan Llew that Christ was crucified by the Romans, and not the Jews, who 'represent the Church. People like you and I'. Dan Llew assumes that he is being called a bad man.

> J. T. shook his head.
> —I'm just as worthless as you are, he said. And as weak.
> It's precisely because we are weak and worthless that we have any value. That is the true measure of our value.
> Dan Llew looked up at Mrs Wilson.
> —What's he talking about? he said.
> —Really, Mr Miles, Mrs Wilson said. That's the last thing anyone would say about Mr Jones. He's not weak and he's certainly not worthless. He still has business interests in both towns. And he has a family that loves him.
> —Which is more than you've got, Dan Llew said.

Unfortunately the rest of the scene is too long to quote, but based on this comic, yet terrible misunderstanding, the argument develops with cruelty and bitterness on Dan Llew's part, and a patient attempt to explain in simple terms on J. T.'s. Only when Dan Llew remembers the words of a hymn does he seem to understand what J. T. is saying about the universality of sin among mankind, and then he knows 'all about that' because he was 'brought up on it'. At the end, when he has said the most wounding things possible to J. T., and broken down remembering his sister, Lydia, and J. T. has begun to leave:

> In the hall Norman turned around to see what J. T. was staring at. Dan Llew's foot was lying in Mrs Wilson's lap as she unlaced his brown boots. The boot fell on the carpet with a thud. Mrs Wilson peeled off Dan Llew's sock and his white foot lay in her hand.

This remarkable image is a grotesque secular *pietà*, but a *pietà* nevertheless.

It is also as it were a touching summary of the dependence depicted in the novel, where the men domineer, cajole, neglect and ill-treat the women, but always turn to find comfort like full-grown babies. Even J. T.'s relationship with Kate is a shadow of this image.

We are left, finally, with the disturbing pathos revealed by a supremely compassionate art, with the heroism of Kate in the mundane world and J. T.'s heroic loyalty. We are left, too, with the enhanced sense of hope that is the gift of works of art that are at once aesthetically and morally good, and that also arises in this instance from the possibilities of individual and national salvation kept alive by loyalty and heroism. The latter observation may be illustrated by a further comparison with Thomas Hardy. J. T.'s father, an alcoholic schoolmaster who ultimately commits suicide, had hoped to advance himself by hard work after the manner of Professor Henry Jones. His situation is reminiscent of Phillotson's and Jude's in *Jude the Obscure* (1896). Hardy, however, unlike Emyr Humphreys, was a tragic novelist. Hardy identifies more obviously with his protagonist, colours his prose with personal views and feelings, comments overtly, and focuses on a crisis which occupies a shorter time span than that of *Outside the House of Baal*. Hardy in this novel is the bitter ironist of a tragedy which is finished within the novel, while society goes on regardless; Emyr Humphreys is concerned with the present, with a continuing crisis, and leaves the possibility of choice which is finally closed by the tragic statement of Hardy's novel. This brief comparison is not, of course, evaluative. It may, however, suggest the different tendencies of two societies as well as two novelists.

Almost the last words we hear J. T. and Kate speak are of death:

> To be completely without fear, J. T. said, would be to arrive at a mystical state. There comes a point where the spirit would have to leave the body behind. Now there is one of the creative functions of death. To put an end to what otherwise would be endless.

In response to her niece's question 'Don't you believe in God, Aunty?' Kate replies:

> —I suppose I have to don't I? The world's in enough of a mess as it is. Nobody seems to want to die when it comes to the push. I don't know what it's all about I'm sure.

Mysticism and the qualified affirmation of doubting common sense seem strangely complementary. Years before, but for an accident that blinded her in one eye and prevented her meeting him, it might have been Kate instead of Lydia who comforted J. T. and received his love.

What did happen, the real history, makes such speculation pointless, although much that is unspoken haunts the novel with a mystery that is the more potent for being other than the easily definable love of power, or its allies, the appetites and material idols symbolized by the public-house which J. T. calls the House of Baal. At last, however, returning to the latest day from the progression of the past, the extent to which J. T. and Kate have always complemented each other has been revealed with as much clarity as a mystery and power of this order will allow.

'A dream of a country'

THERE have been many versions of 'the return of the native' since Hardy's novel, and in our unsettling society there are bound to be many more, but Raymond Williams's *Border Country* is the only one I know which is as intelligent as Hardy's, with an equivalent ability to see the experience as a whole, and to understand and control strong personal feeling without suppressing it. It is this which makes the return a release of energy for living in the present and carrying through, from past to future, a tradition of active social concern, instead of a retreat upon the past. The release is that of the character Matthew Price but also, I believe, of Raymond Williams: a release, perhaps facilitated or even achieved by discovery of the patterns of personal and family experience in the process of writing from within it, which gave fresh impetus to his work and confirmed its direction. For his is a single creative activity, working through different intellectual and imaginative forms, with a common movement: first, back into the past, in order to understand it, then forward, with commitment to certain traditional values and readiness to adapt them to the new conditions of a humane future. The movement in each direction involves a struggle: to distinguish the 'real history' from false versions, and for alternative social relations to those prevailing in modern Britain.

Matthew Price is a university lecturer, in economic history, who returns from London to Glynmawr (the fictional name of a village in a valley on the eastern edge of the Black Mountains) during the last illness of his father, Harry, a railway signalman. Matthew is literally a man with two names, a duality symptomatic of his inner division, the border within him, between local boy, whose feelings are rooted in this community and country, and the man who has returned, who went away to university on a scholarship, acquiring the ability and opportunity to work on 'population movements into the Welsh mining valleys in the middle decades of the nineteenth century', but now, at the time of being called back, uneasily: 'I have moved myself, he objected, and what is it really that I must measure?'

The border is not between abstracted Welsh and English temperaments (as it is in Margiad Evans's *Country Dance* (1932), for example), though Glynmawr is a distinctive community within a recognizable (anglicized) Welsh society, and in this novel, as in the trilogy as a whole, the novelist's positive feelings are engaged more with his Welsh characters and settings than with his English ones. National differences and intermixtures are shown to play an important part in this community, but the border is mainly between internal and external social forces: between English as it is spoken in this place and 'educated' English with its greater capacity for detachment and generalization, between the kinds of personal, family, and social experience on either side of the language divide, and between living the experience of this community and being able to measure and clarify it from outside. Here, in particular, we may see the quality of intelligence in *Border Country* which understands and controls feeling without suppressing it. For Raymond Williams avoids the alternative conventional resolutions of the literature of identity crisis: either rejection of formative influences (often literally family and 'home') and flight into 'freedom' in the present, or retreat upon the past known as inner country or lost community. The border is shown to be both in Matthew and outside him, and to live without either flight or retreat he has to connect what it separates: to measure as a historian, but without abstracting movements from their lived experience: to see the valley with the clear historical patterns which distance discloses, but to know the patterns as the actual life of the place, and as changing with that life. He has to feel what he sees and to see what he feels, as in coming to know his father better as a man, he comes to feel him more deeply in himself, himself in his own children, and 'population' as the body of people of which he is a member.

The experience of returning, which would be difficult for Matthew Price in any case, is naturally made especially painful and critical by its occasion. It is, however, ultimately a release. The values known in his father, in his experience of change and settlement, Matthew is able to carry through into his own life and work. But what makes any sketch of the novel a simplification is also what makes it so fine: the complex reality of Harry Price, of the relationship between father and son, and between Harry Price and Morgan Rosser, and of the lived experience of this community's modern history. There is a good deal of talk in the other novels in the trilogy, talk of a kind which is appropriate to their characters, but here it is the combination in Harry of reserve, wordless or sparsely worded wisdom, and pained inarticulateness that helps to give him the substance and depth of a real, contradictory human being. In his voice, 'always ... there was more than could easily be said, in any feeling'. So is there in the novel, which has also what Morgan Rosser observes in Harry, 'an extraordinary tension between what was felt and what could be said'. Indeed, in *Border Country* much that is felt is shown rather than said, in clear, dignified prose which has very few metaphors and images, and does not need them, since it is enough for such a known world to be shown clearly, for its moving reality to be felt. An example of this is the scene in which Matthew, the boy 'Will', finds his paternal grandfather, Jack Price, lying dead in a field:

'Gran,' he said again, urgently, reaching out and touching the shoulder that lay nearest to him. He hesitated as his fingers felt the rough cloth, and then suddenly pushed hard at the shoulder, trying to turn it, so that he could see the face. But he drew back midway in the effort. He knew now what he would find.

Slowly he stood up and looked around. There was nobody in sight; the field lay empty and desolate. Looking down again, he saw the hand tightly holding two sweetbriars, that were being brought for the garden. Beside the hand lay the big single-bladed pocket knife, with the yellow bone handle carved with initials. The knife had been bought, he remembered his grandfather saying, after his first year's work, when he was twelve. Once he had lost it while hedging, and found it again months later. Narrowing his eyes, Will bent down and again pushed at the shoulder. Then, reluctantly, he touched the clenched hand, which was cold.

On the line, a hundred yards away, the down distant signal dropped to off. He heard distinctly the sharp sound of its movement, and thought of his father's hands on the lever, far up in the box. He looked down, and then broke into a run back across the field.

The connection which the passage shows between the hands of three generations, with those of the dead man and the living man, father and son, closely associated with the tools of their work, presents a profound fact of human experience: individual men are more than their work and family relationships but cannot be separated from these close shaping forms, and whole human beings, known as intimately as children know the feel and look of their parents' hands, implicitly deny identifications in terms of part or function which characterize an inhuman society. In such passages Raymond Williams is at his best as a novelist, but they can occur only in the known community of *Border Country*, where close connections between the generations exist. He can express his profound humanism here in ways that the societies of his other novels do not allow.

The narrative technique of *Border Country* juxtaposes Harry Price's process of settling and living at Glynmawr with his son's gradually unsettling growth and education, and return from his London home to his first settlement. In Raymond Williams's thinking, in which continuity and change are not separable from each other as opposing values, 'settlement' is a keyword, whose full range of meanings he uses. It can mean both particular and general way of life, establishment in life's primary institutions, property or financial arrangement, the material and moral accommodations and terms which people make. However, any listing of its many meanings would be inadequate, because it is their relationships, as social and individual terms, and moral and material values, which his persistent and flexible use of the word signifies. *Border Country* and the following novels in the trilogy realize the complex meanings of 'settlement' in a society which progressively complicates them, as the traditional kinds of settlement, as community and individual or family establishment, increasingly change.

The author's conventional prefatory note to *Border Country* begins unconventionally, with a statement that is also, surely, a boast: 'I know this country'. The novel fully justifies this. Raymond Williams does indeed know 'this country', which is not only the area in which the novel is set but also 'border country', in his special sense of the term. But it is more than these meanings too, because as both his critical writings and his novels show, any 'country' is far more, in its internal and external connections, than the word's isolation of a particular area suggests. Glynmawr and its surroundings are Raymond Williams's country, his 'knowable community'; the venture of his trilogy is to move out from and return to this area in an attempt to disclose and measure our common world, and to carry the values lived in the past into a present and future which cannot be lived in terms of past settlements, but which would not be humanly habitable without the faith of their struggle for a communal order, their 'dream of a country'.

As Matthew Price relearns the country where he was born and brought up, so we too learn to see with him:

> It was one thing to carry its image in his mind, as he did, everywhere, never a day passing but he closed his eyes and saw it again, his only landscape. But it was different to stand and look at the reality. It was not less beautiful; every detail of the land came up with its old excitement. But it was not still, as the image had been. It was no longer a landscape or a view, but a valley that people were using. He realized, as he watched, what had happened in going away. The valley as landscape had been taken, but its work forgotten. The visitor sees beauty; the inhabitant a place where he works and has his friends. Far away, closing his eyes, he had been seeing this valley, but as a visitor sees it, as the guide-book sees it: this valley, in which he had lived more than half his life.

The visitor's way of seeing separates beauty from use and work, the picturesque 'history' of guide-book panoramas from the people's experience in Glynmawr and of movements connecting Glynmawr with our whole industrial society—as the General Strike of 1926 has immediate and lasting effects on the local railwaymen and their families, and as Harry Price with his hands on the lever in the signalbox is literally a transmitter of movement and change. Harry Price with his levers and gardens is a man of many connections, between past and present, nature and culture, settlement and change. Matthew Price has a way of seeing that connects. This is Raymond Williams's way too. He is concerned in all his writings with making connections, and he does so by replacing such conventional antitheses as 'culture' and 'society', 'society' and 'the individual', 'country' and 'city' with their true relationships, the processes of their synthesis, concealed by the rise of interests and habits of thought which divorce them. For such connections to work in the novel, however, he has to create persons and personal relationships, but not as either abstracted from the general social history or as created in the images of an ideology. He has to be both insider and outsider, settled and changing. Seeing and measuring the human world require both attachment and detachment: what Matthew Price needs in his work, Raymond Williams the novelist needs in his. His combination of these in *Border Country* makes it not only the finest novel in the trilogy but also one of the few modern English novels to fulfil his definition, in *The Long Revolution*, of 'the highest realism'.

This definition is worth giving in the context of his conviction that 'parts of our very idea of society are withered at root' and 'it is precisely the lack of an adequate sense of society that is crippling us' (words written of Britain in the 1960s but with even more urgent relevance now):

> The truly creative effort of our time is the struggle for relationships, of a whole kind, and it is possible to see this as both personal and social: the practical learning of *extending* relationships. Realism, as embodied in its great tradition, is a touchstone in this, for it shows, in detail, that vital interpenetration, idea into feeling, person into community, change into settlement, which we need, as growing points, in our own divided time. In the highest realism, society is seen in fundamentally personal terms, and persons, through relationships, in fundamentally social terms.

Now, while *Border Country* cannot have been an easy achievement, it seems to me that the kind of 'extending relationships' he is attempting in the other novels in the trilogy, *Second Generation* and *The Fight for Manod*, are even more difficult to achieve, and in consequence there are times when the reach of both is strained.

Second Generation is concerned with the families of two brothers who moved in the 1930s from the Welsh border country near Glynmawr, and found work in a car factory in a university city. This city with its divisions is, Raymond Williams insists, one city:

> If you stand, today, in Between Towns Road, you can see either way: west to the spires and towers of the cathedral and colleges; east to the yards and sheds of the motor works. You see different worlds, but there is no frontier between them; there is only the movement and traffic of a single city.

Thus, in the opening paragraph, we are told what we will see before we are shown it: 'different worlds', but 'only the movement and traffic of a single city'. Yet the novel does show this, in some respects, very effectively, and particularly in the connection made through Peter Owen, a research student in Sociology, and his father Harold, a shop steward in the motor works. It is the father whom, once again, I feel to be the most substantial presence in the novel. The impressive episodes in and around the factory, of work and negotiations, redundancy and strikes, are not appended documentation but shown as lived by Harold Owen and, to a lesser extent, other characters. The depiction of his tense network of connections, with work and family, and with the communications systems in and between factories, and, through the 'media' with their image-making techniques, between the industrial working class and the 'public', effects a real extension of relationships. This in turn extends the modern novel's range of sympathy and understanding. After all, the life of a signalman with his gardens may be seen to have a kind of romantic appeal (not that Raymond Williams exploits this), but most readers of *Second Generation* will not know much about car factories as institutions or their workers as people. Raymond Williams presents both realistically, and shows how, as with the cars under Harold's hands, they are a critical part of our single, though deeply divided, society with its 'traffic' of movements, images and ideas. His great distinction is that he takes democracy seriously and attempts to see society as a whole, in fact, as a whole way of life, in which a person is more and not less fully human when all his social relations are seen. But it is no part of his intention to suggest that in this society integration may be achieved painlessly, if at all.

Second Generation is a bleaker, harder novel than *Border Country*. It shows more of the capitalist system, with its industry and communications, in a more divided, more complex, and more technologically advanced society. Life at both ends of the 'single city', in the university and the factory and working-class area, is bleaker and harder, more brittle and more nerve-exposed, than life in Glynmawr. Because the connections in this society are more complex and far-reaching, the novel employs far more figurative language to bring them within its scope than was necessary in the known community of Glynmawr; and here there is far more intellectual talk, more open bitterness, insult and class conflict, more analysis and self-analysis. The novel images, in its main characters, the effects of a divided and alienating society: exposure and isolation, disturbance in body and mind, false personal relations and settlements. This is done with disturbing effectiveness, through images of cold, hard light and dry heat, of empty shells, distorted reflections and narrow circles of self-enclosure, in the cases of Peter Owen and his mother, Kate. The images in each instance relate self-alienation and deadlock in personal relations to the crisis they are living, of British society in the early 1960s. But there is also a narrowness in this novel, a claustrophobia which I feel reflects, not the lack of real contact which Kate in particular feels, but the novelist's attitudes. It is the result, I think, of a kind of experience which Raymond Williams treats with unique understanding but so extensively that it excludes other important experiences from his world.

Like Matthew Price, Peter Owen is seeking 'the connection between work and living'. He wants 'to study the social patterns of his own community'. He too is an inhabitant of what Raymond Williams describes, in *The Country and the City*, as 'that border country so many of us have been living in: between custom and education, between work and ideas, between love of place and an experience of change'. In Peter's case, the division between university and factory produces division within him and between himself and others. For him, there are no easy resolutions of the contradictions he is living. Clearly, the experience of 'border country' in his special sense, obviously lived by Raymond Williams, and analysed in his critical writings and dramatized in his novels, is general among people from the working class and the lower middle class who have been highly educated, and therefore offered social mobility and probably geographical mobility also—movements containing the possibilities of class betrayal and disorientation, and of a difficult integration. Similar experiences of division between change and settlement are even more general in our society of changing work, family, and community relations; in our situation of loss of customary forms of human contact and proliferating communications. In this trilogy, however, the strongest light is focused on the working-class academic as borderer, and in consequence his experience not only figures large in the world Raymond Williams presents but also affects its presentation. I feel this to be a limitation on the scope of *Second Generation* and its successor. My criticism of this preoccupation is not that it gives Raymond Williams a sharp eye for class manners—on the contrary, he strikes me as being one of the very few modern writers who really understands, in detail, what class-bound British society does to people—but that so much of the antagonism in *Second Generation* and *The Fight for Manod* is between working-class socialist academics and middle-class socialist or liberal academics. The effect of this is socially, intellectually, and emotionally narrowing. It is as if, while attempting 'the highest realism' as he has defined it, a personal pattern has come to influence his writing so that the range of the trilogy is limited and a version of the 'special pleading' which he has analysed in other writers has entered in.

The Fight for Manod is the novel in the trilogy which gives the broadest view of the political and economic system—of Euro-capitalism and the companies and individuals manipulating it or manipulated by it, of the planners in centralized, high offices and the places and people which are their material. It brings together Peter Owen and Matthew Price as consultants assessing the social effects of a new kind of city which it is proposed to build in mid-Wales. Matthew is now in his late fifties, a sick man who has spent his energies fighting for better social relations. Unfortunately we are granted little insight into his middle years, and the substance of his life even now is largely taken for granted. He seems to me a character with whom the author is thinking and feeling, but with a reserve equivalent to the character's; and there are times when Matthew's thoughts and his conversations with his wife and friends can be fully interpreted only by reference to ideas expounded in Raymond Williams's critical writings. Peter Owen is still in much the same deadlock as he was in *Second Generation:* apparently incapable of love and justifying his personal deficiencies by referring them to a society which must change before he can. He is, as Matthew says, 'within alienation analysing alienation'.

As one would expect, *The Fight for Manod* urgently addresses itself to the crisis of contemporary Britain as Raymond Williams sees it. What is surprising, though, is that it is an underdeveloped novel, with only a few fully realized episodes (notable among which is the rescue of a man trapped in a tractor accident) and few characters who are even partially developed, and with elements of caricature. Indeed, it strikes me as being a novel in which something is being withheld. What this may, perhaps, be deduced from the following conversation between Matthew and Beth, Peter's wife:

'Yes, I feel the pull of the past so strongly, but I think there's something else that belongs to this country: a pure idea, a pure passion, for a different world.'

'In the people around here?'

Matthew looked across at her.

'In what has moved through them. In their religion, in their politics. It's not ever been cynical, not ever resigned. It's been a dream, if you like, but a dream of a country. And if we give up that...'

'I agree with you, Matthew.'

He looked intently into her face.

'If we give up that future... It needn't be this city, but I keep thinking it has to be. That we have to make the leap, get on to new ground. And yet the old ground holds me. It holds us and holds us back.'

Beth held his look.

'You mean giving up the city would be like giving up faith?'

'Yes, I feel that. Past all the arguments, that's exactly what I feel.'

Matthew Price and Raymond Williams are obviously close in feeling and thought, so that what Williams cannot or will not do, Price cannot or will not do either. One thing Matthew will not do is oppose Peter Owen, when he sets out to wreck the scheme of the new city on discovering that it has been, in certain respects, seriously compromised by capitalist interests. As Matthew says, 'in the opposition there's only the opposition. That's why I can't be against him.' Except that Matthew wants a new kind of settlement and Peter, it seems, wants only change, the differences between their ideas of socialism remain largely unexamined. There is, however, an obvious fundamental difference between them as men which must have a bearing on this: Matthew Price is capable of love and Peter Owen is not. Moreover, Welsh border country and the radical tradition of Wales are among the things Matthew loves. His love of the country and the past is obvious in numerous details and even statements throughout the novel, but his feeling for them is largely withheld. In terms of Raymond Williams's intention, here and in the trilogy as a whole, I think it has to be; because the country bearing the marks of its history is there and the new city is not. Love of the country is, as Raymond Williams well knows, difficult to distinguish from nostalgia for an irrecoverable past, and it is easier to feel at home on 'the old ground' than to give oneself imaginatively to the new. I am suggesting, then, that release of this feeling in *The Fight for Manod* might have made it the kind of novel *Border Country* resisted being: a return of the native which is a retreat upon the natal countryside with its lost or mythic community, instead of a release of energy for carrying the values of the real history through to the future. Such a retreat is the kind of settlement Matthew Price and Raymond Williams will not make, but its avoidance in present circumstances, with the new ground both so uncertain and impossible to feel as deeply as the old, requires rigid control of feelings natural to the return. Faith has to be kept: love of the past demands it, demands loyalty to 'a dream of a country', a dream which is now, for Matthew, the new city.

The city is difficult to realize, in fact and in fiction. Matthew's feeling for it is, however, eloquently expressed on one notable occasion, at a critical meeting with the Minister and his advisers, when he brings up the question of where the people of the new city will come from. The passage is worth quoting in full for the quality of its argument:

> 'May I tell you? The feeling in Manod, in that whole district, is against being used from outside. That is also, I needn't say, a very general feeling in Wales. I don't necessarily share Dr Owen's opinions. There were several good things in the original scheme. And on balance there are more in the scheme as now revised. But the crucial factor—you must really appreciate this—is who the people are to be. For this is a country bled dry by prolonged depopulation. Not far away, in the valleys, there is a ravaged and depressed old industrial area. If it can be clearly seen that in these new ways, bringing the two

needs together, a different future becomes possible, a future that settles people, that gives them work and brings them home, then through all the dislocation, through all the understandable losses and pains of change, there could still be approval, significant approval: not just the design of a city but the will of its citizens.'

'You are eloquent, Dr Price, but I don't quite clearly follow. Are you saying that this city should be confined to Welsh?'

'I don't mean nationality. I mean that the storms that have blown through that country—storms with their origin elsewhere—should now be carefully and slowly brought under control. In one place at a time, one move at a time, we should act wholly and consistently in the interests of that country; and those interests, primarily, are the actual people now there, caught between rural depopulation and industrial decline, the end of two separated orders, and there in Manod, if we could see it, is a real way beyond them. But only a real way if it belongs to the people on whose land it is being made.'

Dr Price is indeed eloquent, with an effort which almost costs him his life; but his words, though stirring, are without flesh in the novel, because the history of which he speaks remains largely outside the novel (and a significant part of it is outside the trilogy), while the people of Manod, though given more substantial life than other characters, are still insufficiently developed to give a real, moving presence to his speech on their behalf. Except in such a speech, the new city obviously cannot be realized in a novel which is concerned, not to present a Utopia, but to show the struggle for an opportunity to explore 'new social patterns, new actual social relations'. This dream of a country is a difficult dream, perhaps more difficult now than in its earlier phases, and the energy which might have gone into retreating upon the past is kept for this.

So the trilogy keeps faith, and it does so at a cost to the development of the final novel in particular, which, though admirably tentative, is made thin by its tensions. If, however, my argument is taken as a slighting criticism even of this novel, then I will have failed to show that I regard the movement of the trilogy, from past to present, without retreat upon an idealized past or escape to a future Utopia, as one of the most difficult and necessary ventures of any post-war writer. Matthew Price at the end of *The Fight for Manod* is 'ready to go on'. In a short-sighted yet obsessively retrospective time, this readiness has characterized Raymond Williams too. He goes on with a dream of a country which moved through his people, above all the agricultural and industrial workers of South Wales, not back to any of the dreams which, in fact and in fiction, were used (and are still being used) to romanticize them or exploit them or hold them back from making their chosen settlement.

Edward Thomas

WHEN I first read Edward Thomas, on the periphery of the dominant landscape of his poetry, I already had a deep love of the southern countryside, which I had learnt to see, better than I would otherwise have done, from an early and intensive reading of Richard Jefferies. The affinity between Jefferies and Thomas was at once apparent. What I was principally aware of at that stage was only a part, though an important part, of both writers: the expression of an unique personality, with a plangent but stoical sadness at its brevity and insignificance in the cycles of nature, in ecstatic contemplation of the life-force revealed by even the minutest details of the natural world. Each celebrates that which actually exists, and the quality of perception often reveals the isolated self of the perceiver even more intimately than do the details of Hardy's poems. In speaking of isolation, however, I am referring prematurely to the preoccupation of a later reading; at first, I was more conscious of the details, and peculiar atmospheres, in which the cast of the self is implicit. Of the details of 'But These Things Also', for example:

> The shell of a little snail bleached
> In the grass; chip of flint, and mite
> Of chalk; and the small birds' dung
> In splashes of purest white.

Or the atmosphere of 'Thaw', whose first two lines—'Over the land freckled with snow half-thawed/The speculating rooks at their nests cawed—' recreate the mood of the season when abeyant life is about to quicken, and the lover of such timely sights and sounds is suspended between sadness and expectancy. Aware of the ecstatic voice and delight in activity of Jefferies and Thomas alike, I was more attentive to the hushed quality of suspense between seasons caught by some of Thomas's poems. It was a fact of the country I knew, and recollecting this first reading I cannot easily distinguish between the poems themselves and a way of seeing and feeling that was partly shared with them and partly activated by them.

Reading his work as a whole in the following decade I saw more, without ceasing to appreciate the part perceived earlier. I then read Edward Thomas with an acute sense of the bitterly ironical contrast between the man himself, all that he valued in his England, and the First World War that not only destroyed so much but was made possible, and perhaps inevitable, by forces in the society of which he was an isolated member. I saw, too, that he was a war poet both by virtue of the presence of the war in a number of his poems, and because it was among the events that helped him to find himself as a poet, and made his post-enlistment work—consciously, I believe—a last will and testament. I could then no longer see the south country untouched by the changes wrought since his death, or not undermined by the dark hollow—two of his favourite words, often conjoined—that the tragic history in which he had participated had made immeasurably darker and more hollow. Visiting Steep I was still awed by the country, but thought of Edward Thomas, and Alun Lewis as well, both uniformed, their natural skills adapted to other ends. The change of perspective led me to question the nature of his Nature in relation to the conceptions of other ages based on a changing but vital rural society, and to interpret it as a traditional source of actual and symbolic renewal virtually exhausted in his time. Thomas the 'poor, modern man', as he saw himself, or, like Aurelius in *The Happy-Go-Lucky Morgans*, one of 'the superfluous... who cannot find society with which they are in some sort of harmony', seemed the inheritor of a dying tradition, and the exhaustion, exacerbated by his comprehensively ambiguous position in rural English society, seemed to have given rise to writings in which, for both writer and reader, desire of the unselfconscious being of childhood, and desire of unconsciousness, were difficult to tell apart. At this stage I was most conscious of his harrowing isolation, and my interest centred on such details as his ironical, allusive use of 'merry' and his unironical invocation of Merry England, in 'The Owl' and 'The Manor Farm' respectively, compared with all that those terms had once meant. It seemed to me that Thomas had felt the ironies and ambiguities of his position as keenly, and faced them as bravely, as any person ever could. What was really at issue in this change of perspective, however, was the problem of knowing what England had been in his lifetime, and was now.

The perspective enabled me to see some themes and qualities of the poems at the expense of others, and clouded their subtlety and wholeness. When I read the poems now, the earlier responses are subsumed under an awareness of their irreducibility to a single virtue—their earthliness—or even a complex theory of the poet's 'position'. Thomas is earthly—he uses all his senses—but rarely earthy, in the sense of embodying the generative force of nature, as, for example, some poems by Patrick Kavanagh and Seamus Heaney are. Many of his poems dramatize the difficulty of achieving the balance, let alone union, of opposites. He is a poet conscious of his existence between earth and sky, isolation and society, the ideal and reality, birth and death, and of his impulses divided between opposing tendencies that may at times be united. There is often a corresponding duality in his imagery and settings. Light and dark, black and white, two or more elements, adult and child, the poet and another (whether an actual person or another self), past and present, the living and the dead, ecstasy and melancholy—these are some of the dualisms whose interaction or opposition are dramatized in poem after poem. Accordingly Thomas is often a poet of metamorphosis. Sometimes fancy transforms the actual into the ideal or the unreal until reality is affirmed. 'Sedge-Warblers' and 'The New Year' are two very different poems in which this process occurs, but the classic affirmation is made in 'Wind and Mist':

> I did not know it was the earth I loved
> Until I tried to live there in the clouds
> And the earth turned to cloud.

Sometimes, as in 'The Hollow Wood' and 'The Lofty Sky', the transposition of creatures or elements has a more unsettling and mysterious effect. The 'gloom of whiteness' and 'dusky brightness' of 'Snow' exemplify in a fairly simple way the kind of metaphysical (yet earthly) paradox that is not infrequently of a piece with the totality of a poem.

These observations merely note what I now regard as the prevalent modes of his perception and imagination; the sensitivity required to examine them would have to match the quickness, delicacy and suggestiveness of the imagination at work in the poems, and such an examination would put my earlier responses in their place. That Thomas should perceive so persistently as a man divided, inwardly and outwardly, between real or apparent opposites, that he should sometimes transpose them, often seek and sometimes achieve their balance or union, clearly owes something to the 'position' outlined above, and much to his sense of time, of 'the hollow past' that 'Half yields the dead that never/more than half hidden lie', to his tentative and questing mind, and to his emotional and intellectual honesty that made single-minded commitment impossible; although his love of this earth emerges unambiguously from all his qualifications, and it was, finally, an unabstract but necessarily somewhat idealized England to which he gave himself.

Edward Thomas is, of course, a poet who often uses the first person singular. The variety of his remarkably unified body of work may be seen, not only in his use of different forms but also in the contrast, often present within a single poem, between the virtue which he made of the selfconsciousness that tormented him, and lucid, resonant statement. 'The Glory', for example, can sustain both 'Or must I be content with discontent/As larks and swallows are perhaps with wings?' and the question that follows, and 'I cannot bite the day to the core.'

The same man who wrote:

> What I desired I knew not, but whate'er my choice
> Vain it must be, I knew. Yet naught did my despair

> But sweeten the strange sweetness...
>   'Melancholy'

could begin another poem, 'The Lofty Sky', with 'Today I want the sky', and write 'Adlestrop' and 'Lob'. Here I can only state that his 'I', though broadly within the Romantic tradition and while having certain affinities with Hardy's and George Herbert's, seems to me the most personal, the least affected by transference from the man speaking to the dramatic medium of the poem, of any English poet. If he remains almost as elusive as Hamlet, that is because there is so much of his personality in the poems, and the more effectively a person expresses his essential self the more elusive and mysterious the self becomes; also the more truly common in its manifestation of our shared singularity. But Thomas's 'I' exists either between opposites or in relation to things, creatures and people, and above all in relation to his England, which is as much sky, rain and rivers as earth and its creatures, and in many poems an historical, social world.

Edward Thomas knew the difference between the places he loved and contemporary patriotic ideas of the British Empire or Little England, but at first sight it may still seem paradoxical that one who was 'mainly Welsh' should have become one of the few truly patriotic English poets of this century—by which I mean a poet who could, without rhetoric and sentimentality, if occasionally with a measure of uneasy idealism, express an implicit love of his chosen country. His ability to do so, like that of David Jones, was inseparable from his use of words. To him, words were 'as dear/As the earth which you prove/That we love.' The art of right naming is the art of restoring or drawing attention to the value of the things, people and places named, and only outside literature may a wordless love prove itself genuine. He had this art to a high degree. Further, since there is no real technical revolution or renewal of poetry that is not also a freeing of blocked emotions, and a means of access to old or new subject-matter, the struggle with his own tendencies to be rhetorical and fanciful which Edward Thomas won in his poems—as he had already won it in the best of his prose—has made him a continuing vitalizing influence on British poetry. His work will certainly outlast the stages of any one reader's relationship with it, and remain to say far more than anything that can be said about it.

Honouring Ivor Gurney

FROM December 1922 until his death in 1937 Ivor Gurney was incarcerated in the City of London Mental Hospital at Dartford, in Kent. The story of his life and madness has been told by Michael Hurd with sympathy and understanding in *The Ordeal of Ivor Gurney*. It is neither my intention to rehearse the details or even sketch the outline of that story here, nor to play the amateur psychologist with Gurney's mental state. I want instead to show why I regard Gurney as one of the finest and most significant English poets of this century. I cannot do this, however, without considering his 'world': the world whose composition and eventual breakdown are expressed in his poetry. Madness is always terrible, of course; but in the case of a man greatly gifted as both musician and poet, who is therefore essentially a maker and instrument of order, and a voice of the language which composes and confirms our human world, there is an additionally tragic irony in his descent into the chaos and isolation of insanity. By the same token his personal breakdown, however uniquely individual some of its causes were, must reveal processes of general disintegration in the culture and society to which he belonged.

I

In 'To the Poet Before Battle' Ivor Gurney adjures the poet in the fray to 'Remember thy great craft's honour, that they may say/Nothing in shame of poets.' He is to 'Make/The name of poet terrible in just war,/And like a crown of honour upon the fight.' It is not all surprising, of course, that this poem, written in army camp in England in 1915, before Gurney had experienced actual battle, should have a Brookean rhetoric and exultation at the martial prospect. The poem is only remarkable retrospectively, for expressing crucial attitudes which are virtually the same as those of his later poems, written after he had shown himself to be perhaps the most coolly unillusioned of all English combatant poets as far as the war was concerned.

Michael Hurd quotes a letter in which, writing of his first book of poems (soon to be called *Severn and Somme*), from the trenches in July 1917, Gurney notes its comparative lack of 'the devotion of self-sacrifice, the splendid readiness for death that one finds in Grenfell, Brooke, Nichols, etc'. 'Though I am ready if necessary to die for England,' he continues, 'I do not see the necessity; it being only a hard and fast system which has sent so much of the flower of England's artists to risk death, and a wrong materialistic system.' In the circumstances, this is a remarkably cool and critical assessment of his situation, which might suggest, taken out of context, that he was closer in outlook to Barbusse than the poets he has just named. Gurney goes on, however, 'rightly or wrongly I consider myself able to do work which will do honour to England. Such is my patriotism, and I believe it to be the right kind.' So while treating conventional self-sacrificial idealism with ironical detachment Gurney at the same time states his own ideal—'to do work which will do honour to England'. Here we have the two most emotive words in his poetry, connected as they necessarily were for him: 'Honour' and 'England'.

'Honour' was of course a word with great widespread power in those war years; a power which it would soon lose, at least for serious poetry concerned in any way with 'the condition of England'. It remains to the present one of our great dead words, killed along with others when the language of conventional patriotic idealism met the facts of trench warfare and military politics. It will seem odd at first, therefore, that in Gurney's later poetry 'honour' should actually increase in power, in the feeling with which he charges it, and in its significance within his system of values. It does so, however, not only because he remained attached—indeed became more attached—to a wartime ideal to which he had seemed comparatively immune at the time. Far more important, 'honour' became so central to his love of country that it formed the axis of his world.

The strands of feeling in Gurney's later poetry became a knot that finally broke. But they can be seen more loosely joined in 'To the Poet Before Battle'. Honour in battle is to be received only by those poets who have given honour where it is due—in the conventional terms of this poem, to those of 'might/And strong of mettle'. The poem has just enough substance to sketch Gurney's sense of the poet's role: he has a relationship of mutually binding responsibility with his world: he gives and he receives: he honours and he is honoured.

Gurney's world was his England. His England was essentially Gloucestershire. Such identifications of place or region with nation were common then; with individual and historical differences, they have been common in England from its beginnings as a nation, for England has always been characterized by physical, cultural, and social variousness, forming a mosaic of individual localities within the larger regional differences; and appeals to unified national feeling have invariably used images either of this variousness or of a locality or localities presented in *their* particularity and variety as *essence* of the whole. The identifications of part with whole are naturally felt with special intensity at times of national crisis; and for those who commit their lives and feelings to them, they are fraught with tensions and dangers. Among these at the time of the First World War were the mobilization for destructive purposes of the great power that is love of place and kin, and the subsequent numbing or anger felt towards all patriotic ideas of England as a consequence of disillusionment, when the iron structure of its 'wrong materialistic system' showed through the spiritual and familial ideal for which many had believed they were fighting. This consequence—not experienced by all people, of course, but common among the intelligentsia—has been further complicated by subsequent history to form the tightly, intricately tangled knot which I believe many poets today find their sense of being English is. For Kipling, for example, in a time of much simpler national feelings, the relation between Sussex and England, and England and the atlas of the world, was both morally binding and powerfully emotive. But what is the relation between 'this England' represented by literary tradition, and even more emotively, by a handful of earth, for which such a man as Edward Thomas fought and the actual system which led to the mass slaughter of mechanized war? It is not a question that any English writer with a sense of place, with his own literal or symbolic handful of earth, can avoid living.

The tensions and reactions accompanying identifications of locality and nation—'my place' and 'my country'—are not necessarily conscious; but they will inevitably find direct or indirect expression, at times of national crisis, in a poetry of place. Ivor Gurney's feeling for Gloucester and its countryside would have been strong in any circumstances, but its peculiar intensity and its ultimately tragic strains owed much to the effects on him of the generally devastating history which he lived.

II

The quality of Gurney's feeling for place had other causes, too. In 'On a Memory', an asylum poem first published in *The Ordeal of Ivor Gurney*, the poet reviewing his boyhood speaks of

> Music waking in him, Music outwelling
> From the good soil, That Western land, fulfilling
> All hopes of the mind, all spirit's deep desire.

This is one of several poems to reveal that Gurney, with his strong sense of musical and literary traditions voicing the spirit of England, thought of himself as the medium through which the music inherent in his native land found expression, 'waking in *him*', 'outwelling/*From the good soil*'. Similarly, he was proud to believe himself *the* poet of Gloucester, dedicated

> To my own County where I was born, and the earth
> Entered into my making and into my blood—
> Which I praised better than any ever of Her birth,
> (The City of Gloucester finding in me Her true mood).
> 'To Gloucestershire'

The feeling of being born of England as an expression of her spirit was a convention of Edwardian and Georgian poets, the latter, like Gurney, tending to localize it while the former, with their mock-Elizabethan imperial spirit, could actually feel something maternal about the British Empire. But a similar feeling in relation to one's native earth has been common worldwide from early times, and it would be fascinating to see where a study of its history would lead—certainly to more primitive sources and more responsible and sophisticated manifestations than the Edwardians. In Gurney's case, the contemporary conventional feeling was greatly heightened and individualized by his being an outstanding musician as well as a poet, and therefore having a doubly potent myth of the artist as a voice of his land. And his feeling not only survived the war but was intensified by it. As musician and poet of the county whose very name recalls Shakespeare and the romance of English history, Gurney had far more than most people to protect, and so to lose. Even the good name of his country.

The places of Gurney's poems are not only, or even primarily, scenes in which he figures alone, serving to express an inner drama. They are places coloured by actual friendships, but even more by his ideal community. The latter appears frequently in his poems in an Elizabethan form, which Gurney knows has gone. It is the 'England of madrigal, pipe and tabor—/Merry England again of Daniel', which he evokes in 'Tobacco'. There is, however, a difference between knowing that a particular form of past community has gone, and being able to bear what is felt to be the breakdown of all connection with the past, in a place where the presence of all generations since at least Roman times was sensed. Gurney's community is also, remarkably, an ideal which he sees envisioned by himself and other soldiers in France, as he looks back after the war and simultaneously embodies his vision—seen to be 'romantic'—and places it in a critical perspective. This occurs in 'First Time in'.

> Gone out; Cotswold's Black Mountain edges against august
> August after-suns glow, and air a lit dust
> With motes and streams of gold. Wales her soul visible
> Against all power West Heaven ever could flood full.
> And of songs—the Slumber Song, and the soft Chant
> So beautiful to which Rabelaisian songs were meant;
> Of South and North Wales; and David of the White Rock:

> What an evening! What a first time, what a shock
> So rare of home-pleasure beyond measure
> And always to Time's ending surely a treasure,
> Since After-war so surely hurt, disappointed men
> Who looked for the golden Age to come friendly again.

Despite its conscious romanticism, it would be easy to point out folksy, sentimental elements here and elsewhere in Gurney's poems, and especially in the pleasures he goes on to name—'inn evenings of meetings in warm glows,/Talk: coal and wood fire uttering rosy shows/With beer and "Widdicombe Fair"'—but he shows, for my taste, an attractive ideal of companionship, in a world combining 'high' and 'low' culture. This evidently owed something to his idea of a companionable old England, something to youthful friendships in Gloucestershire, and more to the heightened sense of his home country seen from the trenches, in the glow of *their* comradeship. After the war, however, he could not find his ideal community except as a memory or a dream, and although in some poems the ideal enriches the natural light of his Gloucestershire places, in poems of his mental torment its loss is felt confusedly as chief symptom of England's dishonour:

> In the world's places that honour earth, all men are thinking
> Of centuries: all men of the ages of living and drinking;
> Singing and company of all time till now—
> (When the hate of Hell has this England's state plain).
>
> 'December 30th'

If this movement from a passionately idealized world to a correspondingly bitterly resented chaos were the whole story of Gurney's poetry it would be moving enough; but what I feel makes it more terrible is the poetic recreation of a 'real' external world, which balances his myth-making, and makes the Gloucestershire of his poems one of the most living places in all English poetry.

Gurney's sense of history and of historical continuity contributes greatly to this. He has, for example, a gift for at once naming things and conveying their shapes and textures, which renders place as the presence of historical time, but without conflating widely separated periods or smoothing out their differences:

> One comes across the strangest things in walks;
> Fragments of Abbey tithe-barns fixed in modern
> And Dutch-sort houses where the water baulks
> Weired up, and brick kilns broken among fern,
> Old troughs, great stone cisterns bishops might have blessed
> Ceremonially, and worthy mounting-stones;
> Black timber in red brick, queerly placed

> Where Hill stone was looked for—and a manor's bones
> Spied in the frame of some wisteria'd house
> And mill-falls and sedge pools and Saxon faces...
>   'Cotswold Ways'

Another quality evident here is his evocation of things not only as lived with and used, but also as crafted and made. Gurney finds in his places—in the words of his 'Brown Earth Look'—'revelations/Of beauty in usualty' and 'The sense of myriads tending the needings of life'. His aesthetic feeling for things is firmly allied to his awareness of human uses and needs, and of their character and setting as man's composition. He belongs in this respect with Thomas Hardy, Edward Thomas and, despite fundamental philosophical differences, Gerard Manley Hopkins, rather than with A. E. Housman; for although his landscape is deeply coloured by nostalgia and other personal emotions, it is not primarily a mental space but a long-settled place, humanly shaped and deeply seamed with human experience.

III

Gurney occasionally echoes other poets, notably Hopkins and Edward Thomas among moderns; indeed I think of him as being 'between' these two, not qualitatively—for in his best poems he is not, in my view, a lesser poet than either—not as their mimic, but rather as a poet combining a feeling for the texture and sounds of words, that is akin to Hopkins's, with an apparent naturalness that is closer to Thomas's. He is like them too in the morality of his imagination: his poetic is inseparable from his metaphysic. He expresses this in 'The Escape':

> I believe in the increasing of life whatever
>   Leads to the seeing of small trifles,
> Real, beautiful, is good, and an act never
>   Is worthier than in freeing spirit that stifles
> Under ingratitude's weight, nor is anything done
>   Wiselier than the moving or breaking to sight
> Of a thing hidden under by custom; revealed
>   Fulfilled, used, (sound-fashioned) any way out to delight,
> Trefoil—hedge sparrow—the stars on the edge at night.

It does not matter if Gurney had read the relevant passages in Wordsworth and Coleridge (or Edward Thomas on Richard Jefferies) about the relation between imagination, seeing, and love. For although his beliefs are Romantic, they are expressed with a conviction and stylistic originality that prove their authenticity. 'Awakening the mind's attention to the lethargy of custom' is Coleridge; 'the moving or breaking to sight/Of a thing hidden under by custom' is Gurney. As far as seeing is concerned, Gurney is again with Thomas and Hopkins. He is with them in the sense that all three were with the early English Romantics in their freshness of vision, and not, like many of their contemporaries, prisoners of the Romantic decadence.

'Sound-fashioned' (in a line that is more than usually dependent on Hopkins) has, of course, three principal meanings. The most immediately obvious—soundly or well made—is represented elsewhere by his frequent emphasis on 'square-making'—a feature of Gurney's art which Samuel Hynes notes in his fine essay on him, 'The squaring of human sorrow' (*TLS*, 13 October 1978). There is about both expressions, as about many of his poems, a feeling of the craftsman's hand and eye. A probable cause of this is well brought out by Edmund Blunden in his Introduction to *Poems of Ivor Gurney:* 'Probably much of his style is consonant with the first stages of his quick sensibility awakening among ancient buildings, especially country churches; he grew up with the instances of old craftsmanship in carved work, stone or wood, ever in view and in reach.' Blunden also says, memorably, that his poetry has 'something of the high-poised gargoyle against the flying cloud'. Closely allied to this craftsmanwise meaning of 'sound-fashioned', drawing out its moral connotations, is the sense 'made whole'.

The third meaning—fashioned from sounds—names one of Gurney's greatest gifts as a poet. The reality of his places owes much to his acute sensitivity to weathers, effects of light, movements, physical sensations. These impressions of a world vividly alive and intensely experienced are rendered by his rhythms and syntax, his quick elliptical imagistic detail, and his mastery of patterns of verbal sound. 'Near Vermand' provides a fine example:

> Low woods to left—(Cotswold her spinnies if ever)
> Showed through snow flurries and the clearer star weather,
> And nothing but chill and wonder lived in mind; nothing
> But loathing and fine beauty, and wet loathed clothing.
> Here were thoughts. Cold smothering and fire-desiring,
> A day to follow like this or in the digging or wiring.
> Worry in snow flurrying and lying flat, flesh the earth loathing.

This is a marvellous poetry of bodily experience, with imagination at the tips of all the senses. Gurney's success in making a part of England the world of his poems is also revealed by the parenthetic '(Cotswold her spinnies if ever)', whose existence as a superbly evocative microcosm depends on his creation of that world.

It was Gurney's mastery of sound-fashioning in all its senses that enabled him, in some of the most dynamic modern English poems, to exemplify Coleridge's 'a more than usual state of emotion with more than usual order'. In 'The Sea Borders', for example, Gurney can justify his claim to sympathetic knowledge of the Atlantic battering against its several shores, as if he were that barely contained ocean—

> Not only because I musician have wrestled with the stuff in making,
> And wrought a square thing out of my stubborn mind—
> And gathered a huge surge of spirit as the great barriers bind
> The whole Atlantic at them by Devon or West Ireland.

The surge of energy in the whole poem, like the ocean's within its shores, is the result of great power shaped by its containing form.

Yet for all his making 'a square thing', for all his gathering 'a huge surge of spirit', Ivor Gurney himself eventually broke: a breakdown which is itself 'sound-fashioned' in a number of poems but which pathetically disorders others.

IV

I have suggested that Gurney was highly conscious of, reliant on, and inventive in his use of tradition—tradition in several senses: historical continuity in place, experienced virtually as a comradeship of the generations; musical tradition, both classical and popular—Bach, Beethoven, Schubert, William Byrd, English folk-song, ballads and airs; literary tradition—the Elizabethans, the minor poets of his county and the great poets of the English countryside. In his brief lyrics in particular, Gurney's active participation in musical and literary tradition is plain to see and hear. 'Song' is a beautiful, poignant, example.

> Only the wanderer
>   Knows England's graces,
> Or can anew see clear
>   Familiar faces.
>
> And who loves joy as he
>   That dwells in shadows?
> Do not forget me quite,
>   O Severn meadows.

Such perfect poems are at once wholly his own, as much Gurney in every detail of word and rhythm as his signature, and the essence of a tradition which seems somehow to have produced them *through* the man. This makes even more tragically paradoxical the descent into chaos and isolation of this most companionable man, whose work as poet and musician has a more intimate sense of belonging, to a place and within the traditions of a culture, than that of any other modern English artist. As I have argued, a contributory cause of this was his obsession with 'honour', which ultimately acquired for him the intensity of Lear's obsession with gratitude. For honour was no high-sounding abstraction for Gurney; it was rather the principle of all relationship, binding the poet to others, living and dead, in the country he served. Dishonour meant for him a breach in human nature, in the continuity of truly human order in his country from the time of the Roman settlements; it meant the shattering of his world. But perhaps enough has now been said to bring out the terrible poignancy of the following lines from 'What's in Time', a poem in which Gurney's mind is evidently breaking:

> To make the time's greatest song, and be given
> Dust on the covers for all the pain striven.
> To cast out a shout of love to a far
> Country, long loved, and be given bare
> Silence, and cold unhonouring there.

Self-pity? Certainly. There is plenty of this in the exasperated spirit of his later poems. But it makes a difference to know that his claim to have made 'the time's greatest song' was not a vain boast or empty vanity. Of course, his belief that he would be honoured by Gloucestershire and England according to the honour which he as soldier, musician and poet had given was a sign of his mental instability. He was evidently in some fatal respects a passionately, stubbornly, naive man. But the unreasonable intensity of his love and the quality of the work it produced show up the reason of a culture in which such generous creativity has still to be properly honoured.

It is late enough for this, but still too early for a full assessment of Ivor Gurney's poetry. There is no Collected Poems yet (though it is being prepared for publication by Oxford University Press in 1982); hundreds of poems remain in manuscript and the most recent selection, *Poems of Ivor Gurney,* welcome though it was (it is out of print now), is not well-ordered, while the finality of some poems in their only accessible versions must be in doubt. I am convinced, however, that he will eventually be seen not only as an outstanding modern English poet but also as a crucial figure in the vitally important phase of non-modernist English poetry in the years 1912–22, which produced the initial impact of Hopkins and the greatest poems of Thomas Hardy, the poetry of Wilfred Owen, Isaac Rosenberg and Edward Thomas, and D. H. Lawrence's earlier poetic maturity. With Owen, Rosenberg and Thomas, Gurney was one of the young poets who were highly sensitive to various poetic traditions, and were forced to adapt the gifted poet's normal process of finding his new way in relation to those traditions, to a drastically shortened development and an encounter with unprecedented experience. It was in more than one way a time of breaking down, and for the poets, of attempting to express and comprehend it, while at the same time keeping the language whole, protecting it from all the lies and unrealities to which it was being bent. It was a time of breaking images and failing symbols, of great words abused and rendered impotent. Ideals of England were being shattered, the natural world was proving a source of increasingly diminishing symbolic restoration and renewal, and the sense of community and historical continuity in place was generally under great strain. Gurney lived these movements of disintegration, and the ways he found of writing in spite of them, even as a man of integrity from within them, helped to keep the language alive, but not to hold his huge surge of spirit within the bounds of sanity.

Frances Bellerby in Place

FRANCES BELLERBY was born in Bristol in 1899 and died in 1975. As well as a poet, she was a novelist and essayist, and a fine short story writer. Her *Selected Poems*, published by Enitharmon in 1970, were chosen by Charles Causley from recent uncollected work and from her three previous collections, *Plash Mill, The Brightening Cloud* and *The Stone Angel and the Stone Man*. Her last book, *The First-Known and Other Poems*, was published by Enitharmon in the year of her death.

Charles Causley, in his excellent Introduction to her *Selected Poems*, records that what first drew him to her poetry in the 1940s was, 'above many other outstanding qualities', its secure expression of 'the ambience, and the essence, of place'. The place of much of her poetry is a corner of Bodmin Moor, the surroundings and the interior of her cottage, Plash Mill. This is in some respects familiar ground, recalling the poetic worlds rooted in particular localities of Clare, Hardy and Edward Thomas, and of Charles Causley himself and other English poets since. Frances Bellerby's place is as actual if not as highly individualized as Hardy's and Thomas's, but stranger, with a life outside its history and the poet's consciousness which their beliefs exclude.

'Voices' shows her simultaneously describing a place and revealing the life of the dead:

> I heard those voices today again:
> Voices of women and children, down in that hollow
> Of blazing light into which swoops the tree-darkened lane
> Before it mounts up into the shadow again.
>
> I turned the bend—just as always before
> There was no one at all down there in the sunlit hollow;
> Only ferns in the wall, foxgloves by the hanging door
> Of that blind old desolate cottage. And just as before
>
> I noticed the leaping glitter of light
> Where the stream runs under the lane; in that mine-dark archway
> —Water and stones unseen as though in the gloom of night—
> Like glittering fish slithers and leaps the light.

The lane swoops and mounts, the stream runs, 'slithers and leaps', and the movement is from shadow into blazing light into shadow. There is a central stillness. The light is most alive in the 'mine-dark archway'. All this is sensitively observed, and shows complete control of the mode, perfected by Hardy and Thomas, of presenting a place as at once actual and haunted. In 'Voices', however, imagery of light and darkness, and of movement and stillness and the relation between these conventional opposites, define a precise numinous vision of death-in-life and life-in-death. In the terms of her poem 'The Valley', there is a 'lake of light', but not apart from 'the valley of the shadow'. Here, too, light is comprehended by darkness.

Frances Bellerby's place is where she is always but never alone, always solitary but seeking or finding communion. The house in her poetry, whether Plash Mill or her childhood home, is a particularly haunted place. 'Home' is for her, as for Edward Thomas, a highly charged word. It was where, as a child, she came closest to the understanding for which her whole subsequent life was a quest:

> What the untaught child knew
> Is the sum of all learning.
>   He must walk hand-in-hand
>   With his own understanding
> Who would go down to the grave and lift up the dead.
> 'Resurrection Symphony'

Her place is consequently where she is always homeless, waiting for the day

>   When I shall go on and on and on, my lost home
>   Found in my heart; I, a king bearing his kingdom
>   Within...
> 'Convalescence'

Although the movement of this feeling is similar to that in a number of Thomas's poems, her conception of home in fact differs widely from his. In a crucial passage in *The South Country* Thomas wrote, 'yet is this country [the south of England], though I am mainly Welsh, a kind of home, as I think it is more than any other to those modern people who belong nowhere'. This is central to an understanding of Thomas. He affirms identity ('mainly Welsh'), and a qualified sense of belonging ('a kind of home'), within a context of radical displacement ('those modern people who belong nowhere'). And this precisely defines his modernity, with *home* (not 'a kind of home') standing for all that a radically displaced man lacks—not in *place* as geographical location alone, of course, but comprehensively. In Frances Bellerby, on the other hand, any similar unease is subsumed, in its psychological and social aspects, by a traditional imagery, used with the boldness of a Henry Vaughan or a Traherne, revealing the meaning of life in time. 'Before the Light Fades', one of her finest lyrics, shows her bold yet conditional use of this language:

> Before the light fades
> Someone should be found to explain
> With sufficient wisdom and patience
> Everything I have seen.
>
> And before owl and moth
> Shock by remembered flight
> The deep, tombed, silence
> Of the world of night,
>
> There should appear some linguist
> Hot-blooded as a bird,
> To translate with a single sentence
> Everything I have heard.
>
> Then darkness
> Might prove home,
> And eternal silence
> The kingdom come.

It is evident that Frances Bellerby suffered greatly from bereavements and ill health, and knew physical and spiritual torment. In her novel *Hath the Rain a Father?*, as well as in her stories and poems, there is much to indicate that her relationship with her brother and his death at the age of eighteen in the First World War, during her schooldays, was the source of her quest for understanding. She dedicated her *Selected Poems* 'To the brief and everlasting life of my brother'. The paradoxical truth succinctly expressed here is not affirmed easily in her poetry, however, but arrived at through suffering. The suffering is in the poems, which are at once beautifully shaped and lived through, with experiential reality; they are acts of seeking, not didactic or discursive presentations of truth apart from the struggle to find and express it. (This is true of *Selected Poems* and *The First-Known*, but not always of poems in her earlier books, not selected by Charles Causley, which are passionate but more formularistic workings of her themes of death and resurrection.) It is consequently not necessary to know any biographical facts in order to feel the personal pressure behind her determination 'to learn/Some understanding of a foreign country, in time'.

It is as a poet of suffering, a religious rather than a metaphysical poet, that she differs, I feel, from the contemporary with whom her sense of the life of the dead would at first seem to link her—Vernon Watkins—and is closer in feeling to the poet of absolute loss, Thomas Hardy. For Watkins conveys rather a sense of 'the dead' as an anonymous collective, or at least, a metaphysical problem, than their presence as specific persons; death as separation and loss, and as a cause of terror and anguish to the self, is rarely felt in his poems, though doubtless such feeling accompanied the process by which he arrived at the vision they embody. The strength and clarity of spirit in Frances Bellerby, on the other hand, is felt against the grief from which it was forged, and her understanding comes from her suffering. As she wrote in '1915':

> Grieve no more for the agony of the child.
> She'd have brooked no lighter grief
> Who watched through tears the blackest field
> Against the silverest sky. No thief
> Was pure to snatch such treasure
> From the unmeasured heart that's made your measure.

As a poet who habitually resurrects buried emotions she is at once significantly different from Hardy but with an equivalent poignancy. This poem is called 'Brother and Sister':

> Would you say that field is the one?
> Look, my dear, there's the great
> pink chestnut, and the straight path
> from iron gate to iron gate —
> the old sort, that you wind yourself through.
> Yes, that field is the one.
>
> Then the tree's shadow must still make a tent.
> What are we so troubled about, the two of us?
> There's shelter, freedom, and the whole of time
> whilst that slow sun follows its long course,
> and in and out of the shadow-tent play,
> those deathless children, to our hearts' content.

When Hardy brings to life equivalent moments with lovers or parents or friends it is always on the understanding that his companions are irrevocably dead, but intensely alive for him alone, increasing his isolation; absolute division between the living and the dead determines his characteristic feelings. In this uncanny poem, the intimate tone and the recovery of 'those deathless children' are achieved with no less desolation and no more illusion. Each precise detail of the way to 'hearts' content' is a wound.

Frances Bellerby expresses a strong sense of unity in creation, of Isaiah's peaceable kingdom and holy mountain. Her ultimate hope was evidently in the promise expressed in a passage from St Paul which she quotes in *Hath the Rain a Father?*—'God has made known to us the mystery of His will—that in accordance with his eternal plan He should reunite all things in Christ, both things in Heaven and things in earth'. This is her vision at the end of her powerful long poem 'The Heron'.

> Then will the difference
> Vanish as the God of Love transfigures the everlasting
> Dead that they shine with lively light in the flowing
> Time of forgiveness of all winters, when the Vixen
> Dances with her cubs and the Spider's care is great
> And order has burnt up chaos and the world is calm.

It is impossible to extract passages from her poems without loss, for they are shaped as integral movements of thought and feeling, rhythm and imagery. So, here, the conclusion is validated by all that has gone before, including recognition that the God of Love

> himself offers no protection,
> Guides to no sanctuary, but anneals tenderness
> To a passion, making each individual life a supreme
> Unique dedication, and each individual death
> A tragedy to purge with pity and terror the innocent
> Children of men with their bloodstained hands.

With her passion of tenderness Frances Bellerby would lose nothing that is perfect, and finds perfection in all forms of life. She is accordingly, as Charles Causley says, not a symbolist. Her creatures and things do not represent or intimate something other than themselves. Hers is an art of recognizing and valuing beings for their individuality, and it requires exactness and freshness of perception and expression. This, no doubt, was a quality that enabled her, though beginning to write her durable poetry in the forties and though much preoccupied with themes dear to poets of the New Apocalypse, largely to avoid corrupting influences with a confidence equal to R. S. Thomas's. This, again, places her closer to Edward Thomas and Thomas Hardy, poets with a proper regard for the things of this world, than to any symbolist.

'In Place' shows a young male lizard:

> Now he gleams shell-like, lids drawn
> In the beatific face, jutted elbows
> And firmly spread fingers propping
> The raised torso of this infant son
> Of the god who pulses featherlight as yet
> Through the very young warmth and brightness
> Of the upspringing world.
>
> Here, then, is executed the perfection of a design
> Brought from and through all Time
> Into this moment—into this timed moment

> Out of all Time past and all to come —
> Into this accurate timed moment which being perfect
> Could not be out of place
> In Eternity.

The creature recognized for himself, for his perfect design and the life that has shaped and informs it, is seen transfigured. He is unique and of the one life, briefly incarnate now, and eternal. The art that presents him thus, borrowing nothing from ideas of the immortality of the soul or from Platonic idealism, probably comes as close as any art can to seeing things *sub specie aeternitatis*. In 'Ends Meet' Frances Bellerby reveals her grandmother in the same light, with equal distinctness:

> My grandmother's eyes were blue like the damsels
> Darting and swerving above the stream,
> Or like the kingfisher arrow shot into darkness
> Through the archway's dripping gleam.
>
> My grandmother's hair was silver as sunlight.
> The sun had been poured right over her, I saw,
> And ran down her dress and spread a pool for her shadow
> To float in. And she would live for evermore.

The explicitness of the final sentence of these verses is superfluous; the pervasive light in her poems transfigures beings by revealing the spiritual life informing them, not by dissolving their individuality.

Frances Bellerby's poetry at its best is at once intensely moving and visionary, written from the whole life — body, mind and spirit — of the unique person but preoccupied with themes that a lesser writer would present as abstractions: God, time and eternity, love, life and death; and embodied in a traditional imagery made new by the intensity of the inner life — 'my death-lit life' as she calls it in one poem — informing it, giving an original spirit to familiar forms. Her poetry dramatizes an autobiography not of external events but of emotion and the loss and recovery of vision. The poems are concerned with absolutes sought or known in experience, in primary relationships, in the relationship between past and present, child and adult woman, the living and the dead, and in actual moments of time which 'being perfect/Could not be out of place/In Eternity'. Yet the relationships are broken — by death — and the past present in memory moves the poet to anguish and even despair; not finally, but the first innocence recovered in experience, and the apprehension of final union, are achieved only at the cost of pain, fear and remorse. In 'The Singing Shell' the poet 'raised my eyes to that glittering tree/and its blinding silence questioned me'. She asks what she had glimpsed but 'Life and Love from one fountainhead'.

> Then down came that striding lion the sun
> to quench his thirst; and that gazelle the moon
> poised on the hill's line; and some flown
> fledglings of light sparkled around
> the tree's head, a living crown,
> alert for their turn to swoop and sip,
> whilst flared a fire of jewelled music
> such as stars and birds display, intrinsic
> music in flying fire beyond sound.

Her poetry does not maintain this pitch of ecstasy for long—it is too subtle and dramatic for that; it is a poetry of quest not fixity in assurance; and the quest leads the poet to live and relive the unbearable and face an equivalent desolation. Poignancy is a more characteristic effect and, remarkably, within subtly controlled forms, she recovers an impassioned yet precise language of emotion. But not of emotion alone.

'I like old words', Frances Bellerby writes parenthetically in one poem, immediately after 'brought forth'. It is a nice, humorous touch of literary self-consciousness—though of course quite serious—in a poetry that is highly wrought, but very rarely shows such direct awareness of the reader. For her mind is almost invariably in the poem, totally involved with the movement that it is; her mind is in the language, intent on making the old words live, on creating order and therefore communicating. She very rarely uses any lesser arts to appeal to the reader.

Light and darkness, tree and stream, shell and sea, bread and stone: these, which are among the principal elements of Frances Bellerby's world, are also, of course, traditional religious images, and consequently among the most difficult for a modern poet to use. Poetry without vision eventually perishes, but that which merely assumes traditional images will bring their original life with them is dead from the start. No one needs more than the modern religious poet to create a world which gives flesh to its words. Frances Bellerby in her place quickened the language of that tradition in which she perceived living truth.

English Auden

> The words of a dead man
> Are modified in the guts of the living.

IT IS necessary to say at once that my attitude towards Auden's poetry is deeply divided on certain fundamental issues. For that reason, this essay cannot be a straightforward appreciation, or a basic introduction, despite its very limited scope. It is intended, rather, as an exploration of Auden's attitude towards England, as it is manifested in his work, particularly in its early phase, and as a formative influence on the nature of that work. It must also be, in some respects, a rather querulous appraisal, equivocal in its praise. Yet, what I understand by reverence for an author usually takes one of two forms: either total assent to the central importance of his writing, known as an influence in the reader's life, or a questioning, even quarrelsome, engagement with it, also known as such an influence, but an ambiguous one. If to this latter form, which my attitude to Auden's poetry takes, I add that for more than a decade I have found lines and whole poems by him associated with my feelings and thoughts, then it may explain why I risk writing on this subject now, and why I think of it as an expression of gratitude.

I

'Very soon, it seems, they will be labelling authors, like automobiles, by the year. Already the decade classification is absurd, for it suggests that authors conveniently stop writing at the age of thirty-five or so.' ('Reading', *The Dyer's Hand*, p 12). Of course, Auden was right to criticize the crude forms of classification that most critics adopt, at one time or another, when more concerned to label an author than to enter fully into his work. Right, too, when he said in 'Writing' (*The Dyer's Hand*, p 21), 'When a writer is dead, one ought to be able to see that his various works, taken together, make one consistent *oeuvre*.' Yet it is inevitable that the reader should often isolate one phase of a writer's development as the one he prefers, though whether he is then justified in describing it as the essential one, is another question entirely. For me, by far the most interesting phase of Auden's writing ended with the publication of *Another Time* in 1940, and is represented mainly by *Poems*, *The Orators*, *Look, Stranger!* and the plays written in collaboration with Christopher Isherwood. I believe, however, that his work, from *Paid on Both Sides* to *Epistle to a Godson*, does constitute 'one consistent *oeuvre*'—one that is uneven throughout and in which *Homage to Clio* is the last collection that can be described as major, but which embodies a single, developing, imaginative commitment to an idea of poetry, and to certain attitudes, materials, beliefs. There are also poems in the later collections (*Nones*, *The Shield of Achilles* and *Homage to Clio*), and passages in the longer poems, which I find as admirable, or more so, than the best of the earlier work. For instance, it seems to me that nowhere has he written with more epigrammatic force, compassion and authority than in 'The Shield of Achilles' itself. The following stanzas evoke the scene of the Crucifixion, placed in a modern but universally human context, as it appears on the shield:

> Barbed wire enclosed an arbitrary spot
>   Where bored officials lounged (one cracked a joke)
> And sentries sweated for the day was hot:
>   A crowd of ordinary decent folk
>   Watched from without and neither moved nor spoke
> As three pale figures were led forth and bound
> To three posts driven upright in the ground.
>
> The mass and majesty of this world, all
>   That carries weight and always weighs the same
> Lay in the hands of others; they were small
>   And could not hope for help and no help came:
>   What their foes liked to do was done, their shame
> Was all the worst could wish; they lost their pride
> And died as men before their bodies died.

Characteristically, the changing scenes on the shield, now suggested in their broad aspect, now seen in an emblematic detail, occur in what are primarily moral settings, where man acts out his condition, viewed from above. This technique Auden developed in his attempt to diagnose the condition of English society in the thirties. But, although diagnosis is a necessary word to use when speaking of Auden, throughout his work the diagnostician is conscious of being infected by the sickness he prescribes for and observes.

Of himself at Oxford in the mid-twenties, Auden wrote, in 'Letter to Lord Byron' (*Letters from Iceland*):

> A raw provincial, my good taste was tardy,
>   And Edward Thomas I as yet preferred;
>
> I was still listening to Thomas Hardy
>   Putting divinity about a bird;
>   But Eliot spoke the still unspoken word;
> For gasworks and dried tubers I forsook

The clock at Grantchester, the English rook.

True to the style of this often very witty poem, in its least witty passages, the comment here is slightly revealing but almost wholly superficial. In the thirties Auden did indeed make use of an imagery suggested by 'gasworks and dried tubers', surface features of *The Waste Land*, but derived nothing essential from Eliot or the other great modernists, Pound and Joyce. By the essentials of modernism I mean principles of organization, methods of juxtaposing apparently disparate scenes on the basis of a common archetypal pattern, as in *The Waste Land* and *Ulysses*, and of embodying the past in the present and setting the present in the context of the past. Where Auden uses Joycean techniques, as in parts of *The Orators*, or echoes Eliot, he derives mainly from the surface of their work, from the appearance of their forms and from stylistic mannerisms. Not that *The Orators* is entirely imitative, but it is, as Auden's most self-consciously modernist work, one that combines mimicry of various other writers' styles with distinctly personal preoccupations, rather than a convincing fusion of its eclectic manners and original matter. This is another way of saying that Auden's poetry was never modernist except in appearance—a fact that will be held against him only by those who belittle the alternative traditions still vital in this century. Without maintaining this extreme position, I would still argue that Auden's disregard of the essentials of modernism obstructed his attempt to write a completely convincing long poem, convincing that is as an integrated whole, unifying content and form. It seems to me that all his longer poems, despite superficial ingenuities, and with the exception of 'Paid on Both Sides', are fundamentally discursive. All can be paraphrased in a way that, for example, *The Waste Land* and *The Anathemata* cannot. In other words, he organizes his material—his ideas—on an essentially prosaic basis, and the pleasure his longer poems afford is intellectual, not imaginative: we apprehend the ideas, wittily or idiosyncratically expressed, with the intellect, but in *The Waste Land* different levels of meaning, image echoing image, affect consciousness at a level at which what is experienced cannot be described in other words. The variety within Auden's longer poems, especially *New Year Letter* and *The Age of Anxiety*, is affected by the range from dramatic speech and lyricism to doggerel: we are being talked to, now brilliantly or movingly, now awkwardly. It matters, of course, what the talk is about—that it often touches, intimately, instructively, on questions of first importance—but in my view such a discursive method solves none of the problems of the long poem. Even 'Paid on Both Sides', with its dramatic form, can be appreciated without much loss as a number of concentrated, lyrical passages removed from context.

It is anything but my intention to level these criticisms at Auden's adoption, from the start, of the comic spirit, or his refusal (after a distinctly oratorical beginning) of the bardic role. The criticisms centre entirely on the discursive nature of much of his work. On the other hand, in many of those poems which he called *Songs and Other Musical Pieces*, to my ear Auden is next to Yeats the finest lyrical poet since Tennyson. There are other forms of verbal music than those to be found in, for example, 'As I walked out one Evening', 'Lay your sleeping head, my love', 'Lady, weeping at the crossroads', 'Look stranger, on this island now', 'If I could tell you', but at any time, and especially when prosaic spirits with no sense of rhythm of any kind can set up as poets, Auden's lyrical gift would be something to be profoundly grateful for. Also, when all has been said about his apparently changing allegiances, in how many other poets does one find, expressed so movingly, a deep compassion for the displaced peoples of Hitler's Europe, equal to that of 'Refugee Blues'? It would make no sense for me to write about Auden even in a limited way without acknowledging how moving as well as entertaining I find poems as different from each other in form as 'Roman Wall Blues' and 'In Praise of Limestone'.

II

If Auden owed nothing that was essential to T. S. Eliot, his deeper affinities in the thirties were, I believe, with Hardy and Edward Thomas, to whom he was so condescending in 'Letter to Lord Byron'. More broadly speaking, instead of making use of Eliot's formal innovations Auden developed several lines from that alternative tradition, as it is often called now, which comprises elements from many centuries of English poetry—from Anglo-Saxon elegy and Middle English love song and meditative poem, from the ballads and the Elizabethan dramatic lyric, from the romantic movement and its Victorian heirs—and descends to us, modified, in the highly individual but traditional voices of such poets as Hardy, Edward Thomas and Wilfred Owen. (I do not mean, of course, that all the elements referred to are to be found in each of these poets, only that they formed the language, instincts, and conceptions of poetry from which they wrote.) In *Poems* several elements of this complex tradition are fused, not the least apparent being a deep feeling for landscape and the inanimate which is akin to what we find in Hardy and Edward Thomas. In my view, the common ground of feeling, embodied in landscape, is a peculiarly inward apprehension of death, known in the self, in the English countryside and in nature at large. Although such feeling can be discerned in a great deal of English poetry—probably in all poetry, since death is necessarily one of the primary themes—in Edward Thomas, for example, it was augmented by the sense, intimate as breathing, of living in a society in decline, of failing faith in those powers of renewal traditionally embodied, or symbolized, by the natural world. In fact, I believe it was not only a society in decline, but a dying culture, rooted in the natural world, that influenced the death-haunted poetry of Hardy as well as of Edward Thomas. And it was a similar feeling which Auden inherited, not only from reading them but from his birth and upbringing in pre-war and wartime England. Not exactly in *the* England of these poets, of course, any more than their Englands were identical—too many questions of class, time, and locality arise to allow such an abstraction. Nevertheless, what I believe all had in common was their primal attachment to a world with no potentiality for growth or renewal, no future that did not entail an uncreative return to the past. Eliot too was a death-haunted poet, but for him there was surely no basic experience, in quite that way, of discovering how equivocal was the object of his love, and when he did return to the past it was to the now and always, the pattern of timeless moments.

The sense of doom that shadows Auden's poetry of the thirties obviously derived as much from memories of the First World War as from the slide towards the Second. The war games and sense of guilt prevalent in the poetry of this period derived in part, just as obviously, from the fantasies of a boy who had watched young men of the previous generation being asked to die, and dying, for their country. It is hardly surprising, then, that there should be a good deal of inverted patriotism—or half-inverted patriotism, still equivocal, still attached to the rejected sentiments—in Auden's early verse. This can be seen in the skill with which he mimics the rhetoric of Patriotism in *The Orators* or in 'Paid on Both Sides':

> I know we have and are making terrific sacrifices, but we cannot give in. We cannot betray the dead. As we pass their graves can we be deaf to the simple eloquence of their inscriptions, those who in the glory of their early manhood gave up their lives for us? No, we must fight to the finish.   *Poems*

The confluent influences of Freud (more potently, Groddeck) and Marx on early Auden have been examined by many critics, who have also considered those central figures the spy, the exile and the airman, showing how the diseased bourgeois intellectual is at once inside and outside his doomed class, an agent of the life-force who bears the death-wish in his own person. The complex but coherent dramatization of this predicament, set in a glacial northern landscape with remnants of dead industry, and abandoned mines, provided the singular atmospheric unity of *Poems*. There, Auden or his persona, 'tiny observer of enormous world', is obsessed with the sacrificial death:

> You whom I gladly walk with, touch
> Or wait for as one certain of good,

> We know it, we know that love
> Needs more than the admiring excitement of union,
> More than the abrupt self-confident farewell,
> The heel on the finishing blade of grass,
> The self-confidence of the falling root,
> Needs death, death of the grain, our death.
> Death of the old gang.
>
> *Poems*, XVI

Rendered with more or less subtlety and power, the sacrificial feeling dominates *Poems* and recurs, in an increasingly discursive form, in *Look, Stranger!* To some readers, no doubt the feeling seems hopelessly bourgeois or adolescent. It is certainly more exciting to feel doomed in one's late teens and early twenties than at any later time, and perhaps it is only then that enormous satisfaction can be gained from chanting to one's friends—

> Seekers after happiness, all who follow
> The convolutions of your simple wish,
> It is later than you think; nearer that day
> Far other than that distant afternoon
> Amid rustle of frocks and stamping feet
> They gave the prizes to the ruined boys.
> You cannot be away, then, no
> Not though you pack to leave within an hour,
> Escaping humming down arterial roads:
> The date was yours; the prey to fugues,
> Irregular breathing and alternate ascendancies
> After some haunted migratory years
> To disintegrate on an instant in the explosion of mania
> Or lapse for ever into a classic fatigue.
>
> *Poems*, XXIX

As for adolescence, though, quite a lot of Keats's major poetry appeals directly to that much maligned, but essential stage of growth. And Auden's poetry of doom surely expresses a genuine sense of torment, not of a class alone, or the poet alone, but of all, whatever their origins, who are conscious of being part of a death-haunted, and apparently death-willing, society.

In writing of Edward Thomas I have tried to show that he wrote primarily from the experience of internalized crisis, haunted by his awareness of how much around him, in the English countryside he loved, was dying and by the presence in himself of that death. It is of vital significance, then, to note how in the thirties, for all his talk of 'gasworks and dried tubers', Auden set poem after poem in English landscapes—often against Pennine limestone or other northern uplands, where recent human occupation is evident in its industrial remains. Auden's success in evoking this type of landscape should make us aware of his affinities with Hardy and Edward Thomas, but also, I believe, of the kind of poet he might have become:

> Who stands, the crux left of the watershed,
> On the wet road between the chafing grass
> Below him sees dismantled washing-floors,
> Snatches of tramline running to the wood,
> An industry already comatose,
> Yet sparsely living. A ramshackle engine
> At Cashwell raises water; for ten years
> It lay in flooded workings until this,
> Its latter office, grudgingly performed,
> And further here and there, though many dead
> Lie under the poor soil, some acts are chosen
> Taken from recent winters; two there were
> Cleaned out a damaged shaft by hand, clutching
> The winch the gale would tear them from; one died
> During a storm, the fells impassable,
> Not at his village, but in wooden shape
> Through long abandoned levels nosed his way
> And in his final valley went to ground.
>
> *Poems*, XI

A single place-name is hardly sufficient evidence on which to hang a theory of affinities, but the place itself is rendered lovingly enough to remind us of Hardy and Thomas, especially when we consider that 'many dead lie under the poor soil'. But Auden's rendering of the landscape does not, ostensibly, embody a special relationship between poet and place, but creates a dramatic metaphor for the condition of England. It is also an industrial, humanized landscape, as those of the other poets are rural landscapes enriched by personal and historical associations. Yet, surely, there is enough evidence in this one stanza of Auden's attraction to the inanimate? On one level, this is a love poem which celebrates its small world of inanimate objects, where the machines are really elemental. In fact, the feeling invested in these objects is as primal as any found in Hardy's Wessex. Moreover, Auden may well have thought Wordsworth 'a most bleak old bore', but there is also at least a touch of Wordsworth about his rendering of the inanimate.

III

It is from the sacred encounters of his imagination that a poet's impulse to write a poem arises. Thanks to the language, he need not name them directly unless he wishes; he can describe one in terms of another and translate those that are private or irrational or socially unacceptable into such as are acceptable to reason and society.... Every poem he writes involves his whole past. Every love poem, for instance, is hung with trophies of lovers gone, and among these may be some very peculiar objects indeed. The lovely lady of the present may number among her predecessors an overshot waterwheel.

The Dyer's Hand.

It is my belief that the primary sacred encounter of Auden's imagination was with objects and a landscape akin to those evoked in the poem quoted above. Indeed, he seems to tell us so clearly enough when this statement at the end of his lecture *Making, Knowing and Judging*, together with his affirmation that 'every poem is rooted in imaginative awe', recalls its beginning. There, in speaking of his childhood's 'private world of Sacred Objects', he is obviously referring to such inanimates—machines and minerals—as those described in such books as *Underground Life, Machinery for Metalliferous Mines* and *Lead and Zinc Ores of Northumberland and Alston Moor*. Given such an understandable and attractive imaginative bias, it is not surprising, nevertheless, that it should come into conflict with awareness of human responsibility and his abiding preoccupation with Love, later Eros and Agape. Not surprising that resistance to such a world of sacred objects, and translation of his feelings for it into other terms, should include resistance to a loved landscape and even to nature itself. Further proof of Auden's attraction to the non-human world is provided by the strength of his need to counter it, so that a dominant, even an obsessive, theme of the later poetry contrasts the human world of consciousness and responsibility with the unconscious, creaturely or natural world. Furthermore, in the early poetry the lapse back into the unconsciousness of matter is a theme that provokes strong feelings of attraction and repulsion. For instance John Nower, in 'Paid on Both Sides', experiences the temptation in an acute form:

> Could I have been some simpleton that lived
> Before disaster sent his runners here;
> Younger than worms, worms have too much to bear.
> Yes, mineral were best: could I but see
> These woods, these fields of green, this lively world
> Sterile as moon.

The Chorus echoes his sentiments: 'Better where no one feels,/The out-of-sight, buried too deep for shafts.' The limestone landscape, which is like the tip of an iceberg, is often, throughout the poetry, associated or even identified with the mother, in the form of life's unconscious matrix. It is this to which the 'tiny observer', conscious that social renewal requires the destruction of his class, is tempted to turn in his intolerable predicament. Exile and airman, in working out their strategies for curing the diseased society of which they are infected parts, are tempted by the lapse into unconsciousness. It is a complex theme with which Auden is concerned, expressed in psychological and social terms that are sometimes at variance. Yet the urgency of feeling in these poems is unmistakable, and it often centres on the need to escape a maternal influence identified with the ruined, non-human world. The child's birth in 'Paid on Both Sides' is precipitated by his father's violent death; it is the mothers on each side who keep the feud alive, so that, finally, 'his mother and her mother won'. Naturally, both psychologically and socially the mother can be seen to symbolize a great deal, but I am convinced that the maternal figure also symbolizes that buried world which was the object of the poet's first love, and which now tempts him to resolve an intolerable situation by escaping into it. I am arguing, then, that Auden's translation of this feeling into psychological and social terms, and his resistance to it, provided a great deal of the creative pressure for *Poems*. Moreover, that in his poetry of the thirties, in his most self-evidently English phase, he lived through, reflected, and in one way resolved a general crisis of feeling about England, which was then (and still is to some extent) both a capitalist imperial power and the locality known in childhood. He did not turn towards celebration of an English landscape or locality, because for him that dominant theme of the tradition which he inherited was a dangerous form of escapism. Instead, he sought to understand the society as a whole, viewing it from some high place, like the Malverns, that was both actual and symbolic, physically in England but above English society, or from the vantage point of hawk or airman. In doing so, he developed a rhetoric that is either exciting in its power to suggest a society seen at large, but known in physical and diagnostic detail, or distasteful in its condescension. Thus, addressing Love in the 'Prologue' to *Look, Stranger!*, he wrote:

> Here too on our little reef display your power,
> This fortress perched on the edge of the Atlantic scarp,
> The mole between all Europe and the exile-crowded sea;
>
> And make us as *Newton* was who, in his garden watching
> The apple falling towards *England,* became aware
> Between himself and her of an eternal tie.
>
> For now that dream which so long had contented our will,
> I mean, of uniting the dead into a splendid empire,
> Under whose fertilizing flood the *Lancashire* moss

> Sprouted up chimneys, and *Glamorgan* hid a life
> Grim as a tidal rock-pool's in its glove-shaped valleys,
> Is already retreating into her maternal shadow;
>
> Leaving the furnaces gasping in the impossible air,
> That flotsam at which *Dumbarton* gapes and hungers;
> While upon wind-loved *Rowley* no hammer shakes
>
> The cluster of mounds like a midget golf-course, graves
> Of some who created these intelligible dangerous marvels,
> Affectionate people, but crude their sense of glory.

For the most part, these names are not numinous, sacred from their association with childhood places, but belong to a Britain spread out like a map—a peculiarly Audenesque map which denotes and diagnoses the sickness of the places it names. Such a view was one valid response to the question posed in *The Orators:* 'What do you think about England, this country of ours where nobody is well?', and to the crucial awareness of how easily an idolator of sacred objects might be absorbed into the 'maternal shadow'.

Shortly after the turn of the decade, Auden, resident in New York, discoursed about some of the pressures formative of his powerful early verse, indirectly, in *New Year Letter:*

> Whenever I begin to think
> About the human creature we
> Must nurse to sense and decency,
> An English area comes to mind,
> I see the nature of my kind
> As a locality I love,
> Those limestone moors that stretch from BROUGH
> To HEXHAM and the ROMAN WALL,
> There is my symbol of us all.

A place which has become 'my symbol of us all' is no longer accessory to a 'private world of Sacred Objects'; instead of tempting the idolator, it offers a landscape symbolic of man's faulty nature. The fault is now fallen man's, no longer merely the sickness of English society. To Auden now, England is 'my own tongue,/And what I did when I was young'. The exile with whom many of the earlier poems was concerned has stepped out of the maternal shadow and become the quester, who believes:

> However we decide to act,
> Decision must accept the fact
> That the machine has now destroyed

> The local customs we enjoyed,
> Replaced the bonds of blood and nation
> By personal confederation.
> No longer can we learn our good
> From chances of a neighbourhood
> Or class or party, or refuse
> As individuals to choose
> Our loves, authorities, and friends,
> To judge our means and plan our ends;
> For the machine has cried aloud
> And publicized among the crowd
> The secret that was always true
> But known once only to the few,
> Compelling all to the admission,
> Aloneness is man's real condition,
> That each must travel forth alone
> In search of the Essential Stone,
> 'The Nowhere-without-No' that is
> The justice of societies.

The advantage of discursive poetry, as it may also be one of its defects, is that the reader can always answer back. Aloneness may, or may not, be 'man's real condition'. One could say, it all depends on the man, in the sense that it depends on the man's ideology or metaphysic. It is equally possible to maintain that Auden's idea of 'local customs', 'bonds of blood and nation', and 'neighbourhood' was over-influenced by a middle-class version of English society. Certainly, its portrayal in *The Orators* and *The Dog Beneath the Skin*—indeed, in his work as a whole—convinces me that this was so and that he knew little of what many people still experience as rootedness, though they do not necessarily idealize those roots or falsify them in any other way. Yet it also seems to me that Auden's development was completely honest, and that he did survive one form of sickness inherent in the society and always liable to infect a poet's feeling for English landscape and his childhood idols. If it entailed a loss of intensity, then far better his lonely, compassionate quest than the Georgians' unawareness of the true nature of the dream of Old England with which they were infatuated. Of course, England in its changing countryside, suburbs and cities still remains to be known in depth; others have other ways of humanizing their sacred objects, or find them sacred precisely because they are non-human; but Auden's was one way, a way of rooting himself in the modern rootless experience that was not an escape, but courageous, intellectually honest, and true to the love he consistently invoked.

To Open the Mind

THERE is a contained strength in individual lines ('What does not change/is the will to change') and in certain passages a cadence or a concentration which readers in Britain new to Charles Olson may well single out as the 'poetry' in a thicket of prose:

> In the laden air
> we are no longer cold.
> Birds spring up, and on the fragrant sea
> rafts come toward us lashed of wreckage and young tree.
> They bring the quarried stuff we need to try this new-found strength.
> It will take new stone, new tufa, to finish off this rising tower.
> 'La Torre'

Such qualities are present in *The Maximus Poems* and *Archaeologist of Morning*, but anyone who set out to measure Olson by their prevalence would conclude that alongside, say, Yeats or Eliot he is scarcely a poet at all. And the reader who looks for the wrong thing and finds it to the exclusion of the true nature of what he is being offered, may need some time to discover that he is the prisoner of narrowing critical preconceptions.

In general, quotation comes easily in writing about modern English poetry. Often, partly because of the descriptive bias of the prevalent native tradition, the poem can be illustrated—much as the art of the landscape or portrait painter can be illustrated by isolating a detail from one canvas. But what of the action painting, where the painting is its total action? By selecting a few square inches from a Jackson Pollock the action is arrested and the life of the painting, which is that action, destroyed. So, too, with a poem by Olson: its life is its movement from perception to perception and only by moving with it can the poem be heard.

The problem of hearing is fundamental to 'projective' or 'open' verse, which Olson defines as his own method to distinguish it from 'closed' verse, a set of conventions hallowed in this century by the practice and criticism of Eliot. Action, movement, energy, the terms appropriate to these poems, play havoc with our conventional critical procedures. But perhaps the main difficulty for readers this side of the Atlantic is Olson's 'speech-force':

> That it is simple, what the difference is—
> that a man, men, are now their own wood

>   and thus their own hell and paradise
>   that they are, in hell or in happiness, merely
>   something to be wrought, to be shaped, to be carved, for use, for
>   others
>   does not in the least lessen his, this unhappy man's
>   obscurities, his
>   confrontations
>   He shall step, he
>   will shape, he
>   is already also
>   moving off
>   into the soil, on to his own bones
>   'In Cold Hell, in Thicket'

It takes the full resources of speech natural to the man who uses it to produce the play and force of intelligence in his best poems. But English poetry gets stuck, every generation or so, in a poetic diction and a limited literary conception of movement that deaden the ear to the kind of natural speech-force which American poetry, from Whitman through Pound, Williams and Olson, has retained. And to the ear accustomed to artifice the natural sounds odd—including, initially perhaps, even the naturalness of the superb *Maximus, to Himself:*

>   I have had to learn the simplest things
>   last. Which made for difficulties.
>   Even at sea I was slow, to get the hand out, or to cross
>   a wet deck.
>   The sea was not, finally, my trade.
>   But even my trade, at it, I stood estranged
>   from that which was most familiar. Was delayed,
>   and not content with the man's argument
>   that such postponement
>   is now the nature of
>   obedience,
>   that we are all late
>   in a slow time,
>   that we grow up many
>   And the single
>   is not easily
>   known

In English poetry it is the exploitation of language for visual, sensuous, palpable effects that has produced the dominant modern strain. Although such generalizations are dangerous, it can be seen, surely, that what most poets and their critics, at least since Eliot, have acknowledged as fundamental to the native tradition is a system of movement and arrest: the poem as arrested movement. Rhythm thrusts forward, but paradox, wit, ambiguity, image and description check it, force the mind to dig for layers of meaning, to circle the poem gathering every shade of significance until, circle within circle, it is closed to further exploration. The criticism developed in relation to this kind of poem is adept at connecting item to item in a closed world; but such criticism, helpful in the right place, can do nothing with open verse but hinder access to it. For in the open poem it is the quality of action, the thrust forward from perception to perception, that shows whether the poet's intelligence is really alive to the forces it is part of. We can speak about language in a state of arrest—the poem as object and the primacy within it of image and symbol—but we have yet to learn to talk about speech in the act of movement.

But the challenge Olson poses is not, primarily, an aesthetic one: projective verse depends upon a disposition to reality that underlines the enormous spiritual distance between Europe and America.

It is the claustrophobia of the European, trapped by historical process as by the limitations of space—a claustrophobia felt most acutely by D. H. Lawrence when things had still to get worse—that makes so appealing for him the American's sense of true wilderness (The Plains, the Pacific) to be explored, and of cosmic forces—in the aboriginal Red Indian as in the land. Lawrence's search was for the man beneath the social being, for a society and a form in which to express his sense of man's part in these cosmic forces, and it is with this side of Lawrence that Olson has close affinities. In each case the search is hostile to the burden of an historical conditioning from which the European is never free; it is a search involving myth, the cosmic, non-historical awareness of 'primitive' man, and its image is exploration, the horizon wide enough to allow a new beginning in harmony with the movement its spaces dictate. The poet engaged in this search is an explorer whose domain is space, terrene space—only the technological imagination is happy in the other kind—whereas the European is oppressed by time, by, at best, locality rich in historical experience and, at worst, the hopelessness of an inescapable conditioning by which history becomes nightmare. And in Europe society and the pressures of history upon it force the poet back into private experience, perhaps in part as a refuge from such a public place as the continent has become; so that for the English poet, divided as he is in this century between his European consciousness with its sense of tradition rooted in time, and the appeal of the New World as the domain of exploration, Poland and America are the opposing centres of gravity.

But being defeatist about modern poetry in English on this side of the Atlantic is justified only by ignorance of who the important poets are: David Jones, in *The Anathemata*, and Basil Bunting, in *Briggflatts*

(1966), have both produced work before which all poets should feel humble. Arguably, the most interesting poets now writing in English, outside projective verse or the strong influence of Pound, are those, as in the case of Bunting and Jones, with access to something larger than their own private minds: for example, Geoffrey Hill, a poet with a profound historical sense, and R. S. Thomas, one of the few poets whose circumstances immerse him in the life of a people. Geoffrey Hill and R. S. Thomas bring to traditional forms a world larger than the 'ego-system' Olson was opposed to in the poem (see *The Review*, n.10, January 1964, Robert Creeley in conversation with Charles Tomlinson). And this is an observation which, I believe, focuses attention exactly on the point where the native tradition could die for lack of sustenance. Despite Eliot's idea of impersonality a particular kind of rather limited individual consciousness defines the scope of his own poetry. For lesser poets the 'I' of the poem reduces the whole world to a narrow dance round this focal point. Thus in modern nature poetry we do not get poetry in which nature as force and presence, as in Wordsworth, enters the poem—and enters it because Wordsworth has acknowledged himself as man in nature—but we get instead an increasingly desperate imposition of the ego on the world outside it. In Sylvia Plath's expressionist landscape, objects are distorted by the agonized eye bent on them. And there are some who see this process as the only honest, and heroic, response to the modern world: the ego, having taken upon itself the burden of extreme suffering, warps even the objects of nature by the way in which torment forces it to apprehend them. In one sense the process is true to the metamorphosis of nature in Europe whereby a place named after a birch wood becomes a symbol of horror; but in another it signals the triumph of a deathly past from which the poem cannot break free. For in poets less gifted than Sylvia Plath the process is rife. In fact there is little nature poetry in England now. What has been acclaimed as such is the end-game of anthropomorphism, of the ego as measure of all things.

But in so far as I understand Olson's poetic it expresses a disposition to reality never lost in America as Lawrence's life of searching shows it in retreat from England. It is a disposition whereby the poet attempts to rediscover himself as primal man in nature, as man the creature of cosmos, whose poems are the play of intelligence but with the energy of nature. What man has as a creature distinct amongst creatures, is speech, speech born of the breath that is also life. Attentive to this breath, hearing speech as it derives from the life within, the projective poem emerges as an act true to the laws of nature (as an organism is), unrhetorical, non-descriptive, not a nature poem but a poem that is an object of nature.... But the argument is too easily garbled, though with little excuse: it is expressed with such force and clarity in Olson's essay on projective verse. Doubtless even now there are poets bent on exploiting the poetic as an adjunct to new ego-systems. But these poems, whose speech and movement are alive—like the governing rhythm of Lawrence's prose—are true acts on every level. Ultimately, the acts are an affirmation of life, not a discursive talking about it. Strangest of all to one bred on the native tradition in its modern phase or racked by the sense of living where the past has a habit of suffocating the present, they are an affirmation of 'the pleasure which there is in life itself'.

John Riley: *The Collected Works*

THIS IS NOT a review but a first view of John Riley. I had seen little by him before February 1981, and had only known of him for a short time, as a poet murdered in Leeds in 1978. Now, after one slow reading of *The Collected Works*, with frequent returns to the poems that most delight or baffle me—and there is much here which as yet I can't follow—my only justification for writing about John Riley is that I haven't finished reading him. The openness of this book, in more than one sense, is chiefly what I want to write about here.

'At the Choral Society' is an early poem (1966) that I often return to:

> Then the music like a flower opening
> The skull under cherubs on a marble tomb
> Almost sweating as the fugue beats against it
> Fugue doubtless familiar and known to it
> In its time, tomb of the period, I began
> To think of us all there gathered in that church
> An English church, battle flags and death all round.
>
> And afterwards in the churchyard going home
> Three choir ladies ask now tell us truly
> How it went—they were so pleased to be wearing
> Unfaded roses on their choir ladies' dresses
> So happy but so ready to be cast down
> That I reply with a feeling of release
> So truly, it was a partial opening.

For some reason, John Riley did not collect this poem. He may have mistaken it for the kind of thing he obviously disliked: the poem as self-contained verbal box of tricks, as formal enclosure; or perhaps he felt it didn't quite work, or belong in any of his collections. Whatever the reason, it is to my mind a very fine poem. A closer look at it should have the additional interest of suggesting why he could not rest on the kind of achievement it represents, and which is represented by the more traditionally formal part of his work.

At first glance, 'the music like a flower opening' looks hackneyed and sentimental. What the flower is opening, however, is 'the skull'. Any hint of jaded surrealism picturesquely linking flower and skull is then erased by the organic integration of the life (flower) and death (skull) images in the whole poem. For the poem is a whole, organized by an exceptionally subtle poetic intelligence. 'At the Choral Society' both enacts and defines 'an opening', the word placed ambiguously at the end of its first line and closing the poem with its meaning revealed. The poem has this in common with later Riley—it is not descriptive, picturing a scene, but enacts an experience and its revelation. Its Poundian clarity of precise luminous detail—for example, 'An English church, battle flags and death all round'—also distinguishes, sometimes in a highly elliptical form, all John Riley's writings.

The experience is truly 'a partial opening' because it comes with 'a feeling of release'. The poet's reply to the ladies is exactly truthful, because it arises in response to the total experience, which includes his own humanity: of life invading the material domain of time and death, of human communion, and of the ladies' vulnerable feelings. The cliché of everyday speech—'now tell us truly'—is placed in the context of 'so truly': the truth partially experienced and revealed within an English church with its social, material, and artistic compromises is that life raises a transfigured humanity from death.

Not that such moribund terms can contain the experience of the poem. It is the corruption of our language—our general understanding—that may initially make it difficult to see no contradiction in John Riley being at once a religious poet of great spiritual integrity and intensity, and a profoundly human figure who would probably have responded with a profane, or at least ironic, colloquialism to the terms in which I am describing him and his poem. His poetry establishes, in its terms, truths that, in England today, such words as 'religious' and 'spiritual' mock and obscure. Here we see him redeem 'truth' by giving it a living context. Witness also the naturalness of his speaking voice and its action, with a minimum of punctuation, in the rhythmic and formal control of this poem.

'At the Choral Society' enacts an event; it is also something of a monument—far (yet not all that far) from George Herbert's designs but recognizably of the same world of artefacts as that of the poet whose confidence within his religion and culture enabled him to be, even when most afflicted, an ingenious craftsman in his reshaping of traditional materials and forms. A masterful playing with such materials and forms was for Herbert no obstacle to release of feeling; for the heart recovering greenness a perfect marriage of organic image and established artifice was possible, and Herbert's poems are openings: they received life from a tradition, and they reveal it.

As one would expect from the general situation, with the decay of religious language and artistic forms, there is plenty of internal evidence in *The Collected Works* that for John Riley in the 1970s the case was quite different. As he wrote in 'A Note On Prose', 'The vision has to be established by poetry'. Whatever he believed as a matter of faith and even doctrine, it would not do the work for him. He had to establish the vision.

This meant going beyond the traditional forms that give a somewhat monumental quality—they are marble rather than gifts of Pentecost—to the expression of release and opening in his earlier published poems—in fact, in part 11 of *Ancient and Modern* (1967) and *What Reason Was* (1970); as, for example, in the magnificent 'Poem On These Poems', with its echo of *The Dream of the Rood:*

> Myrtle tree of heaven, white-scented flowers
> Of Venus. Look, I will tell you of a dream that I had
> When speaking men were sleeping: moisture ran down the windows
> Like rain. Outside, the full moon, one day old. It seemed
> I saw another tree, laden with light, the clearest of crosses.
>
> Love, love, the great love, or the unexpected,
> My God, my love I cannot see or sing...

A little further in this direction would have led him to fix on the tree of earthly and divine love a Yeatsian metallic bird. But his vision as he came to establish it demanded real birds, not to oppose but to complete the divine order. His images were to be used, 'not to answer, but to hear'.

During the seventies John Riley progressively opened his forms, in a process simultaneously spiritual and artistic. At the same time, he increased the range and flexibility of his language. Bothered by 'a ringing phrase/even in the correct tongue' he became better able to achieve release, because he could, as in 'travel notes', move without strain between the solemnity of 'ritual of light holds memory of darkness' and the colloquial 'making a bad job of expressing joy'. Consequently he makes an unusually good job of it.

The examples he followed aren't hard to see: most immediately, Pound, Charles Olson and (later, I think) William Bronk. At the same time, he was evidently learning much from translating Mandelshtam and Hölderlin, the latter perhaps giving an added dynamism to his release of feeling. He was thus at the confluence of the two most vital streams of influence on English poetry in the seventies. Influences are rarely heard as echoes in John Riley's work, however; where evident, they are pointers to risks taken, successfully or unsuccessfully—*The Collected Works* includes finished poems at all stages of his writing, but is not chiefly important for its finish. The value he places on welcoming uncertainty within the poem, as an action in which perception fires perception, quick changes of focus occur, and each word is experienced, clearly owes a debt to Black Mountain poetics. The extreme concentration and compounding of image and meaning in Mandelshtam have, I suspect, most affected the poems by John Riley that I can least follow. Yet he is close to Mandelshtam and other Russian poets not as translator alone, or because he emulated an intensity of experience and feeling allegedly unavailable to the modern English poet in his native circumstances, but because he did have an equivalent intensity.

Sobornost and Sophia in Leeds? Why not? John Riley is much closer in thought and feeling to Vladimir Soloviev and Nicolas Berdyaev than to Tony Harrison or even Geoffrey Hill, and therefore to spiritual forces acting on Mandelshtam. Which is to say he lived his belief in 'the positive unity of all' (Sergius Bulgakov), suffered for all that obscures and fragments it, and found his words in his experience. By the same token he is, as he knows, in a living, and therefore continually renewed, tradition of poetry in the English-speaking world. Any reader for whom a sense of exclusive foreignness clings to Orthodoxy and the Russian names might take a look at A. M. Allchin's *The Kingdom of Love and Knowledge* (1979), which shows many connections between Orthodoxy and a deep Anglican tradition from Richard Hooker to F. D. Maurice and beyond. 'Hostile powers, when/Is our nature to restore itself?' John Riley asks in 'The desert Fathers spoke'. It is a concern of all his work, where what is to be restored is not man alone, but the whole creation to its Creator's will. Indeed, the openness of his forms recalls not Olson's models of exploration, but Berdyaev's idea of the eighth day of creation, with man answering God's demand for his creative newness. He shares Berdyaev's conception of knowledge as active, as 'creative transfiguration', and his breaking of traditional forms and refusal to satisfy conventional expectations call to mind Berdyaev's sense of 'the tragedy of human creativeness. Man is not creating a new life, nor a new form of existence, but cultural products.'

Looked at in this light, John Riley's earlier poems may be seen as cultural products impeding creative transfiguration, though as partial openings nevertheless. What he then enters upon is poetry as process of experience and act of discovery. He does not establish a static Byzantium, but rather, as in the dynamic and subtle movements and quick unexpected changes of 'Czargrad', breaks conventional images and mental sets in order to make openings for the life that is always new. It is an act that implies great faith in the divine order and in the capacity of man, freed from his slavery to illusions of reality, to perceive it and play his creative part in it. There are precedents for this in English poetry, of course—Blake for one—and John Riley insists, most refreshingly, that 'truth is eminently possible in poetry now, the tradition of great poetry in the English-speaking world being an unbroken one. Poetry is a glimpse, direct, of truth' ('A Note On Prose'). As a poet John Riley remains, of course, necessarily a 'pattern-maker' but he learns 'the act of changing focus, preparing for what one is unprepared for; and then doing it'.

John Riley is very much of his time and place, especially in his idioms and humour. He writes not so much *about* Leeds and the present, as *from* them, offering experiences not descriptions. He is authentically personal; the opposite of a confessional poet, who leaves us enclosed in the world of his or her own wretched ego, as if we didn't have one of our own, he writes from the centre where he is, which is where for the poet life in all its potentiality alone is. 'To love a land means to look for transfiguration,' he wrote in *Correspondences,* 'and then it is people one is talking about, and to describe this in terms of landscape merely is misleading'. In fact the elements of landscapes—for the most part, Yorkshire, and Cornwall—are present in many of his poems, locating without confining them, but the dominant elements of his poems are those known everywhere, particularly light and the wind.

The context of his work as a whole gives a peculiar poignancy to this brief poem:

> the sadness
> of good poems
>
> consider an estuary
> and expanse of light

His poems are open to the light in which all poems are lost, but which without good poems we might not see. There is a constant sense in his later poems of 'The ungraspable, how near!' (Mandelshtam). Occasionally the imminence of transfiguration is stated—

> a greed of looking, that things
> are on the verge of speech:
>
> boarded cottages give back their lives
> as in some Resurrection picture
>
> significance fully there and all
> our seperate meaningless acts made sense of
> *Between Strangers*

But mostly there are moments in the poems, of light or silence, or when the wind rises or suddenly drops, that are as much openings for the poet as for the reader.

The wind (of Pentecost) is increasingly heard and felt in John Riley's later poems, and the last lines of his 'last completed separate poem' (Tim Longville's editorial note) are

> at the boundary of mind's reach
> at the edge of heart's sensing
> violence of colour
> and the wind rising

Like many of his poems, it comes, very appropriately, to no full stop.

As John Riley himself wrote, in 'Down by the Riverside': 'There is a poetry that goes through life as a strong wind. It puts spaces between words and cleans them and uses them entirely for its own purposes. It makes it less possible for us to get them wholly wrong again without remembering a rightness, or to mimic them without being blown away.'

Living in Wales

FROM LLANGWYRYFON, under the ridge of Mynydd Bach in Cardiganshire, driving east then south, to the area of England encircled by the chalk and the coastal water, we know that we are going home. Not home to England, but to that area of the south. Returning, we feel the same. Not that we are coming home to Wales, but to a part of Cardiganshire. Yet the experiences embodied in the emotive word 'home' are different. This difference is one of my themes in this essay.

In eight years I seem to have made these journeys countless times since I first came for an interview, and got the job which keeps us here and made these thoughts possible. At that time I would have gone anywhere, and might have stayed in Aberdeen, Dublin or Reading, had it offered the opportunity to do the kind of work I wanted to do. Although this work is not my present theme, it is the basic condition of our existence here. Without it, everything would have been different: there would have been another road, which I would not have been describing in this magazine. This road I now travel with my wife and son. He is still too young to be conscious of either place as home, and which place or places he will come to think of as that we do not know, though it will depend to a large extent on our conditions and choices.

From here, we drive over the mountain road to Rhayadr, missing a former way, the steep winding climb to Plynlimmon which in retrospect seems often to have been in mist with long slender hanging streams appearing on the mountainsides when the atmosphere thinned and the aboriginal faces of sheep peered out of it, inaudibly bleating. Returning, I once saw an orange full moon as if detaching itself from the mountain, Plynlimmon in late autumn with the texture and faded colours of a rug left out in the weather for centuries—so fancy pictured it, but the domestic image belied what it was, in its totally non-human state. I have seen a similar moon in Dorset, sliding from the cover of a rounded, manshaped hill; but it was in another world, its homeliness so archaic that it seemed entirely natural. On another occasion, three years ago, I came out of greyness to a vivid orange and red sunset at the mouth of the Rheidol, over the sea. It made me think of a melting pot, and, with an excess of subjectivity, of Aberystwyth as the place in which a former self had been melted down and moulded into the shape it then seemed to have, that five years before I could not have foreseen.

That is not what I want to write about, or at least, not explicitly—at better moments such self-consciousness is itself refined into an equally personal but less private awareness. For what I write must be personal, and to what extent I have been living in part of Cardiganshire, let alone Wales, is not for me to judge. I can only hope that I have not glided over its surface on the magic carpet of class or an alien nationality, which the work of at least one modern Welsh poet has helped me to see as the gravest danger for all English writers today, even at home. But I believe that each person re-creates the place he lives in, at the same time as he is re-created by it. In each case the question for a writer to answer, implicitly, is not, what is the fundamental reality? but what is the reality you have made from the forces that have made you?

But when does any process of making begin? Even with the life of one person it begins neither with his birth nor with what he feels to be the significant stages of his development. If an individual's imagination is inseparable from place, place cannot be separated from the social and historical forces which existed before the individual, and provided the terms of his attachment and the forms in which it can find expression; nor is the individual ever in a position to see the whole of which he is a part. If the identity of person in place were formed even on so definite a principle as the shaping of a stone in the sea it might be easier to write about, but since it is a living process involving conscious and unconscious, historical and unique elements, the best one can do is select, and hope to illuminate, some part which seems significant. Besides, there are things some people cannot write about though they know them to be at least as important as those they can. Allowance must be made for inhibition as well as for other limitations.

On the road south, Herefordshire is a kind of watershed. I find its fat blue shadows claustrophobic, its red fields that look as though the too-green grass has been peeled off them whole like a skin, cloying. It is too far inland; there is no salt in the air. This is sheer prejudice, of course; my only experience there has been of passing through. Gloucestershire likewise. But in Wiltshire the chalk begins. For me, first awareness was of things reminiscent of the beginnings of man in 'Britain', or of the remains that make a certain archaic phase seem like the beginning; tumuli, flints, fossil urchins; cloudshapes corresponding to the shapes of shadowed hills. And of the roots of a city uncovered by air raids, of iron-tinted gravels and clays exposed where shops and houses had been, in craters with blackened grates suspended on their sheer sides, and long-forgotten Norman vaults suddenly thrown open. These became associated with maceheads, stone axes, fossil tree trunks and bones of mammoth and rhinoceros dredged from Solent ooze when the docks were made. In retrospect, awareness of non-human elements, and elements shaped by men so long dead that they appeared to have been a part of them, seems to have preceded my consciousness of the human world. Nevertheless, here, in Wiltshire, where the personal associations begin like dots on a map, they denote an accretion of later experiences and emotions—of being in or out of love, of friendship, of a sense of failure, and vanity, and awe—such as most people are subject to, but against the white ground of this unique landform shaped and re-shaped by man. Later still, from the distance of Wales, and from the greater distance of an experience of radical disconnection, I attempted to recover what I could imagine of ancestral life in relation to this area, of my mother's people, the aptly named Moulds, who had worked the fields much as some of our neighbours still work the Cardiganshire valleys and uplands, dividing their energies unequally among sheep grazing, cattle pasture, and cultivation. This attempt also added its marks to the inner map.

Driving further south, the dots cluster. Then this image falls to pieces. Entering the New Forest and driving towards the Solent, always in view of the Island with its skull-like western end a jagged lump of chalk, I can no longer think of the associations in terms of an image as external as a map. It seems then, curiously, as if there is a fusion of inner and outer, of perceived and perceiver, of memory and the places to which it belongs. Some words of J. C. Powys, about another place, express exactly what I feel: 'it is through the medium of these things that I envisage all the experiences of my life; and so it will be to the end.'

In a way, one's language is the medium of 'these things', and of the people who have shaped one. For instance, when I turn over in my mind the word 'tree' or 'mud' or 'water' I find that it brings with it, sometimes as a shadow, sometimes vividly, sense impressions of particular trees, or of the mud or water of the Solent or Forest streams. Similarly with a kind word like brother or friend, the person who first embodied it is to some degree present whenever it is used. But the words also come fraught with history and legend, so that when I think of 'water' I am aware not just of the green oily Solent with its crabs and goggle-eyed flounders, or of other waters, but of King Canute whom I used to imagine sitting enthroned on the muddy shore near Woolston, of the navies wrought from New Forest timber, of *Mayflower* and *Titanic*, of Queens and ferries and tugs and battleships, of different wars and voyages of plunder or exploration or emigration, and of breakwaters broken by the tides.... And of much, much more. I also used to pronounce the word differently, with a long, flat a, and was 'corrected': this, too, is part of its freight. Perhaps this is all nonsense as far as any respectable philosophy of language is concerned. But I know that I do not need to be told the historical or emotional importance of a language or dialect. Language both shapes identity and is its medium. Always one's words prove, 'what thou lov'st well is thy true heritage'.

Living in Wales has helped to make me intensely aware of most of what I have just written. In a negative sense it has helped me to realize that some people who no longer live in a particular place still carry it inside them, and speak from or through it even when they are not speaking about it. Positively, it has taught me to be unashamed of something that is not, after all, merely nostalgia. More importantly, it has made me aware of where my imaginative commitment lies, where it cannot choose but lie. But here is conflict: since I do not distinguish, finally, between imaginative and social commitment, I must eventually return to the place I draw upon.

I have twice failed to learn Welsh. The second occasion, sitting on a tiny yellow chair, legs stretched under a desk in a Primary School classroom, its walls flaming with dragonish crayons, I realized that, despite a good teacher, the impulse to learn was weak. It involved the recognition that we were living in a community of which we would no more be able to become totally a part than it could have us so. There was also the sadly typical English lack of aptitude for learning languages, to which there are many fine exceptions and which is not necessarily a colonialist trait. But in my case it was also, to some extent, a willed limitation, a concomitant of acceptance of the language barrier as a boundary defining differences. This may seem an ingenious excuse for ignorance and sloth; perhaps it is. Conscious self-justification is no part of my intention. But the tendency for every Englishman in Wales to be assumed guilty of condescension until he has proved his innocence is one which, if I can understand the reasons for it, I also try to resist: not by virtue of an assumed innocence, but in opposition to all stereotypes and caricatures. It is always tempting to generalize about the nature of a people, but that English and Welsh do thrust each other into positions in which each has to play out the role of a national type seems to me one of the saddest outcomes of the historical relationship between England and Wales. It can still be otherwise. The real struggle may be going on elsewhere, but I believe that a small act in the same drama occurs when any person resists the imposition of a stereotype.

A few poems in translation, and one in particular, Gwenallt's 'Rhydcymerau', have deepened my awareness of the relationship that can exist between poet, people and place. With no knowledge of Welsh I have learnt nothing from Welsh poetry but an attitude towards experience, or awareness of an attitude that was innate but could not, I think, have found expression in quite the same way had I remained in England. Not that I can be confident that it has yet found adequate expression, or ever will. Nevertheless I have come to think of imagination as a faculty that can draw upon more than personal experience because it sustains the individual from its source in the larger, conscious and unconscious life of people and place, past and present, to which he belongs. Poems I have read by Gwenallt have this quality, their energies having been drawn through raw, industrial and post-industrial strata of social experience, from the underlying ground. A romantic metaphor, perhaps, but one that indicates a sense of reality at the furthest extreme from the view from the magic carpet. Other writers—David Jones who has said that the Welsh hills, hills such as those I can see from where I write, change all who come under their influence, and John Cowper Powys who lived the latter part of his life in North Wales while continuing to envisage much of his experience through the medium of a place on the Dorset coast, but by no means at the expense of dissociation from his surroundings—have strengthened my belief that differences between peoples are creative and can be bridged creatively.

No, bridge is the wrong word; it is the possibility of the meeting of different cultures and identities, each in some sense defining itself against the other and yet living from its own centre, that I believe in. This is one reason why I do not choose to write about people, whether friends or critics, in this essay: because I am speaking to them, about that process of discovering an identity that their Welshness has helped to activate. Yet this would be a lie if I did not add that there are still times, either among Welsh people or walking alone in the lanes of this area, when I experience dissociation and do not know what I am doing here or what this place is. And this is despite the fact—the paradox I can never forget—that when I write, even when I write of the south of England, whatever few readers I have will be Welsh rather than English. There is then a sense of indebtedness that may tempt me to underplay the severe tensions I am aware of in living in Wales. So, to the foregoing credos I am forced to bring an admission that may invalidate them.

Though I used the word 'centre', it is at least open to suggestion that nothing but a highly personal awareness of place authorizes me to speak for one. I have to admit, therefore, that I can speak confidently only for myself, because my situation makes me consciously individual rather than representative. Such consciousness may indeed be an illusion when seen in its historical context but I am aware, nevertheless, of tension between enforced singularity and the conviction that full identity derives from participation in a common, creative world. Again and again the hard questions have to be confronted. Does isolation on the periphery of an alien culture amount to no more than a form of escapism? If so, escape from what? Of what benefit to anyone, including myself, is such a meditation in this place at this time? The cost of fine sentiments or a credo may be no more than a little ink, but how can anyone discern the real shape that his life is making, apart from its subjective impressions? The shapes one has not chosen may be easier to see. I can imagine making a stronger effort to learn Welsh and to become more fully integrated into this place—yet recoil from it, aware that the tensions referred to were necessary for the kind of making which I really want. It is essential at least to admit the possibility that both one's ideals and miseries are agents as much of the rapacity and exploitation, as of the selflessness and love, that are required to achieve a form.

It was dissociation that brought us here, from Aberystwyth to Llangwyryfon, in the first place. Dissociation, loss of memory, the state of being removed from the stream of contacts and desires that, in health, carries and sustains one. All one summer, seeing the sea slashed with dazzling suntracks, or in storm, printing the window of our third-floor flat with filaments of delicate red algae: being imprisoned in a state of exhaustion and fear was, I suppose, part of the process of growth, the breaking up of dead things attendant upon it, but also of failing to come to terms with the tensions of a small seaside town where the psychic pressures created by conflict between opposing interests can be extreme. To make peace with something inside and outside myself, we bought a small stone house in a third of an acre of ground, bordered on one side by sycamores and open on the other to the hills, in a wedge between two mountain streams, named from its proximity to one of them, the Beidog. It was a beautiful autumn and the grass was more than waist-high. I borrowed a scythe and cut it, clumsily. A cut finger, nettle burn, physical tiredness, the smell of water and earth and dry grass—memory and a sense of touch returned through these things, and self-confidence through friendly contact with neighbours. It was a process of settlement. Vulnerable to self parody, in the manner of one between sickness and health, I convinced myself that I was appeasing generations of labourers whose inherited needs had been neglected by a long period of excessive mentalization. Be that as it may, this is a place of memory, even though what I remember does not belong to it and its memory lives mainly in another tongue.

Nowadays, setting out for the mountain road to Rhayadr, we cross the Garth, one of those high roads from which all north Cardiganshire, and Merionethshire as far as the mountains, can be seen. From there, almost immediately to the south, the bulk of Mynydd Bach with what looks like a perfect round barrow on its back shuts off the view towards the hills above Tregaron. From about the time when I discovered that this was not a barrow, but a rounded outcrop of grass-covered shale, the friable grey rock that everywhere breaks the thin surface of these hills and paves the falling Beidog with flights of irregular water-blackened steps, dates a further stage in my awareness of the total foreignness of Cardiganshire, and the growing wish, still unrealized, that I might express something of its nature. But if I could in any way express it, it would be as an area which, in the culture of its communities no less than its landforms, embodies everything that I am not and, I suppose, no Englishman is. It seems not to exist in English, as if its reality has never been more than a shadow for an English consciousness. It is the most bleakly beautiful area I know, its white, thick-walled farms sparse in the green country dominated by bare hills. At first, one could take it for a largely uncultivated wilderness—which indeed some parts are—whose resistance to man is exhilarating for those who can afford to find it so. Then, observing more closely, one sees the patterns of cultivation, a fence on the barest slope, and realizes that it is an area of intricate boundaries, often with no middle distance, under a vast sky often broken, often moving, and light that from late spring until autumn seems to turn the massive bulk of the hills into fine blue mist. It is an area in which the outsider could develop an exaggerated sense of his own importance, or come to believe in his total insignificance: both are possible reactions when one is made free of so much space, and for a time forgets the existence of cities by whose industry one lives. Here, too, the settlements and the long memories of the people give a body to the illusion of permanence, which the ubiquitous proofs of depopulation or a low-flying jet dissolve.

The images of war which its ruins often bring to mind reveal the truth. Above Hafod the tree skeletons are reminiscent of pictures of the Western Front, of Paul Nash's 'We are Making a New World', for instance; the mines near Cwmystwyth have left the mountainsides a grey desert and among buildings that look like the remnants of a bombed town a rust-red tin roof creaks over obsolete machines. Nor is any place more suggestive of the apparent anonymity of human labour, unless it is the land itself with its earth banks and stone walls. Thomas Johnes of Hafod is remembered on account of books, a broken monument, the vanishing pattern of an estate. But anonymity is, of course, no less an illusion than permanence, as communal memory as well as countless headstones testify. This, too, I have come to realize in Cardiganshire. Finding a memory, attempting to do a measure of justice to the dead: inevitably, this is at once to recover a part of oneself and to lose the most treacherous of all illusions, that the self is autonomous, whereas it is part of a process which it can be in touch with but not fully comprehend. But for any individual, in order to be creative this awareness depends upon his society and its culture having a future that he wants to live for; otherwise, his sense of the past will become essentially morbid, and he will retreat into it, as into childhood memories, because there is nowhere to carry its energies but back into the past. Now, perhaps more than at any other time, the economic and political powers are forcing individual growth downwards, twisting it back on itself, into the darkness where it should be fed for its ascent into the human world. This is why it is so dangerous to have an imaginative commitment that does not or cannot express itself socially. And here, those fields so beautiful in autumn when the blond grasses turn to gold have, in fact, reverted to the wild. The nearest farm to us has come alive with song and laughter and argument only once in the last year, when members of the Welsh Language Society occupied it, and brightened its flaking walls with their red posters.

The end of the ridge is visible from where I am writing. Behind it, the top of the mountain is broader than anyone who has not walked on it would suppose. It is composed of ploughed and grazed fields, of acres of rushes and thistles and a scattering of ruined smallholdings, mostly roofless and choked with nettles, but a few with roofs which give shelter to the diminishing barn owls. Sometimes a kite can be seen there, long ago driven from the London streets by sanitation. Buzzards are more common than sparrows. A cairn looks out over the cold blue water of Llyn Eiddwen, across the bay where the lighthouses at Strumble Head and Bardsey flash after dark. In form it is like a rough sea frozen into crested ridges, not at all like the chalk's smooth, arrested swell. Land hunger induced settlement, and the meagre living killed it. Now, too, there is no community not under threat—one force of change flowing even through these words with which I note it, though it is also possible that Brynbeidog would have become a 'holiday home' like many similar places if we had not bought it. Not that this is in any sense an adequate response to the questions raised by the economic and political system that prices some local buyers out of the market, and drives others away; the system that also makes the wish to reverse the process of social mobility in an individual case more problematic than it may sound.

From Hafod Ithel at the western end of the ridge, Pen Dinas, the hillfort towering over Aberystwyth, appears no bigger than a molehill. I sometimes climb Hafod Ithel to get the place and my activities there into perspective. Even now I know that this place in which I am writing looks from the hill above like a tiny boat. The need to see human settlement, activity and even relationship in that kind of perspective no doubt derives from my beginnings. On the other hand, I know that the hill was not created merely to satisfy such propensities. On Hafod Ithel one is standing on and viewing a human world. The farmers whose sheep graze it are our neighbours. Friends own much of what can be seen in the foreground. There are hills in Dorset which for us are dense with personal associations, though we know nothing of the people to whom they belong. With Aberystwyth minute within a fold in the vast sweep of mid and North Wales, and the Lleyn like a chain of islands embracing Cardigan Bay, it would be easy to imagine oneself voyaging on Planet Earth. But if you know the man on whose bit of land you are standing, it is impossible to forget that you are in a Welsh community where everything you see is a pattern of relationships. Perhaps it is upon a sense of such connections that the real experience of Planet Earth depends.

So a labyrinth of lanes has become a known pattern and against the literal map we have placed another, coloured by personal associations and a sense of the past and of other people's lives. In this way, two areas define the limits of my contactual awareness, and only in relation to these, whether in separation or belonging, can I achieve and project a habitable identity. Yet over-emphasis on such local connections can blind one to others which are far more extensive in space and time. For instance, if I consider a narrow, dung-splashed lane with grass down the middle instead of a white line, concrete milk steps in the hedges and muddy gateways opening into fields with a view of the distant mountains, the lane which passes this place, there is nowhere, finally, to which it does not lead. Similarly there are few influences operative on the world at large that do not reach here by some means and in some form, just as an old lady told me that she had gathered from the television that nowadays some people say that God does not exist, but they are wrong, of course. Consciously or unconsciously, the outsider is an agent of such influences, so that his life has a significance quite apart from what it means to him. It is tempting if one is privileged and temperamentally suited to live in such a place to feel a not altogether justifiable affinity with it, whereas not only has the larger world shaped one, but one's existence here is by virtue of the work it has made available. According to Ned Thomas, 'one can observe the modern world with equal hope of arriving at the truth from a flat in the metropolis or from an isolated farm'. I hope this is so, but would add that the 'observer' is, inevitably, a part of the modern world he sees, whether he dwells on its benefits or destructive influences, or is concerned with creative change or an alternative reality. Consequently, whatever local culture a person in this position has access to has to be seen in the perspective of the civilization that has enabled him to acquire it: the man looking down from the hill remains to be seen in the light of historical and social forces of which he is an agent even if they are outside his field of vision. With Hafod Ithel underfoot, surrounded by the visible signs of neighbourhood and continuity, it would be false for me to identify with the place, or define myself against it, without taking account of this light which is merciless in its exposure of all sentimental illusions. Moreover, there is a considerable difference between the subjective view of a culture held by those who are tangential to it, and the reality of those who experience it from within. I would claim to be aware of the contrast, but not of the reality which the insider experiences, even when he is a friend. And this is where the experience of living in Wales begins and ends for me, with the recognition of differences and the hope that centre might speak to centre. Yet the outsider is to some degree a threat to the other, even if both speak of love of the same things—if things are the same in different languages.

But no, this is not exactly where the experience ends. I have read in an essay on the poet Waldo Williams by Bedwyr Lewis Jones, of 'Tri Bardd o Sais a Lloegr' in which he wrote of areas in England—areas I know well—dear to him 'because poets had lived and suffered and created there' and because he and his wife 'had tasted joy and hope together there'. I did not set out to write an autobiographical sketch because I knew that there was much I would not be able to say, but in lieu of it these words applied to Waldo Williams's feelings about areas in England, especially when extended to include people other than poets, sum up what I have felt about living here. But the pressures are such that it is becoming increasingly difficult for any writer in Wales to express such feelings about both countries equally, when he has them. I can appreciate too well why this should be found no time for speaking about such love, yet to be unable to speak of it, where it exists, seems to me not the least tragic aspect of the situation.

It may or may not be different for our son. He has had many coins put into his hand, in this area whose people one of its most illustrious writers—Caradoc Evans—caricatured for their supposed meanness and other vices, and is known locally as Joe bach. The man who built Brynbeidog, grandfather of one of our neighbours, was called Joe. In memory it is still a living fact. Several people have expressed their pleasure that there is now another Joe in the place. But we cannot say what part it will play in his consciousness to know that he, too, was once called Joe Brynbeidog.

An Autobiographical Essay

> Time, like an ever-rolling stream,
> Bears all its sons away;
> They flie forgotten, as a dream
> Dies at the opening day.

ISAAC WATTS was a Southampton man; perhaps he too had been told that Roman galleys grounded their bottoms on the gravel of the Fleet, and blackened hulls rotting in the estuaries were Viking longships. He may have known the Prayer from Beaulieu Abbey, which we heard in the village church at Evensong, after we had moved from the eastern shore of Southampton Water to the New Forest side: 'O Lord, support us all the day long in this troublous life, until the shades lengthen, and the evening come, and the busy world is hushed, the fever of life is over, and our work done...' If so, he too may have associated it with the tide ebbing from the shingle even before his work was started. These, together with my mother reading from *Laureata,* provided me with my first idea of poetry. In the days when I drew Spitfires shooting down Messerschmitts, and stickmen descending on parachutes, among the poems which I heard were 'Horatius' and 'The Brook', 'The Forsaken Merman' and 'After Blenheim'. We lived in an area where, as in Southey's poem, the ground was said to be as dense with skulls as a potato field with potatoes. I have sometimes thought that many of my poems have been attempts to recreate the awful feelings evoked in me by hearing how the playing child discovered the skull and brought it to her grandfather.

Since I have always thought by making connections among images and ideas, the essays which I wrote from an early age were usually described as poetic or imaginative, and any kind of discipline requiring logic made me seem a fool. I enjoyed writing as a child, and was praised for my efforts: consequently I can barely remember a time when I did not want to be a writer. I did however wish to be an archaeologist, and several other things as well. The kind of writer I wanted to be tended to vary with my reading. When fishing became my first love, I resolved to earn a living by writing for the *Angling Times.*

I now realize that it was largely the absolute attention to a dark or glittering surface, with a constant sense of excitement at being connected to the opaque underwater world from which at any moment some living creature might give a sign, which gave me my abiding metaphor for the poetic process. In fishing there are certain things which one must do well to have any chance of success, but no amount of skill can guarantee that you will catch anything, let alone the one whose image is in your mind. But if I had had the experience, I certainly missed its meaning when I first began to think of myself as a poet, and adopted the preconception whose disabling consequences were to last for at least ten years.

At the age of twelve or so, when I first began to read Richard Jefferies, my natural surroundings were magically transformed. Jefferies has been a lasting presence, one of the half-dozen artists who are, for me, inseparable from the south. It was his essays which I read at that time, in a selection with a dark green cover called *Jefferies' England* (1937). That year, for the first time, nature became all movement, and I was consciously apart from it, observing. I sat about in lonely places and wrote a good deal of lyrical prose, in which the elegiac note was most audible. I saw, through Jefferies' eyes, the uniqueness of each living thing and how it is a drop of the inexhaustible stream. Once, while I was seated on a gate writing in a notebook, a girl crept up behind and pulled me over backwards. Four years later I was writing, for love, imitations of the current A-level texts, Milton, Shakespeare, and T. S. Eliot, to which Keats and Rupert Brooke also added their notes.

My father is a landscape painter. He discovered his gift in boyhood, but was obliged by necessity to start work quite early, and earn his living by other means; it is only in recent years, after retirement, that he has been able to concentrate on his art. Both my parents were determined that I should have the educational advantage that no one else in our family, up to that time, had enjoyed. So after I had twice failed the 11-plus, they sent me to a Roman Catholic grammar school which accepted fee-paying pupils. Nominally a Protestant on admission, I called myself a Communist when, five years later, I scraped into the local university. Although this was political romanticism, it was also rather more than that, for my elder brother, then a carpenter in Oxford, has always been highly conscious politically, and his has been one of the lasting influences on my thought. It was the time of the CND movement, to which I responded with religious fervour. I was utterly convinced that universal destruction was at hand, and this too had a profound effect upon my subsequent intellectual and emotional development: all but the intensity of the living moment was obliterated by that sense of imminent annihilation. My brother encouraged me to read the novels of Gorki, and Marxist and pacifist polemics. At university I worked intermittently at English literature, reading Lawrence and Blake with enthusiasm, but also Kenneth Patchen, Allen Ginsberg and Henry Miller, Kierkegaard, St Augustine and books on Zen Buddhism. My ambition was to write the English *Howl* of my generation.

The poems which I actually wrote, in which I tried to say how stifling and self-destructive I felt my society to be, were all generalized feeling, or else they returned to the objects, and sometimes to the sentiments, of the sketches inspired by Jefferies. But my confidence remained unshaken: being a genius was a way of life, a way of seeing and feeling. In retrospect, I can see that the failure of these poems was due to the fact that I was ignorant of my materials, although they were all around me. My present view is that it is impossible to write about anything without revealing one's social and political convictions, and one's religious doubts or beliefs; if they are not made explicit by the work, they will be implicit in the nature of its materials and the manner in which they have been handled.

The image of the poet which I adopted and finally exhausted belonged to the fag-end of a tradition. It seems probable, however, that no mature poet ever believed all that I believed, and it would be wrong to ascribe emotional romanticism to the Romantic movement. I cannot examine this subject in any detail here, but it seems to me that there are, especially in England, many ideas derived from different ages and from several cultures which the emotional state of the young poet is likely to attract to itself. He may, in making a single assumption about himself, be compounding Rimbaud with Walt Whitman and the shaman of an ancient tribe. Indeed, unless he has an unusual degree of poetic intelligence, something similar to this is likely to be the case, since he does not live in a culture which needs the poet, and which therefore defines his identity. At some stage, then, he will have to define an identity for himself, according to his capacities and beliefs, or else continue to write semi-literately, from the confusion of conflicting ideas, or by borrowing the mannerisms of a modern poetic whose principles he does not understand. The poetic process is, I believe, different in kind from critical thinking. Nevertheless, in so far as critical awareness is a way of seeing the relationships in the poem, between the poet and his idea of poetry and his society, I believe that this is more than ever a time when the poet needs to be critically aware. Not even in cultures which provide a sustaining idea of his identity and his art, let alone in modern England, can he afford to put his trust in instinct alone; although without instinct, without access to that which feels mysteriously 'given' and makes writing an act of discovery and the poem irreducible to prose paraphrase and a statement of conscious intention, critical awareness will make critics not poets.

When, as a student, I thought about my society, I thought about the capitalist state and the American bombers in the stratosphere, the cloudy mass of the islands lying uniform below. This is not a way of thinking which I have abandoned, but in addition I have become aware of what I grew up to know intimately, but often neglected to see from that height above the clouds: an actual part of physical, historical, social

England. By the same movement of consciousness I have come to see a particular history which the books I read at school did not record: for example, not the battle of Blenheim, but my father's father working as a boy in the orchid-house at Blenheim Palace in the days of Churchill's boyhood. But of course it is not only a matter of learning an ancestral history with which one can identify; it is also a way of seeing oneself in relation to that history of people and places which the official national and imperial ideas have always tended either to ignore or falsify. It is a way of coming to know one's 'place', in every sense of that word except the one which the agricultural labourers of the last century would probably have used. But it would be a complete contradiction if this awareness were to be used as an excuse for romanticizing the past in order to avoid seeing the actual present. Moreover, as an Englishman living in Welsh-speaking Wales, I have had to see my concerns in the context of a society for which an English poet is literally not the real thing. Consequently I have had to try to find out not only what I can do, but also for whom, other than myself, it can be said to have any meaning. I do not write this essay in the conviction that I have made either discovery.

Selective as this brief sketch has been, it still provides the only background against which my present thinking can be fully understood. There are, however, many possible self-portraits, each of which will depend upon perspective and the time when it is made. Later, one usually recovers not the actual life-experience of any given period, but the experience as part of a pattern in the light of the present. One may come to see some of the formative relationships while the self which they formed seems like a dream. Inspired by the assumption of an illusive maturity, one may even come to deny much that is really part of one's essential life: it does not accord with the present image, that is all. I do not think that anyone, least of all an artist, is ever in a position to say: I was *that* in those days, and now I am *this*. I am sure, however, that it was only after I had come to live in Wales, in 1965, that I began to think about belonging and relationships. It now seems to me that a person never really sees those things which he takes for granted, and if these happen to be the very things which formed and sustained him, as is usually the case, he will not see himself either. The consciousness of which I have spoken is by no means unusual nowadays: again and again, in writing from England and Wales, from Scotland and Ireland, we see how awareness of a common world begins with its loss.

Thomas Hardy was still alive when my father travelled in Dorset as a young man and met people who thought the author of *Tess of the D'Urbervilles* 'a dirty old man'. To us, he had always seemed a venerable near neighbour, who, although he had been dead for some years, had known more about what would happen to the south of England in this century than many people who still live there. Even the society which I knew in southern Hampshire, which is emphatically not Dorset, reflected aspects of the way of life depicted in the earlier novels, although most of it is after *Jude the Obscure*. In many instances he might have been writing about my own ancestors except for the fact that they worked on the land in Wiltshire and Oxfordshire; again and again I have encountered my own feelings and those of my elder brother and friends in such characters as Clym Yeobright and Jude Fawley. It was inevitable, therefore, that once I began to see the place in which I had been living, I should think increasingly of Hardy. It was equally inevitable that my thinking should become more critical since what I was seeing was not only a place nostalgically remembered, but also the process of education and social mobility reflected in this very way of thinking. I have thought of myself—unjustly—as a Donald Farfrae, who sang sentimental songs about the home which he left in order to better himself; until quite recently I have been obsessed by the idea of returning, to live as Hardy did, close to my place of birth—not to satisfy a theory, but swayed by primary attachments. The social fact, underlying all the ideas and feelings which I bring to it, is that I am living in Wales for the same reason that many Welshmen are living in England. It is an additional fact that I would now find it extremely difficult to leave, should an opportunity to do so arise.

It is unfortunately a common assumption even among poets that creative and critical are mutually exclusive terms. To this way of thinking, a poet who not only writes criticism but also teaches English literature in a university must be positively bent upon destroying his creativity. I do not say this satirically: there have certainly been times, when, in my own experience, the 'poet' could scarcely bear to know what the 'critic' or the 'lecturer' was doing. It is a pity that this should have been so in Wales, where some sense of what a culture is might have been expected to counter an oversimple opposition of faculties within the individual: only when a poet is forced to think of himself as apart from other men, or joyously embraces that illusion, will the fission of himself into various opposing selves begin. It was, however, partly the fault of the romanticism which I brought with me that this tension came about. It is no good relying for survival on a sense of personal integrity if it happens to be founded on a false self-conception. On the other hand, the University of Wales as I have known it does not adequately reflect the culture which might still distinguish it from its English counterparts. In my case, the change from thinking about the place in which I now live as the edge of western Britain, to the realization that it is the centre of a culture, came about more from contact with farmers and with writers, in Welsh and in English, than from working in the university. But of course I work in an English department and, with one or two exceptions, the English departments of the University of Wales are not noted for their interest in Anglo-Welsh literature, the subject which is surely indispensable as an introduction to modern Wales and, for many non-Welsh-speaking people, to Welsh culture as well. If the subject were only one more academic specialization its neglect would not be a matter for concern. But the Anglo-Welsh situation, from which a diverse literature has arisen, is a vital and critical part of the experience of modern Wales, and of Wales as it exemplifies crucial tendencies within the modern world. Study of the literature should therefore involve paying close attention both to works which are rewarding in themselves, and to the interaction and conflict of cultural and social forces which deeply affect the lives of many people within this country and beyond. But perhaps I should simply record the fact that, for me, teaching in Wales has often meant talking exclusively about subjects which have little bearing on the experience of actually living here. Nor can I see this issue as entirely separate from what is ostensibly a far more personal problem. The desire to see poetry and criticism, scholarship and teaching, as diverse parts of a single creative activity does not strike me as being unreasonable; but it is probably true to say that there is no occupation, inside or outside a modern university, that does not make it seem absurdly utopian. In fairness, though, it should be noted that there are now distinct signs of change in the attitude of our English departments in Wales to their location.

If critical thinking and the poetic process are indeed different in kind, they should still serve each other; whether consciously or not, they are united in the individual poet in the form of a relationship that is essential to art and sanity alike. Hostility between bad poets and perceptive critics, or good poets and imperceptive critics, is to be expected at all times, but the assumption of such hostility as a general principle can only indicate that the process of fission within a culture is complete: it will be not only a question of each man for himself; the artist will scarcely know which of several men he is.

Perhaps I have overstated the case. I certainly do not mean to imply that a culture depends for its survival entirely upon a relationship of give and take among its poets and critics. I presume only that to seek wholeness is not only desirable but also the proper human aim, and that it cannot be attained in isolation. Therefore, when a situation arises in which the poet thinks of his sole aim as the exhibition of an unique self, and feels either patronizing or hostile towards the critic for acclaiming or failing to recognize *him*, we will know that something is wrong. We will know that anyway, for other reasons, but if we are poets or critics, or try to be both, we will be especially sensitive to the failure of communication in this form. Apparently, all that remains of our common humanity is the isolation of Adam talking to himself alone—which I take to have been impossible since man and not God created language, and a man would need at least one other before he could learn to talk even to himself. Again I do not say this satirically, but because I have been in the paradoxical position of a poet who thinks that he is talking only to himself. As a critic, however, I now know exactly what I have been doing in Wales: taking advantage of a situation in which people really do talk to each other, where the quality of discourse and the attention to the object often shown in the Anglo-Welsh magazines stand out in welcome contrast to the solipsism and the self-indulgence that bedevil most of the anti-establishment cliques in England, and the mean-spirited dismissiveness all too common in most of the London newspapers and magazines. Of course, this is not invariably true of either centre, and the advantages enjoyed by the Anglo-Welsh writer in his own country are not necessarily going to produce more good poets than a permissive or a restrictive climate of critical opinion. But whether good or bad work is being discussed in the Anglo-Welsh magazines, and whether it is being discussed adequately or inadequately, I always feel that it is a discussion and not a series of unrelated monologues, and that is something to which I wish to contribute. Ideas matter here, and so does poetry: it is not merely a question of members of a clique congratulating each other, or of each specialist having an eye only for his own reputation. There are dangers within this communal situation however, and the chief of these is the temptation to applaud certain views and sentiments irrespective of how well they are expressed. The only service which any writer can do his country as a writer is to write well, though again, it is impossible to write even of earth and stones without disclosing, however obliquely, one's attitude to the land to which they belong. But I would go much further than this since I believe a bodily sympathy with the physical nature of a country, and with a language which roots one's being in a present and historical community of people and things, distinguishes love of country or place from rhetoric and sentimentality.

When such men as T. S. Eliot, Edwin Muir and Herbert Read were alive, it was both possible to respect London as a centre, and understandable that many writers should think of it as *the* centre: not only the centre of publishing, but also the place where reputations were justly made. Although there has always been a lot that is wrong with this idea of the centre, even as far as English poetry is concerned, it could still be justified, to some extent, for as long as at least one or two people of outstanding critical intelligence were in positions of power. For some time now, this has no longer been the case. I did not realize this until after I had come to live in Wales, when the discovery of such poets as Gwenallt and Waldo Williams, and then of David Jones and other Anglo-Welsh poets, made me aware of alternative traditions to those with which I was already familiar, and of a deep seriousness with regard to questions of the relationship between the poet and his society that is totally lacking in fashionable metropolitan criticism. No doubt this realization came rather late: old reverence dies hard, and one may easily transfer it to the new men of influence without questioning the basis of their authority. But having read David Jones and recognized the implication of all his work, that the artist who 'intends life' does not express his private feelings, but shows forth the things which have made and sustained him; and having seen that the great modern Welsh poets write from the depths of their culture and society, which are their personal depths, there was then no further possibility of my being satisfied with my own earlier notions of poetry, or with the ideas current among literary journalists in London and Oxford. The realization was not a particularly novel one, for there are certainly critics who have come to think for themselves earlier than I did; but I still believe it to be less common than it should be. The existence of a limited critical outlook in influential places would not matter very much if it did not mean that there are good Anglo-Welsh poets who are not widely read even in Wales, because a part of their potential readership is affected by the opinions of newspapers (including some in Wales) and periodicals that ignore them, and of teachers who follow suit. But of course the problem is not confined to Wales, since all writers who do not find favour with the literary establishment of their time are bound to be forced into unnecessary isolation; and there is enough real isolation without the addition of this artificially created neglect. In my view, the aim should be, not to persuade metropolitan critics to pay a measure of attention to the literature of Wales, but to strengthen Wales as a centre in such a way that it will command attention everywhere. One practical way in which this aim might be furthered would be for the Welsh publishers to advertise and distribute their books more widely: it is not enough simply to produce good books attractively, and there have been some very good books produced in Wales in recent years; but a good book, an indifferent book, and a downright bad book of poems from a major English publisher will all sell more copies than a good book from a Welsh publisher. I do not understand why, if enough money is available to produce a book well in the first instance, there is not enough to complete the work, by making its existence widely known. My sympathies are therefore entirely with the handful of editors and poets and critics who have devoted their energies to the discussion and dissemination of Anglo-Welsh literature, even to the point at which, in some readers or auditors, yet another attempt to define the term produces voluntary black-out.

It is one thing to write polemically about a general situation, but quite another to write about one's aims as a writer. About two years ago I started to write a sequence of poems called 'Letters to a Brother'. It then seemed that without a language enriched by memory and associations, and shared as a living tongue with at least one other person, I could write from no more than a small part of myself, perhaps from only a specialized 'poetic' self. The idea of the 'Letters' was a strategy devised to solve the problem which has come to preoccupy me: how is it possible to release one's deepest thoughts and feelings, those which remain embedded in the experience of a common world, if the only language commonly available is either standard English or one of the many specialized jargons? The idea of the sequence, in the form in which I conceived it at that time, did not work; nevertheless, most of my more recent writing has been an attempt to find other ways of solving the problem. As an English poet living in Wales there is clearly no question of my trying to play the part of *y bardd* in the Welsh community, or, I now realize, of transferring that role to the place which I come from; nor am I up for adoption, flattering as that idea may be, as an Anglo-Welsh poet. When all the smoke of theory has cleared away, perhaps all that any of my poems can really do, now or later, is to address some words of the chalk giant to the unknown reader: 'My image I leave To whoever it reflects'.

The poetic process is even more difficult to write about, and more dangerous too. Always the writing in which I have found most enjoyment and most confidence has started from something like the sound of shingle crunched underfoot or the feel of a round, chalk-covered flint. That is not to say that the poem will be about those things; only that it may begin from the attempt to make a verbal correspondence to the object or sense-impression, and then connect, or recognize connections among, the images which come to the surface, images of past and present, of geology and history, of one life and other lives. I have latterly written sequences in which this process, working through materials which I call a 'ground', also connects poem to poem. In fact I think of myself as working not so much with words as with the materials which they name, with chalk and flint, or shingle and water and oil. This is not a process that I wish to look into, and what I have said is totally inadequate to indicate the excitement of body and mind that occurs when the materials produce images which signal to each other across time and space. If this is to happen at all, it is usually preceded by days or weeks of will-directed scribbling, when the words feel as if they have been scraped from the surface of the brain. I find that an artist, Paul Nash, has expressed better than any writer, the kind of imagination with which I feel an affinity:

> Last summer, I walked in a field near Avebury where two rough monoliths stand up, sixteen feet high, miraculously patterned with black and orange lichen, remnants of the

avenue of stones which led to the Great Circle. A mile away, a green pyramid casts a gigantic shadow. In the hedge at hand, the white trumpet of a convolvulus turns from its spiral stem, following the sun. In my art I would solve such an equation.

Unit One, 1934

Next to my father's paintings, which are so much of water and of trees and sky in constant movement, like a stream, Nash has had the strongest influence on my way of seeing. It was partly through him that I recovered the sense of awe which first made me want to write. This occurred in Dorset in the autumn of 1969, after a long period in which everything had stood still; then a wheatfield on the side of a hill was suddenly in motion, like a waterfall. Less than two years before, I had begun to write with conviction; but 'Elegy for the Labouring Poor' uncovered a fact of experience whose implications I felt, but whose finality I was not yet ready to admit:

> Under the downs, in countless sites
> Gutted by the exile of their people,
> Others will meet this isolation.
> They will inherit the emptiness.

Once again self-renewal coincided with my response to other artists, this time Nash and the Powys brothers. Now, where I might have seen only chalk dust and the blank unpeopled downs, I saw one vast hill and its prehistoric earthworks as a living form. I reminded myself that the chalk giant was still there, on a neighbouring down. Once more the ground in that place came to feel as deep as when I first saw it, and was told that it was once a sea. There remains, in that landscape, a vast energy, but it is not embodied in any living culture. The landscape changes, of course, both physically and in the way in which it is perceived, but running through it, like a geological fault, is the division between the power which it contains, and the social present. History also remains, so much so that even the earth may sometimes seem exhausted; the monuments to different ages weigh it down; all the air has been breathed, and the young feel as though nothing has been left except dust. Wherever people live there is, of course, a social reality, but, throughout the south, the social reality has shifted its centre. Often the localities appear to be other than they really are: a village seen from above as a huddle of roofs round a church tower, intimate among the rounded downs, might be living in another century, but the greater part of its existence, the things by which it lives and the consciousness of many who live there, is determined elsewhere, manipulated by the lines running south-east.... No, this is not entirely true of any one place, and of some it is true only to a small degree. But in the parts of Wales with which I am familiar the pull in that south-easterly direction still exerts far less influence than it does in the south and west of England. The pull is felt here, of course, as economic and political pressure, in newsprint and a multitude of seductive images, but far more people are able to live within their cultural and social reality, which relates them closely to place. Above all, this world does not belong only to the past; it still contains the possibility of a self-determining future. As with all but one of the poems which I wish to keep, the writing which followed the visit to Dorset was done in Wales. Only a few of my poems have been set in Wales, and these are not the ones I like best. Ten years may have been long enough for me to begin to see what kind of ground this is, but it has not been long enough for me to absorb the experience. Should that be possible in my own language, however, it will demand of me, for reasons which this essay should have made clear, a different approach from that which living in Wales has enabled me to take to southern England.

Poem and Place

THE FOLLOWING reflections have arisen partly from reading Geoffrey Grigson's anthology, *The Faber Book of Poems and Places* (1980), which juxtaposes Wordsworth's 'To the River Duddon: After-thought' with part of Matthew Arnold's 'The Youth of Nature', an elegy for Wordsworth, and includes the closing lines of Lionel Johnson's 'Laleham: Matthew Arnold's Grave'.

Lionel Johnson was recalling Wordsworth when in this poem he wrote: 'Still those waters glide'. The waters are 'the broad, gray Thames' but the line recalls 'Still glides the Stream' from Wordsworth's 'To the River Duddon: After-thought'. Johnson is, therefore, implying a strong tribute to Arnold within a context of explicit homage, since he certainly knew what Wordsworth meant to Arnold, and may have remembered that Arnold on a former elegiac occasion had alluded to the same Wordsworth poem. The stream of Arnold is one, Johnson implies, with the stream of Wordsworth.

Arnold had written, in 'The Youth of Nature':

> So it is, so it will be for aye.
> Nature is fresh as of old,
> Is lovely; a mortal is dead.

Wordsworth in his noble sonnet had written:

> Still glides the Stream, and shall for ever glide;
> The Form remains, the Function never dies;
> While we, the brave, the mighty, and the wise,
> We Men, who in our morn of youth defied
> The elements, must vanish;—be it so!

Arnold in mourning Wordsworth is justly lamenting the incapacity of his own age to rear 'a sacred poet', and the difference between a time of superb poetic confidence and a time self-consciously aware of failing spiritual and cultural powers may be seen in the contrast between Wordsworth's magisterial 'be it so!' and Arnold's mournful, archaic 'so it will be for aye'. 'Be it so!' is, moreover, the hinge on which Wordsworth joins acceptance of man's mortality to a triumphant affirmation of man's power:

> Enough, if something from our hands have power
> To live, and act, and serve the future hour;
> And if, as toward the silent tomb we go,

> Through love, through hope, and faith's transcendent dower,
> We feel that we are greater than we know.

Wordsworth's 'enough' is a sufficiency in comparison with which, in its confidence in a living human tradition, borne by the individual, with a power analogous to the river's to flow through past, present and future, Arnold's and all subsequent periods in England have had nothing or little to offer.

Poetry of place after Wordsworth cannot be understood, I believe, outside a context of loss. The loss is comprehensive, of shared belief in an ideal of order, mainly Christian in derivation, but shaped by local cultural conditions, which include a sense of nationhood, the Church, the English language. Wordsworth, as Arnold says, grew old feeling 'the dissolving throes/Of a social order he loved'. 'To the River Duddon: After-thought' is, however, a great expression of faith in an order transcending the social, which secured Wordsworth's image of Man, God and Nature.

One strength of a living tradition, or at least, of a poet's rooted belief in such a tradition, is that it is common to all. So Wordsworth, for all his introspection and passion for solitude and solitaries, was secure in his shared humanity, as no subsequent English poet has been; he could take for granted his place as a man among men. This sonnet could only have been written by a man for whom poetry was a central human activity, concerned with essential human experience. The individualism of Wordsworth differs from later individualisms, in that it is rooted in a common humanity.

It is no wonder that Arnold, lacking such assurance in himself, his poetic function and his world, should write of Wordsworth: 'The spots which recall him survive,/ For he lent a new life to these hills.' For as the poet's grasp on a common human world has loosened so he has sought to replace it with special relationships, with place in particular, and has come to stress the specialness of other poets, above all in their relation to place. This is both part of the movement by which the English poet has become a specialist talking to specialists, and an effort of one radically displaced within the national culture to place himself.

It is true that Henry Vaughan, writing in the seventeenth century, could affirm:

> Poets (like Angels) where they once appear
> Hallow the place, and each succeeding year
> Adds reverence to't, such as at length doth give
> This aged faith, that there their genii live.

But it is an 'aged faith', and the genial classicism of 'To the River Isca' gives it its provenance. This light-hearted pastoral is far from the darkness in which Arnold, turning to Wordsworth, looks to 'a new life' given to the hills for assurance that there are values in nature—and concludes by virtually losing man against the greatness of nature. The hills belonged to Wordsworth's order, in which man participated; for Arnold they are 'spots which recall him'—and if he means 'spots' to have its Wordsworthian resonance (which I doubt), it is closer here to a limited and even picturesque meaning. Already at Wordsworth's death, in the mind of one of his greatest admirers, his order has become a location imbued with his special relationship, and marginal rather than central.

For all its particular historical variations, a broad movement defining poetry of place may be seen if we consider an anonymous poem of about 1500, 'The Properties of the Shires of England', in which 'property' has its dual meaning and the characteristics of each shire are, often, its inhabitants' products and possessions. Put to increasingly subtle and sophisticated use, 'property' (in the sense of what people are, and have) remained the ground of poetry of place until the advent of places of special relationship, with the loss of a common world. So, in 'The Properties of the Shires of England', '*Herefordshire* shield and spear:/*Worsetshire* wring pear./*Gloucetershire* shoe and nail'; Ben Jonson finds at Penshurst the fruitfulness of England, which expresses his aristocratic ideals; and the 'goodly prospect' of James Thomson's Britannia embraces such virtues as 'liberty' and 'plenty'.

Ben Jonson certainly had his mythic or ideal England, as indeed most poets have. A people's sense of itself is at least as much the creation of its myths and legendary history as of its actual history. Deny the poet myth, and poetry will eventually wither, but no good poet is only an uncritical mouthpiece of the 'matter' into which he has been born, and there are different degrees of reality among myths and ideals. Whereas Penshurst, for example, is real (however Jonson may have embellished the household and the estate, marrying his own generosity with the generosity he found there, to create a great affirmation of this human quality and of other ideals), the Laleham of Lionel Johnson's elegy for Arnold is a dream:

> Half church, half cottage, comely stands
> An holy house, from Norman hands:
> By rustic Time well taught to wear
> Some lowly, meditative air:
> Long ages of a pastoral race
> Have softened sternness into grace;
> And many a touch of simpler use
> From Norman strength hath set it loose.

While it would be mere bloodymindedness to claim not to know what Arnold meant by saying that Wordsworth had given a new life to the hills (though I think we should understand it also in the special sense dictated by Arnold's needs), it is not, I believe, to see in these lines a dream England, all real continuity and change smoothly abstracted, which Johnson, with a more decadent historical and cultural sense than Arnold's, has conjured from Arnold's 'wistful song', in response to a late Empire's escapist longing for the garden of England. Arnold himself had done the same for 'Celtic' Wales, substituting a romantic landscape for the cultural reality which his educational policies and English cultural imperialism gravely threatened, and 'spirit' for the social and cultural properties without which there can be no real national spirit or identity.

From Wordsworth through Arnold to Johnson the Stream changes from a power connecting the poet with his fellows, living, dead and unborn, to a lazy if seductive dream, and the poet from a central human figure addressing himself to the heart of human experience to a culturally peripheral individual misrepresenting another poet's vision.

One impression gained from reading poems of place from the mid-nineteenth century onwards (although the phenomenon does of course occur long before then), is that elegy follows elegy: Arnold on Wordsworth, Arnold on Clough, Johnson on Arnold, and so on. This is only proper, as well as natural. For as Cornelius Varley painted 'Wilson's Pool', Cader Idris, paying tribute to Richard Wilson, the genius of the place, so it is fitting for poets to commemorate those who have taught them to see. As Arnold wrote of Wordsworth, naming one of the chief functions of poetry:

> But he was a priest to us all
> Of the wonder and bloom of the world,
> Which we saw with his eyes, and were glad.

The point I wish to pursue, however, is that poets, with loss of a common world, have tended increasingly to identify other poets, as well as themselves, with place, so that elegies investing particular spots with the poet's spirit have also emphasized the localization of the poetic within an England whose dominant culture has no use for it. A resulting narrowing of focus, in poems as well as ideas of poetry, has transferred its voice from an order embracing man and nature to the hills. Not to the hills as Wordsworth apprehended them, but rather to 'nature' as observed by Elizabeth Barrett Browning among many other poets— 'tamed/ And grown domestic like a barn-door fowl.' This domesticated nature is frequently conceived in terms of personal or social tensions originating elsewhere, and is rarely shown with feeling for either its otherness or the human processes in its making. Or rather this has been the case until quite recently in England, and is still a strong convention.

The poet's special relationship with a place is represented splendidly by Arnold, again, when in 'Thyrsis' he writes: 'Who, if not I, for questing here hath power?' and 'I know these slopes; who knows them if not I?' The intensely possessive note expresses the cultural isolation (if in some cases, social elevation) of the English poet since Wordsworth. This has less to do with temperament, except in so far as temperament is influenced by the world into which one is born, than with his culturally marginal role. (*His*, because it is obvious that additional factors concerning male dominance of the media of communication, culturally and spiritually null though they mainly are, affect the female poet.) The effects of this isolation on poetry of place are many and various, including concentration on place as a refuge or escape from an unmanageable or unlovable society or nation, or to provide imagery for an inner world. Housman powerfully exemplifies the latter tendency, with a landscape whose reality meant little to him, but which gave body to a peculiar range of emotion, while Clare and Hardy are among the poets who have written the most authentic poetry of place in relatively recent times, and have more in common with Wordsworth than with Housman or Arnold. In Clare and Hardy places can be said to receive a voice, in that an actual local community achieves its first public articulation through one of its members. Irrespective of the fact that both poets were in some sense dislocated, with an ambiguous and even strained relationship with their community, voiceless generations speak for the first time through them. When all has been said about their special individuality, it is not to be thought that the world of feeling they unlock is rare, rather than their gift for unlocking it. The range from located to dislocated expression is great in both, but particularly in Hardy, who could both write as a commoner and achieve the extreme sophistication of 'the spot's unconsciousness of you'. The latter was only possible for one who habitually identified all human significance with place, indeed felt and envisioned with place; which is not likely in one so secure in his belonging that he remains unconscious of it.

It was at a moment of great tension between defensive patriotism and recognition of his country's grave offences that Coleridge wrote, with tell-tale shrill vibrancy, in 'Fears in Solitude':

> O native Britain! O my Mother Isle!
> How shouldst thou prove aught else but dear and holy
> To me, who from thy lakes and mountain-hills,
> Thy clouds, thy quiet dales, thy rocks and seas,
> Have drunk in all my intellectual life,
> All sweet sensations, all ennobling thoughts,
> All adoration of the God in nature,
> All lovely and all honourable things,
> Whatever makes this mortal spirit feel
> The joy and greatness of its future being?

The sentiment was ominous, too, not because it is inherently unsympathetic, (which it is not; love of country is a primary theme of any developed national culture, and will find distorted or oblique expression if the direct channels are, for any reason, obstructed), but because Coleridge's reason for loving Britain, that he has derived virtually his whole being from her natural forms, must inevitably lead to yet greater strain when Britain can no longer be identified with these forms, but has to be seen as a polity inimical to their spirit and her own best traditions. By the same token, the potency of the identification has made it a convention of feeling through a long history with episodes in which automatic response to it has been, at least, a highly questionable virtue. The strain of the identification is apparent in Edward Thomas's wartime image of England, and surfaces in 'This is No Case of Petty Right or Wrong'. It has led to contradictions, when the poet has either held to Coleridge's sentiment while knowing that his country and its polity are not a single harmonious ideal, as in the case of Edward Thomas, or pretended that they are one, in the face of the evidence, as Thomas's Edwardian and Georgian contemporaries tended to do. The dishonesty of the latter tendency degraded the language of patriotic sentiment, which the war poets then did much to revalue, but it still carries forward dream Englands which continue, in some quarters, to betray the people and their history. Poetry of place has often been implicated in this betrayal. Indeed 'Fears in Solitude' itself, though fraught with felt and acknowledged tensions that make it a moving personal testimony, not any kind of betrayal, is a notable instance of the poet finally sinking such tensions, unresolved, in his loving contemplation of a home landscape. This is the more notable for Coleridge's acute awareness of the capacity of 'dainty terms', images and abstractions to falsify reality and atrophy the moral sense. The strain may also be seen, of course, in the contrast between Coleridge's solitude and fearful self-communing in his womb-like spot, and the public address to his fellow Britons that his bold and ambitious oratory assumes. Edward Thomas was also to 'resolve' in an elemental scene an historical predicament that could not in fact be thus resolved:

> Dinned
> With war and argument I read no more
> Than in the storm smoking along the wind
> Athwart the wood. Two witches' cauldrons roar.
> From one the weather shall rise clear and gay;
> Out of the other an England beautiful
> And like her mother that died yesterday.

For others there has been no such resolution. For example, it was a terrible moment when Ivor Gurney wrote 'The High Hills':

> The high hills have a bitterness
> Now they are not known,
> And memory is poor enough consolation
> For the soul hopeless gone.
> Up in the air there beech tangles widely in the wind—
> That I can imagine.
> But the speed, the swiftness, walking into clarity,
> Like last year's briony, are gone.

Terrible for Gurney in his bitterness and hopelessness, but terrible for England too, for the culture one of whose most cherished self-images could not be expressed more succinctly than by poem-and-place, and of which Ivor Gurney was so sensitive a representative.

What is this 'soul hopeless gone'? Not the essence of man as a spiritual being, but rather Gurney's innermost self, once secured by identification with the place from which he is now excluded. It is his Cotswolds, the hills themselves, but also the essence of his England, that Gurney depends on for his very life. The identification may recall Wordsworth's relationship with the River Duddon, 'my partner and my guide', which is on the robust side of a visionary tradition whose rarer spirit is represented by Thomas Vaughan's 'What a clear, running crystal here I find:/Sure I will strive to gain as clear a mind.' Gurney's marvellous 'walking into clarity' is reminiscent of the latter. Both Wordsworth and Vaughan, however, were grounded in an order, sacred and communal, whereas Gurney had nothing but the place, which was absolutely his partner and his guide, as the Duddon to Wordsworth was not. 'Walking into clarity', the equivalent of a spiritual exercise, on which Gurney's soul depends, requires freedom to walk in a loved place. But Gurney no longer has access to the place, except poorly in memory and tormentingly in imagination. 'Gone... gone' echoes across the poem. This is one possible outcome of a special relationship with place. When the place becomes everything, its loss will leave nothing.

The intention of Geoffrey Grigson's *Faber Book of Poems and Places* is not responsible for these reflections. He illustrates rather the varieties of place in Britain and beyond, arranging the poems, so to speak, geographically, not chronologically, with views of the South of England being followed by views of the South-West and so on, through Scotland and Ireland to France and Italy. Several pleasures are to be had from this ordering of things. There are, for example, the pleasures of any Grigson anthology, of fresh and exact observation in the works chosen, and of meeting piquant, out of the way items which the reader might otherwise not have found; few modern anthologists and critics have had as honourable a career as Geoffrey Grigson's in redeeming the unjustly neglected from obscurity. There is also the pleasure, which will no doubt occur with different poems for different readers, of finding again, perhaps after many years, poems that first raised hairs on the back of the neck; Charles Kingsley's 'The Sands of Dee' was among the poems that did this for me. There is however another pleasure, which I think requires a look at what its source may otherwise obscure.

This is the pleasure of variety, of both seeing in poems the local, regional and national differences distinguishing the anthology's geographical areas, and of finding different views of the same place side by side. An obvious example of the latter is the juxtaposition of the 'Dover' scene from *King Lear* with 'Dover Beach'. Such juxtapositions afford the opportunity to look closely at different uses of the same place by different poets. Their danger on the other hand is that superficial variety may conceal real differences, and the book serve as yet another literary excursion which charms the reader with local colours. After all, what a yawning gap there is between Shakespeare's samphire cliff and Arnold's 'the cliffs of England'. No use denying that for many, in many different circumstances, seeing the white cliffs has drawn an additional poignancy from these and other stratified literary images superimposed upon them, or that even for the most iconoclastic literary mind England can ever be only a bare history. No use denying, either, the possibility inherent in such potent images of betraying the reality of people and place at a particular historical moment. The reality always has, in any case, its own authentic poetry, which a poet may have to break cherished literary or mythic images in order to reveal.

The capacity of images to obscure and even to falsify is illustrated by the section 'Wales and the Marches'. This includes poems by Henry and Thomas Vaughan, 'Grongar Hill', 'Fern Hill' and poems by Gerard Manley Hopkins and W. H. Davies. There is nothing else by anyone who has, to my knowledge, lived in Wales for any length of time, let alone by another Welsh poet, whether writing in English or in Welsh. Omission of the latter may be due to Geoffrey Grigson's objection to what he calls 'the thin prosiness of contemporary verse translation, on the after-track of Ezra Pound' (although he includes a translation from the early Irish by Kenneth Jackson, in a section, 'Scotland and Ireland', which may be criticized largely on the same ground as that representing Wales). But what about this, for example, from Anthony Conran's translation of David Gwenallt Jones's 'Rhydcymerau'?

>   Near Rhydcymerau,
>   On the land of Esgeir-ceir and the fields of Tir-bach,
>   They have planted the saplings
>   to be trees of the third war.

★ ★ ★

> And by this time there's nothing there but trees.
> Impertinent roots suck dry the old soil:
> Trees where neighbourhood was,
> And a forest that once was farmland.
> Where was verse-writing and scripture
>   is the South's bastardized English.
> The fox barks where once cried lambs and children,
> And there, in the dark midst,
> Is the den of the English minotaur.

The anger here is grounded on a sharp delineation, at the heart of the poem, of a familial neighbourhood, now destroyed, in which a particular poetic tradition in the native language was the expression of a whole way of life.

It is a matter, then, of the exclusion not only of eligible Welsh poems, but of a whole dimension of the country's lived experience. Indeed there is much, in good translations of medieval and modern Welsh poems, that could have been used to arrest the English literary tourist, and show him where he is. The section begins, however, with the magnificent Snowdon sunrise passage from *The Prelude,* and includes 'Tintern Abbey'. The delight of reading these again is vitiated by the strong impression, to which they innocently contribute, that Wales is being presented largely as a source of visionary experience for English poets. However, not only is there nowhere in these islands, and possibly in the world, where place and native poetry are more closely identified, but the retention of some Welsh poets into the twentieth century of a common world shared with their readers offers an alternative relation between poet and people and place that English readers might benefit greatly from observing. The omission of R. S. Thomas, David Jones and other Welsh poets writing in English contributes further to an Arnoldian dissolution of Wales in the mists of English romanticism.

I am the more inclined to dwell on this in the light of Geoffrey Grigson's fine understanding, revealed in many books, that place and people form reciprocal relationships, and shown by such observations in his Introduction as that: 'Our feeling flows into places, and an accumulation of feeling, historical, cultural and personal, flows back from places into our consciousness.' I was particularly struck by his words concerning Verlaine writing '"about" the fen village in Lincolnshire where he was so happy'—'how "about" requires the extension of those inverted commas'.

For the weak 'writing about' I would substitute, in the case of some poetry of place, 'writing *from*'. Some Welsh poets of European stature have in this century continued to write from place, from deep within a communal experience, with a poetic confidence equal to Wordsworth's. Waldo Williams is a modern instance of the visionary poet in a sustained and sustaining relationship with a living tradition, who wrote from a countryside which was also the ground of his culture.

A passage from a recent brilliant short book by Ned Thomas, *Derek Walcott: Poet of the Islands* (1980), is relevant to this subject:

> Those who have read J. R. Jones's book *Prydeindod* will be familiar with his notion of *cydymdreiddiad*—that subtle knot of interpenetration, which, he says, grows in time (in people's consciousness) between a territory and its people and their language, creating a sense of belonging to a particular stretch of the earth's surface. From the point of view of an established and secure culture such as that of England, this may seem a rather vague and mystical notion. The secure culture takes it largely for granted and therefore leaves it undefined. But in various parts of the world, the absence or loss of this *cydymdreiddiad* focuses the mind powerfully upon the idea.

There is an illusion abroad among some Welsh writers that England still has 'an established and secure culture', and one even hears, from time to time, the image of 'a great rooted oak'. While it is understandable why this should be felt to be so in a country which suffers much from her dominant neighbour, it is plain that an old image is having its life artificially prolonged by economic, political and communicative powers that are, in the main, destructive of culture, in the sense in which Ned Thomas is using the word. A sense of belonging in England has for some time been largely to a locality or region, and also to a class, institution or group, while writers with such a sense have often gained or recovered it, as a result of dislocation. In fact, in a situation of radical general disintegration, England has in recent years become one of the parts of the world where 'loss of this *cydymdreiddiad* focuses the mind powerfully upon the idea'.

It is all the more of a pity, then, that *The Faber Book of Poems and Places* fails to represent some of our most vital poetry of the last twenty years, which has arisen from an involvement with place, and shows strongly contrasting responses to this loss. It includes no Bunting, Jones, Hill, Fisher, Harrison, Tomlinson, Davie, Silkin or Sisson, to name some of the principal omissions. None of these is a poet of place in the sense of either having a tourist's or exclusively pictorial eye, or being only local (though in view of William Carlos Williams's sense of the local and Patrick Kavanagh's definition of the parochial 'only' needs inverted commas as much as 'about'). They are rather poets who have, in their different ways, redeemed poem-and-place from its association with dream Englands. There is an exactitude in their care for their subjects, shown in their care for their language, that obviates the betrayal of people and place which has occurred widely in the long romantic twilight beginning before Wordsworth's death and still prevailing over much of Britain. It may be long before any English poet has earned the knowledge of a Crabbe, or can feel as Hopkins did about Oxford—'All mine, yet common to my every peer.' But the care these and other poets show at their best for what David Jones called 'the very things of which one is oneself made' promises re-vision of our common places.

Bibliography of books discussed in the text

Matthew Arnold

On the Study of Celtic Literature (1867; Dent Everyman Library, 1976)

W. H. Auden

Poems (1930)
The Orators: an English study (1932)
(with Christopher Isherwood) *The Dog Beneath the Skin; or Where is Francis?*, a play in three acts (1935)
Look, Stranger! (1936)
(with Louis MacNeice) *Letters from Iceland* (1937)
Another Time (1940)
New Year Letter (1941)
The Age of Anxiety: a baroque eclogue (1948)
Nones (1951)
The Shield of Achilles (1955)
Homage to Clio (1960)
The Dyer's Hand, and other essays (1963; Paperback, 1975)
Epistle to a godson, and other poems (1972)
All published by Faber & Faber Ltd.

Frances Bellerby

Hath the Rain a Father? (P. Davies, 1946)
Plash Mill: poems (P. Davies, 1946)
The Brightening Cloud (P. Davies, 1949)
The Stone Angel and the Stone Man: poems (Ted Williams, Plymouth, 1958)
The First-Known, and other poems (Enitharmon, 1975)
Selected poems of Frances Bellerby, chosen and introduced by Charles Causley (Enitharmon, 1970)

Ivor Gurney

Poems of Ivor Gurney (Chatto & Windus, 1973)
The Ordeal of Ivor Gurney, Michael Hurd (Oxford University Press, 1978)

Seamus Heaney

Wintering Out (1972; Paperback, 1973)
North (1975)
Both published by Faber & Faber Ltd.

Emyr Humphreys

The Little Kingdom (Eyre & Spottiswoode, 1946)
Outside the House of Baal (Eyre & Spottiswoode, 1965)
National Winner (Macdonald, 1971)

David Jones

In Parenthesis (1937; Paperback 1975)
The Anathemata: fragments of an attempted writing (1952; Paperback, 1972)
Epoch and Artist: selected writings (1959; Paperback, 1973)
The Sleeping Lord and other fragments (1974)
All published by Faber & Faber Ltd.
David Jones: artist and writer, David Blamires (Manchester University Press, 1971)

Charles Olson

The Maximus Poems (Jargon, 1960)
Archaeologist of Morning (Cape Goliard, 1970)

Philip Pacey

Charged Landscapes (Enitharmon, 1978)

John Cowper Powys

A Glastonbury Romance (John Lane, 1933; Pan, 1975)
Autobiography (John Lane, 1934; Macdonald, 1967; Pan, 1981)
Maiden Castle (Cassell, 1937; Pan, 1979)
Owen Glendower (John Lane, 1941; Pan, 1978)
Porius: a romance of the Dark Ages (Macdonald, 1951; Village Press)
Rodmoor: a romance (Shaw, New York, 1916; Macdonald, 1973)

T. F. Powys

Soliloquies of a Hermit (A. Melrose, 1918; Village Press 1975)
Black Bryony (1923)
Mark Only (1924)
Mockery Gap (1925)
Mr Tasker's Gods (1925; Trigon, 1978)

Innocent Birds (1926)
Mr Weston's Good Wine (1927; Penguin, 1976)
The Dewpond (Elkin Matthews, 1928)
An Interpretation of Genesis (1929)
Fables (1929; reissued as *No Painted Plumage*, 1934)
Kindness in a Corner (1930)
The Only Penitent (1931)
The Two Thieves (1932)
Captain Patch (1935)
All published by Chatto & Windus except where shown.
Welsh Ambassadors—Powys lives and letters, Louis Marlow (Chapman & Hall, 1936; Bertram Rota, 1971)

John Riley

The Collected Works. ed Tim Longville (Grosseteste, Leeds)

Edward Thomas

Richard Jefferies (Hutchinson, 1909; Faber Paperback, 1978)
The South Country (Dent, 1909)
The Happy-Go-Lucky Morgans (Duckworth, 1913)
Keats (T. C. & E. C. Jack, 1916)
Collected Poems (Selwyn & Blount, 1920; Faber, 1936; 1949; Paperback, 1979)

Raymond Williams

Border Country (1960; 1978)
The Long Revolution (1961; Penguin, 1965)
Second Generation (1964; 1978)
The Country and the City (1973; Paladin, 1975)
The Fight for Manod (1979)
All published by Chatto & Windus.

Index

Allchin, A. M., 156
Arnold, Matthew, 13, 14, 17-19, 78, 180-4, 187
Auden, W. H., 14, 137-47
Augustine, St, 170
Austen, Jane, 87

Bach, J. S., 127
Barbusse, Henri, 121
Beckett, Samuel, 74
Beethoven, L. van, 127
Bellerby, Frances, 14, 130-36
Bennett, Arnold, 101
Berdyaev, Nicolas, 12, 156
Blake, William, 13, 43, 53, 54, 55, 56, 59, 67, 156, 170
Blamires, David, 45
Blunden, Edmund, 126
Bradley, F. H., 38
Breughel, 71
Bromwich, Rachel, 18
Bronk, William, 195
Brooke, Rupert, 120, 170
Browning, E. B., 183
Bulgakov, Sergius, 156
Bunting, Basil, 150-51, 189
Bunyan, John, 87
Byrd, William, 127

Causley, Charles, 130, 132, 134
Clare, John, 67, 184
Clough, A. H., 183
Coleridge, S. T., 43, 67, 125, 127, 184-5
Conran, Anthony, 187
Constable, John, 67
Cowper, William, 87
Crabbe, George, 190
Creeley, Robert, 151

Davie, Donald, 189
Darwin, Charles, 36

Davies, W. H., 187
Dix, Gregory, 38
Dostoevsky, F., 97
Drayton, Michael, 55, 56, 58
Drinkwater, John, 29

Eliade, Mircéa, 39
Eliot, T. S., 28, 34, 38, 41, 50, 52, 56, 79, 139, 140, 148, 149, 151, 170, 175
Emerson, R. W., 67
Evans, Caradoc, 94, 101, 168
Evans, Margiad, 106

Farjeon, Eleanor, 30
Fisher, Roy, 11, 12, 67, 189
Freud, Sigmund, 141
Frost, Robert, 20

Geoffrey of Monmouth, 55, 56
Ginsberg, Allen, 170
Gorki, Maxim, 170
Goya, F. de, 71
Graves, Robert, 49
Grenfell, Julian, 120
Groddeck, G., 141
Grigson, Geoffrey, 180, 186-89
Gwenallt (D. Gwenallt Jones), 162, 180, 186, 187, 188
Gurney, Ivor, 14, 120-29, 185-6

Hardy, Thomas, 13, 22, 28, 29, 67, 75, 76, 85, 89, 98-9, 106, 119, 125, 128, 130-31, 132, 134, 140, 143, 172-3, 184
Harrison, Tony, 156, 189
Heaney, Seamus, 12, 13, 71-4, 117
Herbert, George, 119, 154
Hill, Geoffrey, 12, 67, 151, 156, 189
Hölderlin, Friedrich, 155
Hooker, Richard, 156

Index

Hopkins, G. Manley, 67, 125-6, 187, 190
Hopkins, Kenneth, 91
Hoskins, W. G., 67, 69
Housman, A. E., 125, 184
Hughes, Ted, 12, 67
Humphreys, Emyr, 14, 83-105
Hurd, Michael, 120
Hynes, Samuel, 126

Isherwood, Christopher, 137

Jackson, Kenneth, 187
Jefferies, Richard, 21-2, 30, 67, 116, 125, 170
Johnes, Thomas, 165
Johnson, Lionel, 180, 182-3
Johnson, Ronald, 66, 67
Jones, Bedwyr Lewis, 167
Jones, David, 12, 13, 14, 32-65, 66, 67, 78, 119, 150-51, 163, 176, 188, 189, 190
Jones, J. R., 189
Jonson, Ben, 182
Joyce, James, 50, 79, 94, 96, 139

Kavanagh, Patrick, 72, 117, 189
Keats, John, 20, 27, 170
Kierkegaard, Søren, 170
Kilvert, Francis, 67
Kingsley, Charles, 187
Kipling, Rudyard, 122
Knight, W. F. Jackson, 57

Larkin, Philip, 12, 67
Lawrence, D. H., 13, 22, 79, 85, 128, 150, 151-2, 170
Leavis, F. R., 50
Levy, G. Rachel, 47
Lewis, Alun, 117
Lewis, Saunders, 12, 38, 44
Littlewood, J. C. F., 49
Longville, Tim, 157
Lowell, Robert, 67

Maeterlinck, Maurice, 31
Malory, Thomas, 55
Mandelshtam, Osip, 155-6

Marlow, Lewis, 75, 76
Marx, Karl, 141
Maurice, F. D., 156
MacDiarmid, Hugh, 12
Miller, Henry, 170
Milton, John, 53, 170
Moore, Henry, 79
Muir, Edwin, 175

Nash, Paul, 67, 165, 178
Nichols, Robert, 120

Olson, Charles, 14, 66, 148-52, 155, 156
Owen, Wilfred, 128, 140

Pacey, Philip, 66-70
Palmer, Samuel, 67
Patchen, Kenneth, 170
Pater, Walter, 31
Paul, St, 133
Picasso, Pablo, 79
Piggott, Stuart, 61
Plath, Sylvia, 151
Plutarch, 54
Pollock, Jackson, 148
Pound, Ezra, 67, 139, 149, 155, 187
Powys, Rev. C. F., 75
Powys, J. C., 14, 75-9, 85, 87, 89, 161, 163
Powys, Llewellyn, 75-6
Powys, T. F., 14, 75, 80-92

Raleigh, Walter, 56, 73
Read, Herbert, 175
Rimbaud, Arthur, 171
Riley, John, 153-58-
Rosenberg, Isaac, 36, 128
Ruskin, John, 67

Schubert, Franz, 127
Selden, John, 57, 60
Shakespeare, William, 23, 56, 28, 53, 56, 170, 187
Shelley, P. B., 26
Silkin, Jon, 189
Sisson, C. H., 189
Snyder, Gary, 67

Soloviev, V., 156
Southey, Robert, 169
Spenser, Edmund, 56, 73

Tennyson, Alfred, 140
Thomas, Dylan, 78
Thomas, Edward, 13, 14, 20-31, 67, 78, 116-19, 125-26 128, 130-31, 134, 140-41, 142-3, 185
Thomas, Ned, 167, 189
Thomas, R. S., 78, 134, 151, 188
Thompson, E. P., 67
Thomson, James, 182
Thoreau, H. D., 67
Tolstoy, Leo, 97
Tomlinson, Charles, 67, 151, 189
Traherne, Thomas, 131

Varley, Cornelius, 183
Vaughan, Henry, 131, 181, 187

Vaughan, Thomas, 186, 187
Verlaine, Paul, 188
Virgil, 57

Walcott, Derek, 189
Warner, Sylvia Townsend, 91
Watkins, Vernon, 132
Watts, Isaac, 169
Whitman, Walt, 67, 149, 171
Wilkinson, Louis, (See Marlow, Louis)
Williams, Raymond, 12, 67, 106-15
Williams, Waldo, 167-8, 175, 188
Williams, W. Carlos, 12, 67, 149, 189
Wilson, Richard, 183
Wordsworth, William, 22, 28, 67, 125, 143, 151, 182-4, 186, 188

Yeats, W. B., 12, 21, 72, 140, 148